'Leadership makes the difference in the field of human services. Peter Gilbert, our experienced and highly regarded leader in his own right, has done a great job with this text. Bringing together ideas, theory and practical examples of leadership in action, Peter has delivered a text that which will be of enormous benefit to everyone holding or aspiring to leadership positions.'

Professor Antony Sheehan, Director of Care Services, DoH

'This book addresses some of the critical issues to be faced with regard to leadership in the 21st century. Growing diverse leadership skills is a major priority for developing holistic services fit for the future.'

Jane Campbell, MBE, Chair SCIE

'Leadership is the vital spark in creating and maintaining value-based and effective services at a time of unprecedented change. Peter Gilbert has used his own considerable experience, and a wide range of sources, to give practical help in ethical-based leadership to managers of human services at all levels'

Jo Williams, CEO, Royal Mencap,
and former DSS of Wigan and Cheshire

'Leaders are accused of stating vacuous claims and hollow soundbites. A perception persists that leaders are intent purely on serving their own interests. This is as true in health and social care as anywhere *else so* it is particularly good to see the emergence of a rallying cry to more reflective leadership based on integrity. Peter Gilbert has earned the right to speak with authority on this subject, as he does so well here.'

Hari Sewell, Director of Social care and Substance Misuse
for Camden and Islington Care Trust

'Leadership has become an important subject for exploration in all areas of public life and not least in the churches. This timely exploration is linked to a range of questions about how authority is understood and received today. Peter Gilbert's wide experience of 'hands on' leadership from the armed forces to health care informs what he has to share in this book. He has become a leader in helping a range of Christian denominations and training organizations to understand the implications of new forms of leadership for their members. This comprehensive book comes at just the right time to help develop and provoke a debate which should be at the heartbeat of the life of our major public institutions and faith communities.'

Malcolm Grundy, Director, Foundation for Church Leadership

'A truly timely and readable book about a subject area that is crucial to the health and social care field – leadership, and one which significantly encompasses the fundamental issues of tackling discrimination and acknowledges the notion of full humanity – written by an inspirational leader in his own right.'

Professor Kamlesh Patel OBE, Head of Centre for Ethnicity and Health, Chairman of MHAC and Director of BME MH Prog Dept of Health

'Leadership and Spirituality are both highly topical issues. A very interesting read.'

Rev. Dr Peter Sedgwick, Principal, St Michael's College, Llandaff

'Leadership can be a science and it can be an art: Peter Gilbert shows us how it can be a way of looking at and living our lives. Leadership can be about leaders and it can be about the people they lead: Peter Gilbert explores with us how in the various parts of our lives we are all leaders. With his wide range of experience and with his own very special brand of wisdom and humility, Peter leads us on a journey of discovery that has meaning for all of us.'

Professor Christine King, Vice Chancellor, Staffordshire University

Leadership

Being Effective and Remaining Human

Peter Gilbert

Russell House Publishing

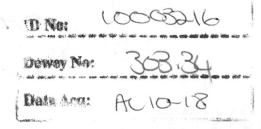
First published in 2005 by:
Russell House Publishing Ltd.
4 St George's House
Uplyme Road
Lyme Regis
Dorset DT7 3LS

Tel: 01297-443948
Fax: 01297-442722
e-mail: help@russellhouse.co.uk
www.russellhouse.co.uk

British Library Cataloguing-in-publication Data:
A catalogue record for this book is available from the British Library.

ISBN: 1-903855-76-4, 978-1-903855-76-8

Typeset by TW Typesetting, Plymouth, Devon

Printed by Cromwell Press, Trowbridge

Russell House Publishing
is a group of social work, probation, education and
youth and community work practitioners and
academics working in collaboration with a professional
publishing team.
Our aim is to work closely with the field to produce
innovative and valuable materials to help managers,
trainers, practitioners and students.
We are keen to receive feedback on publications and
new ideas for future projects.
For details of our other publications please visit our
website or ask us for a catalogue. Contact details
are on this page.

Contents

Introduction

Leadership is a word much in vogue at present. The problem with being a concept in current favour, is that it can be over-used, misused and then abused! We only have to think of that ancient and very persuasive word *community*, and the concept of 'care in the community', to know how easy it is for a useful and positive construct to fall into disapproval and disuse.

It is vitally important that this does not happen with *leadership*; as nearly all international and national reports, public and private sector documents, inquiries and investigations carry the injunction that more and better leadership at all levels in organisations is an urgent imperative.

What is leadership?

One might be forgiven for thinking, looking at the shelves in bookshops and airport bookstalls, that leadership is something newly-discovered by management gurus in the USA. Not so! Leadership has been around since the dawn of time, and has been a necessary part of the human condition because it speaks of discovering and giving a sense of direction, and walking with people on a journey. Leadership is to do with path finding, steering a boat full of fellow human beings on a stormy sea – either literally or metaphorically; it is about 'we' more than 'I'; and it is about both the courage to stick with a certain direction against all the odds, and also, paradoxically, sometimes having the courage to acknowledge that the current focus is wrong and a new path needs to be sought.

Leadership is never something that you arrogate to yourself, but it is a privilege and a gift, ultimately conferred on us by those we serve.

About this book

Working with people and their challenges is difficult and demanding work. The text succinctly introduces sets of theoretical ideas, relates them clearly to practice issues, and guides the reader to further learning. Exercising true leadership as a professional, or as a manager at an operational or strategic level, is a challenge which calls for self-awareness and a willingness to take on new learning. Taking on these challenges without a sound knowledge base is a very risky strategy indeed and, potentially, a disastrous one.

This book examines leadership and its purposes in depth.

Part One considers why we need leaders even more profoundly in the modern world; looks together with the reader at the need to lead oneself before one attempts to lead others; and then at the theoretical base of leadership.

In **Part Two**, the accent is on practice, with special consideration of leadership in the context of changing organisational configurations, especially in the public sector; and the part that organisational culture plays in helping us get the right 'recipe' for an organisation or team.

Part Three looks at some of the possible dangers for leaders when they lose their sense of values and direction, and engage in discrimination and oppression. It considers what might be the factors in creating a person-centred organisation which manages to be both effective and humane.

This book is not just for people 'at the top'

Everybody acknowledges that the pace of life and work has become more frenetic over recent years, but although technological improvements have taken place, the health of organisations is still primarily founded on the quality of the people working in them. Leadership today, as it has always been, in truth, is about helping to elicit the qualities from those we work with, so that leadership can be there *at all levels*.

I hope that this book will be helpful for leaders at any level in an organisation. This very much includes practitioners who do not always see themselves as leaders; and also for those working as a lone practitioner, manager, consultant; but provide leadership through their independent perspective provided to formal organisations. The book is intended to be a resource for people working across the human services, including social work and social care; youth and community work; criminal and community justice work; counselling; advice work; housing; and aspects of healthcare.

Currently, in my roles for NIMHE and SCIE, I find myself working across the United Kingdom, so whether you find this book useful, or not, or if you have comments about how I could have written something more useful to you, then please let me know when you meet me! I wish you every success because your effectiveness and humanity creates better services for all of us.

To Dominic Gaisford O.S.B.
An inspiration in life and death.

About the Author

Peter Gilbert is NIMHE/SCIE Fellow in Social Care (Policy and Practice), Project Lead for the National Institute on Spirituality and Mental Health and Visiting Professor in Health and Social Care at Staffordshire University. He was formerly Director of Operations with Staffordshire County Council, and Director of Social Services for Worcestershire.

Following a first career in the army, Peter qualified in Social Work at Sussex University, and then worked as a generic social worker, mainly in the field of child care. In 1981 he took up post as the first team leader in West Sussex with responsibility for services for people with learning disabilities and their families; working out of one of the old long stay hospitals to build up community teams and services. During this time as a frontline manager Peter carried a caseload and practised as an Approved Social Worker. Thus he had thirteen years in direct practice, and believes passionately in the frontline worker as leader.

Substantial management experience has come in leading services in West Sussex, LB Merton and Kent in the whole range of client groups, services and partnerships. Multi-disciplinary and multi-agency working has also been a marked feature throughout Peter's career. In 1992 he went to Staffordshire SSD to implement the NHS and Community Care Act, and was involved in major reorganisations of services with a range of partners, both statutory and voluntary. He also supported the advent of user, carer and advocacy organisations, as he did as Director of Worcestershire, when he had to work in the context of major reconfigurations of social care and also health services, as the 'Kidderminster' factor came into play. In this later role Peter experienced an episode of depression which reinforced his personal and professional commitment to an holistic approach to mental health.

Since retiring from local government in April 2001, Peter has been a Core Group Member, helping to set up the National Institute for Mental Health in England. He has also been Senior Adviser on Social Care for the Sainsbury Centre for Mental Health, and is currently an Associate Consultant with the National Development Team. Recent national policy publications are *Briefing for Directors of Social Services on the Integration of Mental Health Services* (ADSS/NIMHE, with David Joannides, October, 2003) and *Inspiring Hope: Recognising the Importance of Spirituality in a Whole Person Approach to Mental Health* (NIMHE/MHF, with Vicky Nicholls, MHF, November, 2003). Peter is author and co-author of a number of books on policy, practice and leadership, including: *Managing to Care*, written with Terry Scragg, in 1992.

Other national roles: inaugural member of C.S.C.I.'s Mental Health Improvement Board; Board member of C.O.P.C.A.; member of Social Perspectives Network Executive; facilitator for the national learning sets for Directors of Social Care and Senior Managers; work for the DoH on changing workforce practice for psychiatrists, social workers and nurses.

As Visiting Professor at Staffordshire University and Visiting Research Fellow at the University of Sussex, Peter is committed to ensuring the integration of theory with practice. He has recently co-authored a Pack on *Supervision and Leadership* with Professor Neil Thompson, and runs regular workshops at Worth Abbey, in Sussex, on 'Spirituality and Leadership in the Workplace'. In June 2003 Peter published *The Value of Everything: Social Work and Its Importance in Mental Health*, with Russell House Publishing, which is regarded as the standard text in its field.

Acknowledgements

One of the many positives and negatives of getting older is that there are more people to thank, and even more people that one should thank, but are limited by reasons of space. The first people inevitably are my mother and father, who were both leaders in their own way, my father having a combat command in one of the most difficult sectors of the Second World War and acquitting himself admirably, and my mother as the first European woman to venture into areas of the Indian subcontinent previously unexplored.

In the book, I write, amongst other things, about 'servant leadership' as a concept, and I have gained insight into this through my time as a student and then co-worker at the Benedictine Abbey of Worth in Sussex. I am particularly indebted to Fathers Dominic, Bernard, Stephen, Christopher and Luke, but the whole of the community in effect. I saw combat service in the army and was privileged to serve with many fine individuals of all ranks, mentioning especially Lieutenant General Sir John Wilsey, a fellow Jerseyman, Lieutenant General Sir Cedric Delves, and Major-General Bryan Dutton, now Director-General of the Leonard Cheshire Foundation.

When I came into social services, I was very fortunate to work for one of the noriginal children's officers, Bridget Ogden, in an office full of highly committed and development-orientated people such as the late Jean Carruthers, Ian Gates and Bob Phipps. I worked for a number of social services directors coming from a professional background: Helen Seed, Peter Smallridge, Christine Walby and Robert Lake; and others who came from different spheres of activity: Roger Mortimore, Trevor Knowles and Norman, now Lord Warner; and I learnt different aspects of leadership from all of them.

I have been fortunate, since leaving local government, to work for some outstanding leaders in some of the new agencies that have sprung up to develop services in the 21st century. It has been a pleasure working for Professor Antony Sheehan, Paddy Cooney, Jan Wallcraft and Malcolm Rae and others from NIMHE; Jane Campbell, Bill Kilgallon, Amanda Edwards and colleagues from SCIE; Richard Humphries, CSIP and my partner in the Social Care Fellowship, Professor Nick Gould of Bath University, Christina Pond, NHS Leadership Centre, Dame Denise Platt, David Behan, Judith Thomas and Gerald O'Hagan from CSCI.

It has been a privilege to work with Staffordshire University, Vice-Chancellor Professor Christine King, Dr Teeranlall Ramgopal, Professor Paul Kingston, Bernard Moss and colleagues. I am also indebted to a number of others: Jennifer Bernard and Joan Maughan, and colleagues from the National Development Team; Jo Williams, Chief Executive of Mencap; Dr Linda Holbeche and Chris Lake from Roffey Park Institute; Members of the National Learning Set for Directors of Social Care: Hari Sewell, Mary Clifton, Philip Douglas, Hazel Murphy, James Sinclair, Kate Dawson, Neil Perkins; many other colleagues including Leroy Lewis, Colin Williams, Jo Gray, Dr Karen Linde, Bill Robinson, Andy Nash, Albert Persaud; Ian Dyer, Karen Wood, Julian Clyde-Smith and colleagues from Jersey; Professors Steve Onyett, Terry Scragg and Adam Fairclough; Dr Ray Jones and Ian Wilson; Dr Andrew McCulloch, Vicky Nicholls, Mary Ellen Coyte and colleagues from the Mental Health Foundation, Professor Sheila Hollins, Dr Mike Shooter and Professor Bill Fulford from the Royal

College of Psychiatrists. Also the reverend Dr Peter Sedgwick, Principal of St Michael's College; and Profesor John Adair for his lifelong inspiration on the essentials of leadership.

My thanks also to members of my running club, Worcester Joggers, for keeping me sane(!), or reasonably sane, especially Mike Sell, Vicki Hasler, Nigel Stinton, and Richard and Min Sowden.

I would also like to thank those pathological leaders I have worked for, who taught me what kind of leader I do not wish to be!

This book would not have been written without the dedicated typing and collating of Maggie Holloway and Carole Smallwood.

Lastly, I would like to thank my long-suffering wife Sue, and my daughters for putting up with me spreading books, articles, papers and case examples all over the house, and I hope to fulfil my promise to clear the dining room table at some stage in the future when 'the five tests' have been met, and presuming that the promise was really a promise and not an aspiration!

Peter Gilbert
5 January 2005

PART ONE

Leadership: What is it?

Think about the leaders you've been impressed with over the course of your working life. Almost without exception they will be people with high self-esteem, whose actions are congruent with their espoused views, who understand their own beliefs and values and who have a strong sense of their own direction. To be truly effective as a leader, you've got to be comfortable with who you are and what you are about. Essentially, concentrating on leading yourself is a powerful way to grow your ability to lead others.

(Chris Lake, Former Programme Director,
Roffey Park Management Institute.)

CHAPTER 1

Leadership: Description and Purpose

More than anyone, leaders should welcome being held accountable. Nothing builds confidence in a leader more than a willingness to take responsibility for what happens during his [sic] watch.

(Rudy Giuliani, 2002)

It is not good enough just to preach the doctrines; you have to live the life.

(Victoria Woodhull, 1872, US Presidential Candidate)

I was brought up to believe I could do anything.

(Tanni Grey-Thompson, 2004)

Leadership is a priceless gift which you have to earn from the people who work with you and you have constantly to earn that right.

(Sir John Harvey-Jones, 1988 former Chair of ICI and BBC's *Troubleshooter*)

He has all the intangibles of what it takes to produce team work in Ryder Cup matches.

(Hal Sutton, 2004, US Team Captain, on Bernhard Langer, winning European Ryder Cup Team Captain)

I am still searching myself, I don't have all the answers and I certainly have no pretence to omniscience.

(Martin Luther King, quoted in Fairclough, 1995: 139)

Introduction

In Britain we have a tendency to overuse words which have a profound meaning, so too often devaluing them. What happened to the word 'community'?! The same could easily happen to 'leadership', as every time there is a report in the realm of politics, business, sport, public services, questions are always posed about leadership. No sooner has a business or sports leader, or a health and social care executive, been appointed, and seen as a leader to take the business/service/sports team forward, than issues are raised about their leadership ability.

At the time of writing this book, there are questions in the run-up to the US Presidential elections of November 2004, as to whether George W. Bush or John Kerry has the leadership history and requisite qualities to be President of the most powerful nation on earth; Brian Clough, the football manager, has his reputation raked over in the obituaries; and Stuart Rose, the new Chief Executive of Marks and Spencer, that icon of high street retailing, is facing more poor turnover figures.

In any national or international report, questions of leadership are likely to be at the fore, for instance, the recent report by the Cabinet Office Performance and Innovation Unit

(PIU), *Strengthening Leadership in the Public Sector*, puts leadership at the heart of the modernisation agenda, thus:

> *Britain's public services face unprecedented challenges at the start of the 21st century. They include: demands to modernise public services, and orient them more closely to the needs and wishes of customers; higher expectations on the part of the general public, who expect public services to keep up with private ones; increasing opportunities, and requirements, for partnerships both across the public sector and with private and voluntary organisations.*

(Cabinet Office, PIU, 2001, quoted in Alimo-Metcalfe and Alban-Metcalfe, 2004: 173)

It has become something of a truism, but is nevertheless true, that the political, social and economic environment has become increasingly difficult over the last few decades. The general pace of change; technological innovations; the demands of citizens, and those of government to satisfy citizens; the dictats of globalisation; multi-culturalism and trans-culturalism (see Chapter 2) all create an environment which is more and more complex to manage.

As Lawrence and Elliott comment in one of the foundation management texts:

The anarchic context of much management activity underlines the need for leadership, because it is the essence of the leader that such a person has objectives, has an idea of desired states of affairs that may be both planned and striven for.

(Lawrence and Elliott, 1988: 16)

It certainly seems that in a complex environment, 'leadership' is a necessary and helpful entity. But what is it? And do we have the right conception of it? There are indeed quite a number of common misunderstandings about leadership:

- That 'leadership' and 'management' are the same.
- 'Leadership' is so superior to 'management' that once you have the former you do not need the latter.
- 'Leadership' is tied to specific roles, rather than being a quality required at all levels and in all groups: e.g. users, carers, professionals and all staff.
- Leaders have to be a charismatic hybrid of Alexander the Great, Queen Elizabeth I, General Norman Schwartzkopf and Florence Nightingale!

Exercise 1: Images of leadership

Please spend some time to allow yourself to think of the images that the word and concept of leadership conjures up in your mind.

If possible, try not to think of word-based definitions. See if you can tune into emotions, colours, images, music, pictures, memories, sensory experiences, which the word 'leadership' brings into your mind. We are a very 'wordy' culture, in general, and it is sometimes useful to remove ourselves from the complexities of the written word, and think more laterally.

Sometimes it is helpful to get away from words entirely, and think in images, sounds, memories, experiences (see Exercise 1).

The etymology of leadership

It can also be helpful to go back to etymology, to the original roots of words. 'Leadership' is derived from the Old English *laedan*. The Oxford English Dictionary defines 'lead' as: 'to show the way to (an individual or a group) by going with or ahead; to guide, control and direct; to direct the course of; to give an example for others to follow'. This definition points the way to something very visceral in our history as human beings, and a perception which is very necessary in today's world. The Anglo-Saxon *laed* means a path or road, related to the verb *lithan*, to travel or to proceed. The Anglo-Saxons who gave us our only King with the appellation 'Great', Alfred, with his emphasis on both protecting his people in times of crisis (battles to protect his people, not foreign adventures) and looking forward to the education and enlightenment of his people, where people used to travel by land and sea. So their concepts of leader would be around: pathfinder, helmsperson, navigator, steersperson, explorer, educator.

'Management' comes from two words: the Latin noun *manus* – hand, and its derivative, the Italian verb *maneggiare* – to handle or train. It epitomises control, but also a 'hands-on' coaching to increase skills, to produce from something or someone with raw talent a controlled source of power and skill. Although this has many positive connotations it has a more static ethos than leadership.

John Adair (2002) in his recent book, *Inspiring Leadership*, points out that neither the metaphorical basis nor the word itself are unique to the English language. Adair states that the metaphor of a journey can be found in the Mashona language in Zimbabwe, as well as in Persian and Egyptian. The Ancient Greek word for a leader, *hegemon* (whose derivative, *hegemony*, is seen in modern usage as a concept of attempting to control and dominate), probably rested on the same image of a road or journey. Adair makes a similar claim for the Roman word for leader, *dux*, from which we derive *education* – leaders being educators as well as direction-finders. The Latin word for governor, *gubernator*, literally meant the helmsperson of a ship. In Hindi, the word *rajah* also derives from the word for helmsman.

Adair goes on to point out that some of the 'etymological cousins' to the root word laed also bear our consideration. Leaders are expected to shoulder the burden, or *load*, of a role which carries responsibility. The word 'lode-stone', literally weigh-stone, was so named because the magnetic oxide of iron acted as a magnet in guiding mariners, just as the Lode-Star (or North Star) was so called because it led them. *Lodeman* was in fact an Old English word, now completely extinct, for leader (Adair, 2002: 61).

Adair goes on to consider some of the other Northern European nations which also have versions of the 'leader' word in their language; but it is not present in all languages. The French, for example, look not towards the horizontal imagery of moving forward along a path, or steering a ship, but rather more to the vertical, related with words to do with the head – body size and intellect. Leadership has a much more democratic value of walking with, and this notion of leadership as a way of doing things together, rather than being a loner or going in circles within one's own intellect, is reinforced by the old Latin roots of *con*, and *com*.

All the *con* words give the meaning *with*, e.g. the two meanings of conduct: to lead someone while walking with them, and proper behaviour. It is literally leading *with*.

There are so many *com* words: community, camaraderie, compassion, communication, command, commission, commitment, which again give us a concept of working as a team rather than as a set of individuals however talented they may be.

So where does our study of the words lead us?

In short, leadership throughout the centuries seems to be about a small, but essential, number of aspects:

- **Integrity, authenticity and trust.** Unless people feel that the person leading them is someone who is trustworthy and whom they can trust; is trusting of them to do their bit, and not only says the right things but acts them out as well (in the jargon: 'walks the talk', not just 'talks the talk'), then **why** should anyone follow them?
- **Values.** Related to the above, the leader needs to have an explicit value base which links with their personal integrity. Would you wish to work for a manager in human services who believed that people with disabilities were essentially inferior? Or for a retailer who thought that selling suits and skirts which fell to pieces after a couple of hours was an ethical way of doing their business?
  Of course, values can be problematic as well. The horrendous consequences of the warped value-base of Hitler and the Nazi party are referred to in Gilbert and Scragg's *Managing to Care* (1992, Chapter 1).
- **Providing direction.** Sometimes referred to as 'vision', which can sound rather ephemeral –

or as one psychiatrist said to me, 'as a psychiatrist, I always get worried when managers start talking about visions'! But essentially, this is giving people a picture of a desired future state, which needs to be better in some ways than the current situation, or necessary to avoid the current situation deteriorating.

- **Inspiration and empowerment.** The ability to engage people's hearts and minds so that they move along a path to achieve that desired future. Empowerment is important because, as we will see in future chapters, the current situation requires individuals and groups within the organisation to fulfil aspects of the mission, without constantly referring back to the overall leader. We have all known managers who have micro-managed. In terms of global strategy, one of the reasons for Alexander the Great's success (see Bose, 2003 and Keegan, 1987) was that, despite a very charismatic leadership style, he was excellent at handing independent commands to competent generals. Adolf Hitler, on the other hand, had the majority of the outstanding generals in the Second World War, but negated their effect by attempting to micro-manage whole areas of operations.
- **Delivery.** Ultimately, leaders must deliver what they set out to do, or to redefine the objectives in the light of experience. Ernest Shackleton, the explorer, whom many people cite as a leader they admire (Morrell and Capparell, 2001) never reached the South Pole, but redefined his objectives when his ship became trapped in the ice, so that saving the entirety of his crew and bringing them safely home became his vision and mission.

One obvious historical figure to encapsulate all these essentials is Alfred the Great. Taking over as King of Wessex at a time when Danish invasions threatened to overrun the whole of England and thus destabilise and destroy a nascent civilisation which was rising out of the ashes of Romano-British (Celtic) culture, Alfred's first and essential mission was to halt and if possible throw back the invaders. This he did, but not before coming within an ace of defeat, and having to hide in a remote area of Wessex. The well-known story of Alfred burning the cakes, is clearly an illustration of his essential humanity. Despite being very nearly completely defeated, Alfred still retained the trust of his people because of his integrity and

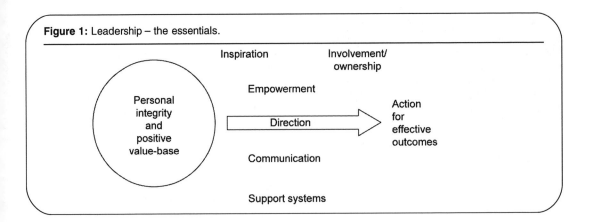

Figure 1: Leadership – the essentials.

abilities. He was able to inspire his people; throw back the invasion; offer the invaders an alternative cultural tradition which they took on board; and then set about enunciating and creating a different vision, which was to educate his people. It is said that Alfred himself translated some of the ancient Latin texts into Anglo-Saxon, and he brought in educators to lay the foundations for a new civilization. (See Brooke, 1971, Chapters 2 and 7; see also David Starkey's Channel 4 Series on *Monarchy*, 2004.)

Historical, or even recent examples of leaders from the public sphere can be highly inspirational. The danger is that we think that it is only these people who are leaders. **This is not so.** We can **all** be leaders in our own way, at work and in different spheres of our daily lives, and we see examples of leadership every day of our lives. We only need to open our local paper to see people acting heroically to save a child who has fallen into a river; running a marathon to raise money for charity, after recovering from cancer; managing a shop for Mencap, Help the Aged, Mind, etc; coming back from being 'on the ropes' after illness, injury or oppression, saving an historic building – and so on. In the domestic sphere, parents of children, young carers looking after their disabled parents, those who care for sick relatives, or take in adoptive or foster children, are all displaying qualities of leadership. Perhaps the greatest exemplar of leadership is the parent who gives a child/children a vision of the future that can be theirs, who educates and inspires, nurtures and protects, empowers them to take risks and responsibility, sets attainable goals within the overall vision for life, transmits values and a sense of value and valuing, and integrates the inevitable failures and successes. This is leadership.

The person so ambitious for advancement that they forget their own children's birthday, is not a leader!

> *Exercise 2: Leaders I have known*
>
> Please spend some time thinking about leaders at any level that you have known and worked with in your career, and what qualities and behaviours made them leaders to follow.

Exercise 2 is one well worth doing with other people. In leadership training I have been doing with a number of authorities, I found it (and Exercise 3) an excellent way of getting into practical examples of what leadership is about. In one recent training programme, some of the following examples and points were made:

- Emily Pankhurst, the suffragette leader, was mentioned as an example, because in the words of the participant, 'she made a difference. She had the courage of her convictions and was prepared to go to jail. She had charisma, but was perhaps seen as a bit fanatical which may have alienated some people who would have been temperamentally inclined to support her. She targeted change-agents within society to change opinion, and used events to assist that change process.'
- A new manager had come in to take charge of a residential home for older people. They had had to be both authoritative and supportive because the existing staff felt very uneasy with her challenge to the way things had been done for so many years, because although they had not been happy with the autocratic

---

CASE STUDY 1: THE AREA SOCIAL WORK OFFICE

I was very fortunate to start my career in social work in an office where there were a number of people I consider leaders. Bridget Ogden (see also Gilbert, 2004b) had been a Wren during the Second World War, and was in the chart room during the D-Day landings. She had trained as one of the first wave of childcare officers under the 1948 Children Act, following the Curtis Committee's Report. Bridget was an exemplar of the highest professional standards. She was utterly dedicated to providing and promoting an exceptional social work service across all client groups within her district in West Sussex. She would educate, support, nurture and encourage, but she expected the best, and if you fell below those standards, it only needed a raised eyebrow from Bridget to make you vow never to slip again!

Bridget's reputation was not simply internal: she was respected throughout the wider department, and by all the other relevant agencies. I remember visiting a Crown Court Judge in chambers. I was a bit early so I expected to wait outside. Instead, he waved me in with the remark, 'Ah, you're one of Bridget's boys. I'm happy for you to sit in while I finish off what I'm doing'. He proceeded to send packing two solicitors who had brought in a proposed divorce settlement which spoke a lot about property and nothing about the children, and turned to me with a smile to say, 'Bridget would approve of my doing that!'

Bridget was not the only leader within the office. My team manager, Jean, was an example for me throughout my career of how to deliver professional supervision (see Figure 20), and combine goals with education and support. She was constantly trying to improve our practice and our minds. To the cry, 'we are feeling very stretched', her response was, 'not stretched enough!' Not happy with our simply undertaking casework, she expected every social worker in her team to fulfil a community role, e.g. liaison with the special school, GP surgery, etc. I took on the role of working with a special school for children with learning disabilities, and in many ways that push from Jean shaped my career.

Bob and Ian were senior practitioners who provided leadership at the frontline. It was to them that we went with queries when we did not want to bother Jean or Bridget. They were experienced, thoughtful, well-read, and happy to impart knowledge in an accessible way. You knew that their value-base was sound and consistent. They were available and they never let you down.

So in this office, there was leadership at all levels, and there was also a helpful gender balance. Unfortunately, some commentators today give an impression that men who are in leadership roles or lead, will only do so in a way which smacks of machismo; whereas women are invariably intuitive, nurturing, educative and empowering. This is a difficult myth to challenge but it is a myth, and we know that from our own experience. This area office had very high morale and delivered a very high quality of service. A neighbouring office also had an experienced woman manager as area director, but with a very different style, which was cold, distant, detached and disempowering. Bridget also had detachment (see Parikh, 1991) – she was never a 'pal', it was quite clear who was boss, but she wished to make sure that the people she had appointed to her team had the support necessary to do the job to the best of their ability. Good work was noticed and explicitly acknowledged. She was not the uninvolved short-term performance manager whose response to good work is simply to demand a ratcheting up of performance!

---

approach, in many ways, it did make them feel 'safe', and for a time they were reluctant to move to a new way of doing things.

- Martin Luther King was another example, and the group member described King as, 'charismatic, passionate, committed and a

motivator. He had a vision with forward thinking, and challenged people to do new things. His inner strength and bravery assisted people to own and share a common vision', (see Historical Leadership Example 3).

As we have seen, leadership is not necessarily a function of a particular managerial role. You can be appointed to manage a position and a team, but that does not necessarily make you a leader as such.

A leader can be defined as the 'person who is appointed, elected, or informally chosen to direct and co-ordinate the work of others in a group' (Feidler, 1967: 43).

Penny Humphries, Director of the NHS Leadership Centre, defines leadership as: 'working through others to achieve a vision' (Speech to NHS Confederation, 2004).

Leadership is defined as the process of moving a group (or groups) in some direction through mostly non-coercive means. Effective leadership is defined as 'leadership that produces movement in the long-term best interest of the group(s)' (Kotter, 1988: 32).

We will look shortly at why leadership is required in today's world (reports in the private and public spheres, and the writings of the students of organisational efficacy have no doubt that leadership is required). John Adair, who has written consistently on leadership since the 1960s, has no doubts:

> The importance of good leadership today hardly needs to be stressed, for it is widely recognised that a democratic society cannot work effectively without it. Leaders are needed in all fields and at all levels to give direction, create team work and inspire people to give of their best.
>
> (Adair, 2002: 1)

If this is so, then:

What do organisations want from their leaders?

Setting (or maintaining) a vision for a desired future

For industry, commerce and private practice, this might well be seizing or maintaining competitive advantage (see Porter, 1985).

For the public sector, it would be achieving or maintaining excellence in relation to a set framework, for example national standards, star rating systems.

Marks and Spencer and Sainsburys are perhaps some of the best examples of retailers who have lost competitive advantage to such an extent that they are struggling to re-assert their competitiveness against Tesco, Asda etc. even though they have prime retailing sites.

Since the late 1990s there has been a lot of talk about 'a primary care led NHS' but to achieve that, Primary Care Teams have to be effective in their clinical practice, their commissioning and their partnership working, both in building an effective Primary Care Team and making the appropriate links with other agencies.

Creating (and maintaining) partnerships

In the private sector, this is often work towards vertical integration through procuring consistent quality in goods and services.

In the public sector, with the changing nature of structures, for example Children's Trusts, Mental Health Partnership Trusts, Connexions, Sure Start, Primary Care Teams, etc. (see Harrison et al., 2003) this means effective working within and across new boundaries.

As has been pointed out consistently by organisational development experts such as Professor Edward Peck and Bob Hudson (see Glasby and Peck, 2004) successful partnership approaches are primarily based on **relationships** not just **structures**.

The example I gave of case partnership in *The Value of Everything*, in working with Mrs S. and her daughter, where both mental health and child protection were an issue (see Gilbert, 2003b: 37–8) demonstrated that effective partnership can take place without formal integration of structures.

Performance and delivery

Organisations will expect leaders to provide the highest possible level of performance and delivery. The greater the investment by shareholders, financial backers, government, local councillors and citizens, the greater the expectations.

In the case of sport, for example, the papers will often state that Mr X, football manager of Melcaster Rovers, has spent X million pounds on Y number of home grown and foreign players yet the Rovers are still languishing in the bottom half of the premiership. One can almost see a mathematical formula which balances money spent, the reputation of the manager, the expectations of the shareholders, board and supporters, the expected recovery process; past versus future glories in a graph which inevitably leads to the parting of the ways for the manager.

At an operational as well as at a strategic level, managers must innovate so that they do

CASE STUDY 2: THE NORTH SUSSEX COMMUNITY LEARNING DISABILITY TEAM

The team, the first of its kind in West Sussex, was set up in 1981 in unpromising circumstances. The Forest Hospital, where the team was generated was a converted workhouse, the frontage of which had been built in 1815, just after the Battle of Waterloo, and the organisational culture seemed to be from that era as well!

The Management Board was riven with disputes over the basic direction and value-base of care, and the senior nurse conducted his 'supervision' sessions by shouting at his staff at the top of his voice!

I came into post as Principal Social Worker. At the same time as I was appointed, Barry Spooner, an experienced Learning Disability and Mental Health qualified nurse was appointed to set up a community nursing team, something which the hospital management were reluctant to do, but had been pressured into by the Health Authority. The Board, however, were quite determined not to have a multi-disciplinary team which would open it up to all kinds of subversive professions such as psychology, social work etc. Little did they realise, however, that they had a Trojan horse within the nursing profession in Barry, who immediately he got his contract, announced that he was setting up, in conjunction with colleagues, a multi-disciplinary community team which would be a first for the county.

The first thing to say about Barry was that he showed enormous courage in defying his organisational masters. The second challenge was how to prevent the whole idea being subverted by powerful interest groups. Barry's idea was to invite the senior consultant, who had been vehemently opposed to such an innovation, to be Chair of the team, and therefore both assist the medical interface with other specialists and general practice, and at the same time neutralise hostility.

In the longer term, there were at least two major cultural obstacles to overcome. The first was within the hospital, though this was much easier than anticipated. The vast majority of the nursing staff wanted to see a revolution in care and attitudinal values, and bearing in mind that all the new nursing staff on the team had spent many years in hospital ward settings, their conversion into effective community practitioners was astounding. When I see the way some community mental health teams appear to struggle with these issues more than 20 years on, I am even more impressed with the practitioners within that Sussex team. One major way into the organisational culture was the teaching input that community workers gave to the nursing school, and the subsequent placements, which meant that every new member of staff coming from the training school had been positively influenced by the community team and the community setting.

The second cultural obstacle was making links between a hospital that had a very poor reputation, and a variety of communities and community groups. As somebody who had worked in the area for seven years before moving into the Principal's role, I took the lead on this and Barry and I worked in partnership to meet with user and carer groups, local Mencap societies, GP practices etc.

More detailed information on the team is contained in Gilbert and Spooner (1982) and Gilbert (1983 and 1985), but the experience of the Community Learning Disability Team in North Sussex demonstrated that even the most entrenched attitudes could be challenged, and if not completely changed, then at least got round by opening up other methods and channels. Cultural change is extremely complex, as we see in Chapter 6, but it can be done!

---

not stagnate. Recent work on the management of multi-disciplinary teams in integrated Health and Social Care organisations (see Scragg, 2001) shows that too often managers are engaging in routine tasks rather than moving the service forward. Chris Payne, one of the most incisive thinkers on residential care, wrote as long ago as 1988:

It is a sad fact that there are many residential managers who interpret their role either in terms

---

Historical Leadership Example 1: Eleanor Rathbone

Many people in social care and related settings will probably be familiar with the work of the Rathbone Society. But Eleanor Rathbone herself was an unsung hero of the 1930s and the Second World War. Like Winston Churchill, she was an early identifier of Hitler's tyrannical designs on the rest of Europe. When Neville Chamberlain, then Prime Minister, returned from Munich on the 30 September 1938, brandishing his piece of paper with Hitler's name on it, Rathbone (1872 to 1946) denounced it as not 'peace with honour' but one of a series of betrayals of vulnerable countries by the British Government.

Born in 1872 into a prosperous Liverpool family with a Unitarian faith, she gained her values in social responsibility from her father who was a Liverpool MP, dedicated to researching and alleviating the poverty in the city. After university, she threw herself into a number of feminist organisations and those to assist the dispossessed, and in 1929 she was elected an MP – one of only 14 women in parliament. With an astounding breadth of vision, Eleanor Rathbone campaigned on behalf of more equality and justice in England but also abroad, championing causes of women's rights in India and Africa, and raising awareness to a level which had not been seen before.

From 1933, when the Nazi regime came to power in Germany, Rathbone turned her attention to that phenomenon, which she described as, 'it was difficult to get the stench out of one's nostrils, the sights of horror out of one's mind' (quoted in Pedersen, 2004: 43). Much of Rathbone's energies were poured into helping refugees, and she still had the energy and vision to influence ministers, who respected her, despite the hard time she gave them, to pass a comprehensive Family Allowances Act at the end of the war.

A driven and visionary woman who it was said was difficult to get close to because all her energies were poured into those she served, she wrote in a pamphlet in January 1938, a comment on leadership still most pertinent today: 'there is little hope for freedom, justice and peace unless there can be roused in the peoples of the surviving democracies as vigorous a faith and a self-sacrificing devotion to these great ends as the Dictators have succeeded in mobilising for their false ends' (See Pederson, 2004: 45).

---

of 'doing' all the things for which their staff are paid to do, or who become administrators pure and simple. Instead of which, they should be building on their knowledge and understanding of practice to take a more rounded and prospective view of the services being offered; to initiate sensitive programmes of, for example, staff recruitment and selection, development, supervision, training and stress management; to create a sound 'foreign policy' for their establishment; and most importantly to offer skilled professional leadership to staff.
(Payne, 1988, quoted in Gilbert, 2003b: 90)

Building and enhancing reputation

It has been said that reputations take years to make and seconds to destroy. Depending on the nature and size of the organisation, a reputation needs to be built up on a global, national or local basis. We all know that our local hospital, for example, or the neighbourhood school has a very clear reputation.

- When I moved to one job in the West Midlands, a colleague of mine in the Health Service said to me: 'Peter, I valued your expertise this morning and I'm going to give you some advice in return. If you're involved in a crash on the motorway, your first words, should you have breath enough, are 'take me to hospital X'. Your next breath should be a very emphatic 'do **not** take me to hospital Y''. That is a broad local reputation.

- Listening to a group of parents you will often hear the words: 'school z is absolutely hopeless; the teachers are dispirited, there are high truancy rates; fights in the playground etc.' But another parent may respond: 'your information is out of date. Mrs J, the new Head who arrived eighteen months ago, has

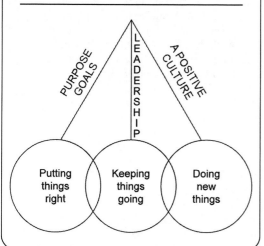

Figure 2: Leading to, and managing, positive change.

turned the place around. Academic results are going up, the kids are happier, there's less bullying etc.' Unfortunately for Mrs J., she is still working with a local reputation which says do not go to school z, because 'everybody knows' that it's no good.

- Clothing retailers may be known for the quality of their products; but gain a reputation for, e.g., unimaginative women's clothing, and even if you bring in new buyers and product ranges, shoppers have already gone elsewhere. Tesco is now recognised as the leading food supermarket retailer. But it took about two years between the improvements in its product range and in the attitude of its staff before swathes of shoppers who habitually went to other retailers moved to Tesco. Morrisons, who recently bought Safeway, are, according to business analysts, having more difficulty than anticipated in turning the ailing retailer round.

Recruiting, retaining, educating and inspiring people

However technological the world becomes, there are always going to be people in key positions; and of course, in the human services, we are talking about delivering services to people through people, where the recruitment and retention of the right people is absolutely crucial. As new forms of public service are introduced in education, health and social care; and the preparedness of government, of

whatever hue, radically to change the configuration of services, public services need to look at the lessons – both good and bad – from the private sector. We all shop, buy insurance, use public services ourselves. What annoys us is likely to annoy the people we serve. If you are tired of ringing your insurance company and hearing 'press button 57 if you want to readjust your policy', then no doubt those who use your service will be similarly irritated if they get such a response from your switchboard!

The quality of our people at all levels indicates the quality of service to the user/customer.

What do people want from their leaders?

In the light of the increasing mobility of scarce labour resources, all of us have to ask the question why would anybody be led by us?! The theory of leadership will be dealt with later on in Part 1, but essentially leadership studies now tend to be focused on:

- Leaders in successful organisations (e.g. Collins and Porras, 2000 and Collins, 2001).
- What people have to say about their leaders (e.g. Alimo-Metcalfe, 2003, Kouzes and Posner, 1990).

James Kouzes and Barry Posner talk about leadership 'credibility', and state that 'Leadership is in the eye of the follower', or as somebody else put it, 'Frontline staff are the consumers of management'.

Kouzes and Posner identify a number of attributes in a leader which make other people wish to work with and for them:

- **Integrity** – people want to work with someone they believe is honest and truthful, and has character and conviction. We do not want to serve someone who is only fuelling their own career. As an ex-army officer, who saw combat, I have a very simple view on this: i.e. when the chips are down, and the shots ring out, do you and your colleagues cover your own backs or protect those of your comrades?!

  John Storey's recent book on Leadership in Organisations, looking at current issues and key trends, contains a whole chapter on 'leadership and integrity', homing in on the Enron scandal. (Storey, 2004: 41–57).

Often what we want to see from our leaders can be gleaned from the historical and/or public

---

CASE STUDY 3: THE ABDICATION, NOT DELEGATION OF POWER – UK ATHLETICS

Much management writing today is to do with the effective delegation of power. As we shall see as we go through this book, authority in large organisations cannot possibly be held by one or a small group of people, there needs to be shared and dispersed leadership throughout the organisation. Unfortunately, people often confuse delegation with abdication!

A good example of this is athletics within the United Kingdom where decision-making has been devolved down to bodies which may be inclined to make decisions in line with vested interests rather than the future of the sport, and little or no authority is retained at the centre to challenge and overturn such decisions and create more rational decision-making.

One minor leadership role which I have very much appreciated over the last few years was being Chair of my local, non-affiliated running club, Worcester Joggers. The Joggers have been in existence since 1984 (see Gilbert, 2005), and have provided a social environment for encouraging physical fitness to a group which has a good gender, age and ethnic make-up.

Unfortunately, when the Joggers applied to become affiliated to UK Athletics, the Regional Association refused for the strange reason that there was an athletics club (a very different animal than a jogging club) in the city, also called Worcester. When it was pointed out that not only are there two football clubs in Manchester, both with the appellation Manchester, and these are not often confused (!), but that there are plenty of running clubs from the same city within the environs of the same Midlands Authority, both bearing the name of the relevant town or city, the application was still rejected.

Enquiry elicited the strange admission that the regional committees were in effect 'the prisoner of the existing clubs'. All efforts to appeal to higher authorities were met by the response that all powers are vested in the regional associations, which are apparently geared towards serving existing clubs rather than welcoming new ones.

At a time when government ministers are stating clearly that a rising tide of obesity is threatening to swamp the health service of the future with cases of heart disease, diabetes and problems with body structure, the major athletics organisations within the UK are apparently geared more towards preserving the status quo than serving the health of the nation.

When carried forward on a wave of enthusiasm for delegating, ask yourself whether you are delegating powers to others or abdicating powers from yourself? Also, whether you have appropriately devolved responsibility and resources or just created additional burdens for those below you!

---

figures we mention when we are talking about the subject. Do you instinctively think of founders of professions or social movements like Florence Nightingale for nursing, Octavia Hill for social housing, Elizabeth Fry for prison reform? Political leaders such as Winston Churchill, Nelson Mandela, Mikhail Gorbachev? Religious leaders such as the Dalai Lama, Mother Teresa of Calcutta, Rabbi Jonathon Sacks? Military strategists such as 'Bill' Slim, the Duke of Wellington, Napoleon, Boadicea, Joan of Arc, etc.

Fiona Wilson, one of the most accessible writers on gender and leadership (Wilson, 2003: 136) points out that, 'very little research has looked at the relationship between masculinity or femininity and leadership'. Women may often find themselves, as Wilson points out (142) 'in a cultural trap. There is a lack of appropriate female role models and so the male role model prevails in which women are at a cultural disadvantage appearing either as failing to conform or as unfeminine'. Recent research by Ryan and Haslam (2005) indicates that women not only confront a 'glass ceiling' while their male colleagues benefit from a 'glass escalator', but, increasingly, women are gaining leadership roles in precarious positions – the 'glass cliff', where, if they fail, they can be singled out for blame. As an individual, leaders need to consider role models which can guide them, and in organisational terms, they need to encourage

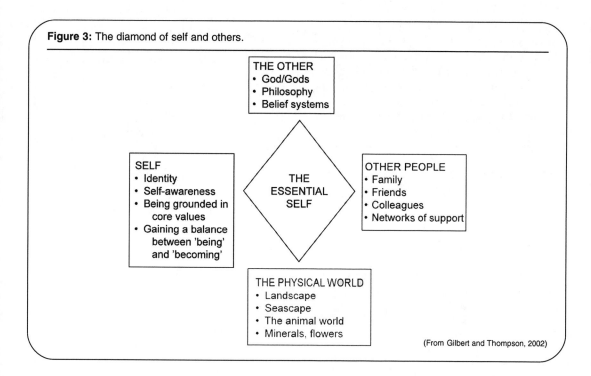

Figure 3: The diamond of self and others.

THE OTHER
• God/Gods
• Philosophy
• Belief systems

SELF
• Identity
• Self-awareness
• Being grounded in
  core values
• Gaining a balance
  between 'being'
  and 'becoming'

THE
ESSENTIAL
SELF

OTHER PEOPLE
• Family
• Friends
• Colleagues
• Networks of support

THE PHYSICAL WORLD
• Landscape
• Seascape
• The animal world
• Minerals, flowers

(From Gilbert and Thompson, 2002)

appropriate role models as Jo Williams has striven to do in her tenures as a Director of Social Services and Chief Executive of Mencap (see Leadership Example 2, Chapter 2).

It may be helpful to look at Exercise 3 and see which historical/public figures you would pick as leadership examples. Kouzes and Posner (1990: 11) write that:

If a leader behaves in ways consistent with his or her stated values and beliefs, then we believe we can entrust to that person our careers, our security, even our lives.

In the round the world yacht race, written up in *Inspiring Leadership: Staying Afloat in Turbulent Times* (Cranwell-Ward et al., 2002) the issue about who you would wish to sail with is placed in stark contrast.

Tom Peters (1989: 518) puts it in a similar way when he writes:

Trust and credibility comes through everyone's observation of the manager's symbolic integrity, not his or her 'policy document'.

In all of this, leaders need to know who they are, so that those they lead know who they are and what they stand for. The diagrammatic representation in Figure 3 encourages us to think through issues of our own essential integrity: who we are, what we stand for, what

are our beliefs and values (see Chapter 3), and how we stand in terms of relation to those we work with, e.g. are we just exploiting them for our own ends?

• **Competence** – this may mean technical competence in certain leadership roles, but, in more senior positions within an organisation, it will be about a general competence and ensuring that the organisation as a whole is competent and that one part of it is not driving the other e.g. sales, H.R., finance.
• **The ability to create a vision** – as we saw in the discussion about where leadership comes from as a concept, leaders must know where they are going and to what horizon they are pathfinding people.

Of course, there are often creations of warped visions and false dawns. The vision of Adolf Hitler and his extraordinary ability to create the symbolism which promoted it (see Burleigh, 2000) is the obvious example of pathological leadership. In the business world, Marconi's switch into majoring on telecommunications led to their marked decline during 2001. On the other hand, in a world of change, to do nothing can be disastrous, with the added problem of complacency, and a lack of awareness when danger surfaces.

The modern manager needs to have the capacity for 'helicopter vision', to get above the ground level and scan the wider horizon, **but** must also be aware of the need to 'land' and communicate the vision to those still 'on the ground'!

- **Inspiration** – both to keep going when things get tough or remain a daily grind, or to cope with the seismic shift required at times of radical change, the leader must create a climate of inspiration (as well as perspiration) and generate excitement and passion.

To go back to the original question at the beginning of this chapter: if the leader is not expressing a passion for the project, why should anybody else?!

Kouzes and Posner add five fundamental actions which people said built the credibility of those they wanted to lead them:

- Know your constituents.
- Stand up for your beliefs.
- Speak with passion.
- Lead by example.
- Conquer yourself.

They quote the Himalayan climber, Jim Whitaker, as saying 'You never conquer a mountain. Mountains can't be conquered, you conquer yourself, your hopes, your fears'.

You may well be aware of John Adair's classic three circle model of Mission, Team and Individual interlinked (see Adair, 1983). This model is still a most helpful aide-mémoire to all leaders. But modern leadership needs to go further now, in that people desire to understand their working life within a broader framework of meaning. The classic story told of President John F. Kennedy holds true. When Kennedy visited the NASA Base during his presidency, he asked a janitor what he did. The janitor did not say 'I'm sweeping the floor', though he had a broom in hand, but he told the President, 'I'm helping to get men into space'!

We therefore need an additional three interlocking circles to give the why as well as the what:

The Rule of St. Benedict (6th century) which has created and sustained communities across the centuries, is very strong on the personal quality of humility. Benedict is clear that the leader must always remember who they are, what role of stewardship they hold and who they represent (Benedict, edition 1982,

Figure 4: Developing the concept of action-centred leadership.

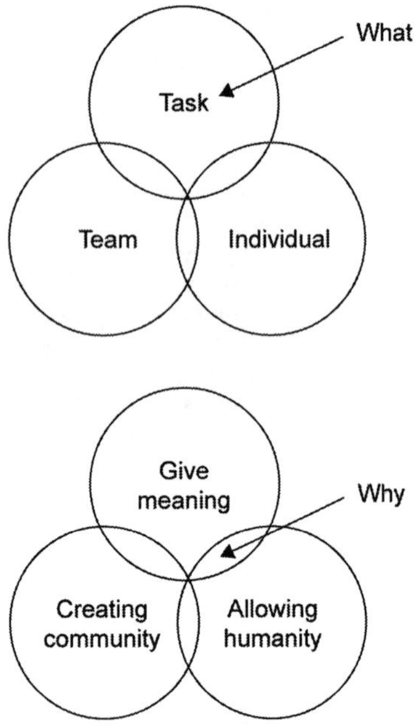

(From Gilbert, 2003, derived from Adair, 1983, and expanded upon)

Chapter 2). The Abbot must 'distrust his own frailty', and he therefore leads through humility.

As the notes to the 1981 translation of the Rule of St. Benedict state, 'The Abbot is one who has already made the journey, and is therefore able to guide others along the right path' (8). This is not a journey of complacency or all knowing, but of one who is skilled in exploration and able to act as a guide, while listening all the time both to God, and to each and every one in the community. As Benedict points out in Chapter 3 of his Rule: 'The Lord often reveals what is better to the younger' so that **all** should be called for counsel.

Stephen Covey (1992), in his work on *Principle-centred Leadership* has integrity and trust as a major foundation of everything else. In four levels: personal, interpersonal, managerial and organisational, Covey relates four matching principles:

- Trustworthiness at the personal level.
- Trust at the interpersonal level.
- Empowerment at the managerial level.
- Alignment in terms of the whole organisation.

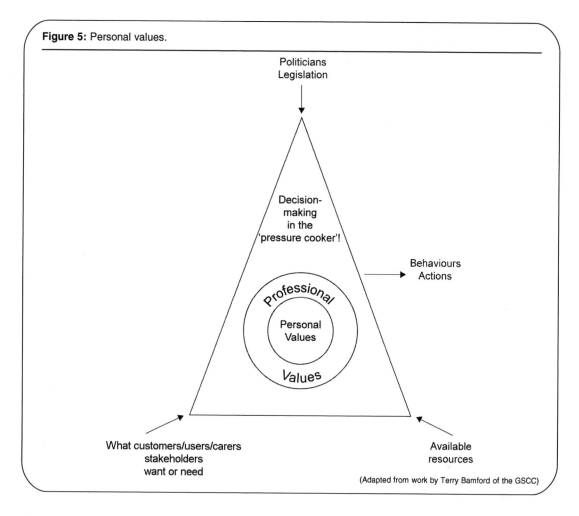

Figure 5: Personal values.

(Adapted from work by Terry Bamford of the GSCC)

Certainly people will not be willing to be guided along a path towards a visionary goal, if they believe that their leader is only after self-aggrandisement.

Jim Collins, in his comprehensive study of the most successful private sector organisations in the USA, talks about 'level five leadership' (Collins, 2001) and lays side by side issues of professional will and personal humility. In a neat phrase, he talks about leaders looking in the mirror, not out of the window, to apportion responsibility for poor results, and looking out of the window, not in the mirror, to apportion credit for the success of the company. The pathological leader is always, as the wicked queen in *Snow White*, neurotically looking in the mirror to protect and promote their own ambition, and hunting down rivals.

In a highly pressured world of business, public service, political government, the armed services etc., people look to see whether their leader has both personal and professional values which inform their behaviours.

'Values' sounds a simple concept, but of course it is not. Christopher Pollitt (2003) in his recent text on *The Essential Public Manager*, talks about:

- **Values:** an enduring belief that a specific mode of conduct or end-state of existence is personally or socially preferable to an opposite or converse mode of conduct or end-state existence.
- **Ethics:** rules of conduct and behaviour.

And these are quite often shaped by motives, and/or psychological drivers, and the norms which we have grown up with. Professor Fulford et al. (Fulford and Woodbridge, October 2004) discuss the diversity of values which we may encounter and the need to bring them into some form of congruence (see Chapter 3).

Pathological Leadership Example 1: The 'bean counter' mentality

Ms B. took over as Chair of Blankshire Health Authority at a time when the Health Authority, the Trusts and Partner organisations were all in financial difficulties. Someone with accountancy skills seemed to be the right appointment as Chair, but unfortunately Ms B. knew, in Oscar Wilde's dictum, the price of everything and the value of nothing. To do her credit, she knew that difficult decisions had to be taken and had the willingness to take action. Unfortunately, she did not have the skills in relationships and partnership building which might have carried through the changes with a degree of unity, if not unanimity. Her concept of partnership working was to set out a very definite plan, and then engage on a 'consultation' exercise which was, in effect, the authority telling everybody else what would happen. On large scale projects such as hospital reconfiguration, this ran into major difficulties and had some long-term political consequences both locally and nationally.

Even on a relatively smaller scale the bean counter mentality created unnecessary difficulties. Faced with some short-term budgetary issues, Ms B. decided to cut the majority of grants to the voluntary sector. Advised privately and helpfully by partners in the local authority against this course of action, she persevered with her scheme and was surprised that the furore which had been predicted by her partners duly fell about her ears. Eventually relationships, with considerable help from partners, were sufficiently repaired for work to continue, but Ms B. did not seem to appreciate that once you lose people's trust they are reluctant to give you that trust again. Her concept of relationships was speaking to somebody about a matter, and then presuming that she never had to speak to them again because she had a relationship with them. She would have been better advised to read Jane Austen's novels where the partnership relationship is forged over time and in a way which leads up to and beyond the actual contract!

Cranwell-Ward et al. (2002) use another set of interlocking circles composed of personal attributes, management skills and leadership attributes (more on this in Chapter 5).

Put together they create a series of powerful effects whereby the motivating personal attributes together with the management skills produce what Cranwell-Ward and her colleagues call the 'x factor' around performance drivers; while a different set of personal and leadership attributes combined create the 'y factor' which is around the kind of emotional intelligence and inspiration, also figuring strongly in the work of Daniel Goleman et al. (2002).

The round the world yacht race was a particular 'pressure cooker' example of leadership, where the attributes, qualities and skills stood out in sharp focus. One of the most interesting aspects of the presentation (Roffey Park Management Institute, 2004) was the revelation that the crew of the winning yacht greatly respected their skipper, were very pleased to have won, but would not wish to sail with him again! The crew of the second boat home, whose performance was also remarkable, said that they were quite prepared to sail round the world with their skipper again after a hot bath and a warm meal!

Organisational leadership, therefore, has to be there for the long run, not just for a sprint. Benedict (1982) also perceives this when he states in Chapter 64 (88):

> *Therefore, drawing on this and other examples of discretion, the mother of virtues, he must so arrange everything that the strong have something to yearn for and the weak nothing to run from.*

A performance management regime which has stood the test of time!

Exercise 3: Historical/public figures as leaders

You are invited to set down historical or current figures who you see as a leader who inspires you.

Leadership and management

'I keep six honest serving men
(They taught me all I know)
Their names are what *and* why *and* when
And how *and* where *and* who'.

(Rudyard Kipling)

In the 1950s most organisations in the UK were administered, not managed, and certainly not led. The inter-war years saw a profound sense of disillusionment with the economic and social optimism of the Victorian era and the liberal reforms of the early 20th century. The loss during the Great War of so many natural leaders, and often whole communities in the 'pals battalions', coupled with the class conflict in the 1920s and a sense of betrayal about the perceived breach of the post First World War social contract, bred cynicism and stagnation. The aftermath of the Second World War saw a greater sense of social cohesion, and a belief in an underpinning welfare state. In many ways the war against fascism and social reforms went hand in hand; the victory at El Alamein taking place coincidentally on the same day that the Beveridge Report on Social Reforms was launched. But the aftermath of the Second World War also bred complacency and the sense that the war had been the great effort, and therefore leadership need not be taken into the peacetime era. Britain was seen as a leader in 'administration': the civil service, the judiciary, colonial administration, the professions – all fields in which the UK saw itself as a world leader. But as North America, Western Europe and the Far East moved forward in radically different ways, Britain found itself left behind, not only in wealth creation but in social welfare as well.

Although Britain made the right decision in trying to 'win the peace' at the same time as driving to 'win the war', through the support given to the work of Sir William Beveridge, the development of the NHS, social insurance, national assistance, the passing of the 1948 Children Act etc., the country made the fundamental mistake of not *rethinking its role* in the world. The government still saw Britain as a world power and its expenditure and commitment to those aims undermined progress in other fields. The commitment to the Korean war, for example, misdirected much of the drive that could have gone into social development. Midwinter (1994: 93), in his excellent *Overview of Social History in Britain*, claims that 'The nation was now in the position of the [wo]man with champagne tastes and beer pockets'!

While foreign commentators praised, 'the very English way of reconciling respect for liberty with a very high degree of public order and co-operation' (Martin Wiener, US academic quoted in Midwinter, 1994: 106) the reforms were essentially gradualist, and where they were more radical, as in housing policy with the proliferation of high-rise ghettos, the approach was mistaken, with long-term adverse social and economic consequences. Midwinter comments on the role of women in society:

The welfare state improved *the lot of women without* changing *it*

(page 108, my emphasis)

and this is a constant complaint of the post-war years, as indeed it is today.

In British industry the most often quoted example is that of British Leyland, with its reputation for shoddy work – the 'Friday car', and divisive industrial relations. But just as undermining in the long-term was a failure within senior management to plan ahead a viable range of models that the public wanted to buy. With a lack of customer responsiveness in models and reliability, pleas to buy 'British' (reinforced by films such as *The Italian Job*) fell on deaf ears.

The country was alarmed to find that it seemed to have 'won the war' but 'lost the peace', both in economic terms and then in what its economy could purchase in terms of health and welfare. Technological innovation was often spectacular but undeveloped, while institutions and professions went unreformed, without adequate internal and external scrutiny. As Leadbeater (2000) remarks: 'We are timid and cautious where the Victorians were confident and innovative. We live within the shell of institutions the 19th century handed down to us. Our highly uneven capacity for innovation is the source of our unease. We are scientific and technological revolutionaries, but political and institutional conservatives'. Sound administration came to be seen as useful but insufficient in itself and belatedly, Britain began to consider management as a way of coping with the increasing complexity of organisational change.

Management was seen as more active than administration, setting broad strategic aims and

Table 1: Administration and management compared

	Administration	Management
Objectives	Stated in general terms and reviewed or changed infrequently.	Stated as broad strategic aims supported by more detailed short-term goals and targets reviewed.
Success criteria	Mistake avoiding. Performance rarely measurable.	Success seeking. Performance mostly measurable.
Resource use	Secondary task.	Primary task.
Decision-making	Has to make few decisions but affecting many and can take time over it.	Has to make many decisions affecting few and has to make them quickly.
Structure	Roles defined in terms of areas of responsibility. Long hierarchies; limited delegation.	Shorter hierarchies; maximum delegation.
Roles	Arbitration.	Protagonist.
Attitudes	Passive: workload determined outside the system. Best people used to solve problems. Time-insensitive. Risk avoiding. Emphasis on procedure. Doing things rightly. Conformity. Uniformity.	Active: seeking to influence the environment. Best people used to find and exploit opportunities. Time-sensitive. Risk accepting but minimising it. Emphasis on results. Doing the right things. Local experiments: need for conformity to be proved. Independence.

(Gilbert and Scragg, 1992, p. 118, derived from Rees, 1984)

backing this up with sound planning, organising, briefing, monitoring, controlling and evaluating, as set out by the Work Foundation (formerly known as the Industrial Society) in various pamphlets and its pocket cards for managers, which are still a useful aide-mémoire today (see Figure 16).

As the pace of innovation and change increased, however, as we will look at in more detail in Chapter 2, the ancient concept of leadership was seen as the vital spark to assist soundly managed organisations make the necessary quantum leaps forward to keep ahead of the game.

Sir John Harvey-Jones, Chair of ICI, during a period of major change, and later renowned as BBC TV's *Troubleshooter*, wrote that:

The business that has not been purposefully led in a clear direction, which is understood by its people, is not going to survive, and all of history shows that that is the case.

(Quoted in Gilbert and Scragg, 1992: 132)

American management guru, Tom Peters, in his work with Nancy Austin, went further in arguing almost for a replacement of management by leadership:

For the last 25 years, we have carried around with us the image of manager as cop, referee, devil's advocate, dispassionate analyst, professional, decision-maker, naysayer, pronouncer. The alternative we now propose is leader (not manager) as cheerleader, enthusiast, nurturer of champions, herofinder, wanderer, dramatist, coach, facilitator, builder.

(Peters and Austin, 1985: 265)

This model, which relates back to our earliest traditions, as we saw at the beginning of this chapter, is attractive, but tends to neglect the fact that complex organisations, as John Kotter (1988 and 1996) points out, need both leadership and management combined. As Kotter asserts 'The real challenge is to combine strong leadership and strong management, and use each to balance the other' (quoted in Gilbert, 2003b: 95). Table 2 takes the issues of Table 1 and moves them forward.

Of course, it is not always easy to combine the attributes of management and leadership in

Table 2: The balancing foci of management and leadership

The manager focuses on systems and structure	The leader focuses on people
The manager maintains	The leader develops
The manager asks how and when	The leader asks what and why
The manager concentrates on planning and budgeting	The leader sets a direction and aligns people
The manager has his eye on the bottom line	The leader has his eye on the horizon
The manager is deductive and rational	The leader is inductive and intuitive
The manager ensures the accomplishment of plans by controlling and problem solving	The leader achieves goals through motivating and inspiring people
Good management copes with current complexity	Leadership is about coping with change
The manager does things right	The leader does the right thing

Both facets are required for the organisation to flourish

Peter Gilbert, adapted from Kotter, 'What Leaders Really Do', *Harvard Business Review*, May/June 1990 and Bennis, 'Leadership in the 21st Century', *Journal of Organisational Change Management*, I: 1, 1989.
(See also Gilbert and Thompson, 2002)

one person, though that may well be the ideal. In fact, to drive change forward, leaders may have deliberately to break away from the cycle of organising and controlling, leave those to others and get out to do the listening, empowering and inspiring. In a profile, Antony Sheehan, former Chief Executive of NIMHE, and now Director of Care Services for the DH, is quoted as saying:

There may be many reasons why I fail in this job, but it won't be for lack of talking with people, networking with people. I don't think I could do this job from behind a desk'.

('It's time to look at the big picture'.
The Guardian, 14 July 2004)

Effective leaders need to stand back and fix their eye upon the horizon, while at the same time being in touch with the views of those they serve, be they customers, service users, carers or

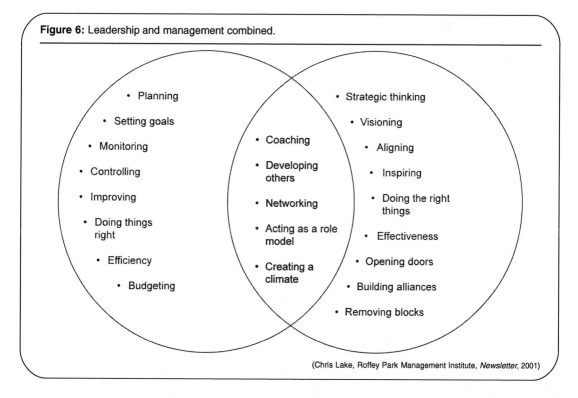

Figure 6: Leadership and management combined.

- Planning
- Setting goals
- Monitoring
- Controlling
- Improving
- Doing things right
- Efficiency
- Budgeting

- Coaching
- Developing others
- Networking
- Acting as a role model
- Creating a climate

- Strategic thinking
- Visioning
- Aligning
- Inspiring
- Doing the right things
- Effectiveness
- Opening doors
- Building alliances
- Removing blocks

(Chris Lake, Roffey Park Management Institute, *Newsletter*, 2001) consumers. Somehow, leadership must be twinned with management, so that if the leader is looking at the horizon, someone is looking at the bottom line. Chris Lake of Roffey Park Management Institute, has a helpful diagram which shows management and leadership not in opposition to each other, but congruent.

Linking right back to our consideration of the roots of leadership, management is the necessary ability to ensure that the ship is sound, well supplied with the correct amount of sails, oars, etc., and that the crew are competent to undertake the journey. Leadership is about pathfinding, setting the direction and inspiring people – most especially when the going gets tough.

The Need for Leaders in Today's World

This President likes to say he is a leader. Mr President, look behind you. There's no-one there. It's not leadership if no-one follows.

(Senator John Kerry, Presidential Candidate, 2004, on President Bush's lack of international support)

It is not so much that capitalism has delivered the goods to the people, as that the people have been increasingly delivered to the goods.

(Jeremy Seabrook, 1988: 183)

World, world, Oh world!
But that thy strange mutations makes us hate thee,
Life would not yield to age.

(Edgar in Shakespeare's *King Lear* IV ix)

The world is a comedy to those who think, a tragedy to those who feel.
(Horace Walpole, *Letter to Sir Horace Mann*, 1769, quoted in Bauman, 2000: 54)

The system (health services) hasn't ever been designed around the patient whereas almost every business these days is having to design itself around whatever you call them – customers or clients or whatever.
(Derek Wanless, author of the Wanless Report on the NHS, quoted in the *Health Service Journal*, 25 April 2002)

Introduction

In this chapter we will pick up the threads of the end of Chapter 1, when we saw how the changing nature of the world of work moved the need for the activity carried out by managers from 'administration' to 'management', and then to 'leadership'. In Chapter 2 we consider in a little more detail the state of the world in which we live and work, and the nature of organisations.

The world we live in

My father-in-law was a director of the major UK battery firm Chloride through the 1960s. He worked hard at a demanding job and had very little annual holiday. Stressful as it was, however, his job was analogous to steering a large barge down a canal; while for today's executives, it is much more like taking a small craft white water rafting down some treacherous rapids, with rocks, shoals, eddies, falling boulders from the attendant cliffs, and treacherous currents.

To continue the analogy, the modern leader in the public or private sector has to:

- Know where the boat is going to.

- Recruit the right people and skills for the crew, and provide incentives (not necessarily financial) for them to remain with them, and not step out at the next bank saying: 'I've had a better offer elsewhere – I am a scarce resource, you know'!
- Build the team, train and inspire them.
- Gain the requisite resources for the journey.
- Steer the boat, negotiating the rapids.
- Look out for and adjust to the cross currents.

Leadership today is truly managing in white water!

At whatever stage in their career, a manager needs to consider a variety of issues that are pertinent to the immediate environment they are working in. Managing the internal organisation of the boat without paying attention to the currents will see the craft overturned or drifting up a creek; only viewing the environment, without managing the crew and their equipment, will leave the raft unable to complete its task of driving down river.

One way of achieving this synthesis is to consider the STEP process: the Social, Technological, Economic and Political factors which shape your immediate and wider world (see Exercise 4). Some of these factors will intertwine, e.g. how much of the welfare state central government in the UK wishes to deliver by mainstream statutory agencies; by special partnerships, e.g. Sure Start, Connexions, etc; by the voluntary or not-for-profit sector; by the private sector?

A daily reading of the newspapers demonstrates actual or perceived divisions between England, and an increasingly divergent Scotland and Wales, on policy issues; and between different elements in government. The manager of a local branch of NCH, Mind, Mencap, Barnardo's, RNIB etc., would need to be aware of the **national** (this will be increasingly important following the effects of devolution where Scotland now has its own Parliament, and a diverging social policy from England, and Wales has its Assembly, which will usually wish to give a Welsh ethos to policy which emanates from England) picture on this issue, but also how their **local** statutory commissioners wish to balance provision by the statutory and other sectors.

In 2004, the issue of specialist treatment centres for, for example, hip replacements and cataracts, raised its head. Some argued that this was privatisation of the NHS by the back door; ministers responded that local authorities had been more 'enabling' rather than purely 'providing' bodies since the full implementation of the NHS and Community Care Act, 1990 in April 1993, and that the private sector complemented the NHS rather than replacing it.

Much of what we do and how we do it depends on how we look at humankind and the individuals which make it up within the overall context of global and national society. As Kathleen Jones (1972: xiii) the social historian puts it:

> It is important to recognise that the way in which the mentally ill [sic] . . . are defined and cared for is primarily a social response to a very basic set of human problems . . . How do we define [mental health]? What forms of care should the community provide? Who should be responsible for adminis-tering them? What is liberty, and how can it best be safeguarded? All societies have these problems. How they answer them depends on what they are, and the values they hold.

And, after all, not only does mental health affect us all, but the issues around health, safety and liberty are crucial in all events, and have been seen as such throughout British history. The fact that the USA, 'the land of the free', has begun unprecedented restrictions on individual liberty following the events of 11 September 2001 (see e.g. BBC2, *The Power of Nightmares*, 20 October 2004) is bound to have a knock-on effect in the UK where we now sit, perched uneasily on a fence, between the individualistic and atomised ethos of the USA and the more communitarian approach of Western Europe. We can get into these issues in various ways: through newspaper reports, sociological texts (such as the eminently readable *Bowling Alone* by Robert Putnam, 2000) or indeed through novels and autobiographies. Eva Hoffman's beautifully crafted autobiography, *Lost in Translation* (1989) considers cultural dissonance, as she moves with her family from a Jewish community in Poland to a new life in Canada and the USA. Hoffman's remarks concerning identity strike at the heart of the matter:

> Well . . . I say it's hard to explain [why Americans go to psychiatrists]. It's a problem of identity. Many of my American friends feel that they don't have enough of it. They often feel worthless, or they don't know how they feel. Identity is the number one national problem here. There seems to be a shortage of it in the land, a dearth of self-hood amidst other plenty – maybe because there are so many individual egos trying to outdo each other and enlarge themselves . . . or maybe it's because everyone is always on the move and undergoing enormous changes, so they lose track of who they've been and have to keep tabs on who they're becoming all the time (262).

Let us now look at four main frameworks in turn.

Social

The society we live in has not just come into being in a puff of smoke! It has evolved through the influence of Greek and Roman civilisations and their rediscovery in the Renaissance; the Anglo-Saxon and Scandinavian invasions and their melding with Romano-British culture; constant interaction with the Continent; the early onset of the Industrial Revolution and the influence of scientific thinking through Englishmen such as Isaac Newton and others; British imperialism and its consequences; and the ideological conflict between individualism and communitarianism, neatly summed up in Margaret Thatcher's famous dictum: 'There is no such thing as society. There are individuals and families and nothing else.'

The nature of society today

We are said to be living in a post-modern world. What does that mean? It is simply that we have moved from eras where there was an acknowledged world view, expressed as 'truths', whether of science, religion or social systems, to one where there are no certainties. David Harvey (1990: 9) describes post-modernism thus:

> *We are our own little story-tellers, living among the ruins of our former grand narratives . . . today we tell one story and tomorrow we will tell another.*

Zygmunt Bauman's motif is to see the move from modernism to post-modernism in terms of a transition from solid structures to free-flowingness – or what he terms 'liquid modernity' (Bauman, 2000, see Figure 7).

While Peter Vardy (2003: 12) gives us an image of a 'constant sea of change', where humans are adrift in 'tossing and raging waters and reality is merely their own perspective', and there are no 'rocks of certainty' on which one can stand firm.

Bauman uses a variation on the historical time-line I have given above, in his postulation that in pre-modern times the settled civilisations were at risk from the nomadic tribes; and this often led to victimisation and exclusion of outsiders – a mindset operating against the outsiders of our modern world today. But now he sees the 'revenge of nomadism' over settlement and stability. The 'global elite' of opinion formers, globalised businesses and media barons, are what Bauman describes as 'absentee landlords', ruling without burdening themselves with the need to manage, reform or lead societies.

Exercise 4: The STEP exercise

Social	Technological
Economic	Political

Please use this exercise to look either at the overall STEP issues for the business you are in, or those factors facing your organisation, or both.

Many of my generation were brought up on George Orwell's *1984* and Aldous Huxley's *Brave New World* with their forecasts of a rigidly controlled society, structured and administered by an elite. Modern science fiction films often pick up the theme with an individual breaking the system and leading their people to freedom (e.g. *Logan's Run*). What the films and the modern concepts of individuality fail to address, however, is: if modern humans are free, what can they do with their freedom?!

In fact, modern society appears to show a number of characteristics:

- **Anxiousness.** Fears concerning the Cold War and nuclear annihilation have been replaced by a more random state of anxiety. Before the fall of the Berlin Wall there was fear of a specific enemy. Now, interviews with mid-westerners in the lead-up to the USA Presidential election of November 2004 seem to demonstrate that we fear everyone!

  The public space, which in the Greek city state or polis was a scene of discourse and communality, is now full of fear and moral panics, so even when crime levels fall, levels of anxiety rise. An example for me was the investment by Stoke City Council in quite a large-scale sheltered housing scheme in the mid 1990s, of an enclosed variety, which was mainly in response to a breakdown in trust of older people in their social environment in one part of the city.

  Alain De Botton in his book *Status Anxiety* considers how the modern world increases our anxiety as we become increasingly conscious of our gradated place in the pecking order. As De Botton (2004: 15) puts it: 'the attentions of others might be said to matter to us principally because we are afflicted by a congenital uncertainty as to our own value . . . Our sense of identity is held captive by the judgements of those we live among'.

- **Atomisation.** Our emancipation from past certainties and beliefs has left us all individually in charge of our own destinies, with very little family, community or societal backup. We are masters and mistresses of our own little ship, but when that vessel becomes becalmed or wrecked, then we have nobody to blame or rely on but ourselves. The existential meaning of angst is 'the dread caused by humanity's awareness that an individual's future is not determined, but

Leadership Example 1: Karen Wood

Karen Wood is chair of the One-in-Four Service User Forum in Mental Health in Jersey, Channel Islands.

A survivor of mental ill-health, Karen cites the non-judgemental support of family and friends, medication, and regaining a spiritual perspective as important components of her recovery.

Mental Health professionals in England were not seen by her as engaging with her as a person with unique strengths and needs and her own opinions. Her road back into employment was aided by a sympathetic manager and colleagues, and she gained in confidence and self-esteem to progress within that role and then later become self-employed before moving to the Channel Islands.

Karen sees leadership in the user movement 'as bringing people in organisations back to their 'roots', reminding them of their own fragility and common humanity. These vital therapeutic components are often lost in the power-ridden hierarchies and protocols employed by corporate institutions'.

Her belief is that leadership needs to grasp this concept of common humanity and articulate it. 'Leaders should lead from knowledge of their own vulnerability and a clear sense of their own beliefs and values'.

One-in-Four is the first user forum for mental health users and survivors in Jersey, and already that voice is being heard here in formal planning mechanisms with the statutory and voluntary sector; the group is looking at issues such as joining in the interviewing process for professional staff; it has a clear mission statement and publicity; and is combating stigma through the media.

The qualities Karen believes are needed to lead in this role are:

- Clarity of vision and the ability to impart that to others.
- Humour, energy, perseverance, forbearance and sensitivity.
- Honesty and empathy.
- The ability to bring out the best in others.
- Self-reflection.

The One-in-Four group believe they can help each other in developing leadership skills through:

- Undertaking delegated tasks so as to boost self-esteem and self-confidence, which in turn enables individuals to tackle larger objectives.
- Communicating hope and dealing sensitively with perceived 'setbacks'.
- Helping members to make the connections between skills that are used within the group and those outside.
- A mutual sense of 'journeying' – we're all in it together!
- Helping people to 'uncover' gifts and talents that have lain dormant from previous training and occupations. These only become transparent if people feel good about their membership of their group.

---

must be freely chosen'. (Oxford English Dictionary definition)

In a study of social housing policy in Brighton (Dickens and Gilbert, 1979) we were able to show that the now much-reviled council housing schemes, with all their faults, were often, as Aneurin Bevan and others had described them, examples of a range of skills, roles and classes working together and bonding in solidarity at times of crisis.

Putnam's work on the USA charts a worrying decline in 'social capital', which has seen considerable decline in America since the 1960s. Surveys show that North Americans are now less content than they were in the 1950s and 1960s (see also Hutchinson et al., 2002).

- **Having or being?** Over the past 30 years we have seen our transmogrification from 'individuals' into 'consumers'! This sounds quite an innocent, even positive development, but it means that our value is not so much related to our uniqueness as human beings as to what we consume. This, of course, partly or wholly, disenfranchises many of the people we work with: elderly people who are mentally frail, abused children, people with learning disabilities, youth at the margins of society, etc. As Hutchinson et al. (2002: 5)

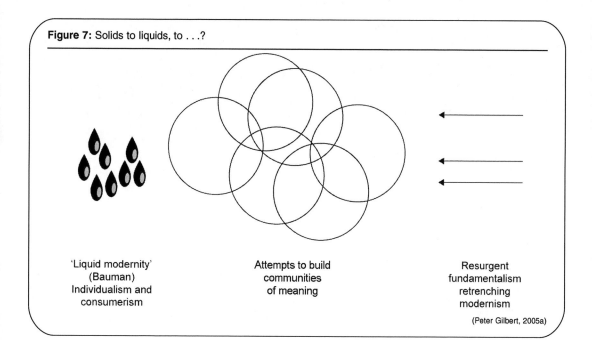

Figure 7: Solids to liquids, to . . .?

'Liquid modernity'
(Bauman)
Individualism and
consumerism

Attempts to build
communities
of meaning

Resurgent
fundamentalism
retrenching
modernism

(Peter Gilbert, 2005a)

point out, in capitalised market economies, having money means belonging, particularly in the US and the UK. 'Lack of money brings real hardship and refusal of access to money is indicative of exclusion from citizenship.'

The acquisitive society has not brought an increase in happiness and well-being.

The psychoanalyst and philosopher Erich Fromm (1976) suggests in his work *To Have or to Be?* that our kind of pursuit of happiness does not produce well-being. Looking at well-being 30 years on, Hutchinson et al. (2002: 7) remark that 'rich populations seem not much happier than poor ones, certainly not as happy as their relative wealth would indicate' (see also Layard, 2005). Recovery rates from psychotic disorders in a number of the countries of the developing world, where there is effective social capital, are actually better than those in the developed world where expenditure on formal mental health services is exponentially higher. Frank Furedi (2004) in his dissection of the formalised therapeutic approach to human emotion, makes some similar points that as social capital declines, formal therapeutic professionals move into the vacuum, but in a way that is as likely to create dependency as healing and autonomy. In studying some reactions to major social traumas, Furedi discovers an important shift towards people being encouraged to find

meaning purely through their individual selves rather than through the individual and community process, and states that: 'This move from a bereaved community to a community of bereaved expresses the individualising imperative at work in society' (15).

In a recent paper, entitled 'The McDonaldization of Social Work' (Lovelock et al., 2004: 39), Adrian James speaks of a McDonaldized service as being 'driven by the need to produce, as quickly, as efficiently, and as cheaply as possible, a product of uniform size, quality and acceptability, rather than by the need to produce the *best* product or, more significantly, to produce something that caters for a range of individual consumers, in different settings and with different needs'. This standardisation, which often negates professional skills, and leaves the professional and the professional leader stranded as 'a stranger in a strange land', is part of the alienation of modern society. One of the skills of a modern leader is to be able to celebrate diversity, including professional diversity (see for example Case Study 2, Chapter 1) within an overall vision for the organisation as a whole.

● The counter-reaction from modernists and fundamentalists is attempting to impose a newly fashioned grand narrative (see BBC 2, *The Power of Nightmares*, 20 October 2004) to, as David Tacey (2004: 5) puts it, 'mimic the past'.

Figure 7 attempts to describe the competing trends which squeeze our attempts to take the best from an ethos which allows us our own story, rather than impose one upon us, while at the same time providing us with enough communal structure so that we are not de-stabilised and overwhelmed by global forces.

Technical

You only have to stand by a coffee machine – certainly a beneficial technological improvement in my opinion – in any office, to learn how technological improvements are seen to help or hinder the workforce.

Speed of communication has both increased our responsiveness and added to our pressure. As a colleague said recently: 'I had an email at 8.30 a.m. this morning asking why I hadn't replied to theirs of 7 a.m.!'

Faster communication does not necessarily mean better communication, but the ability to set up email and internet groups, agree complex documentation, disseminate papers etc., has made it easier to formulate decisions.

On the other hand, it is noticeable that even major businesses and defence contractors, with large budgets, suffer from technological problems. For instance, in October 2004, Sainsbury, the retailers, announced more poor trading figures, and part of their downturn in the retail war with Tesco and Asda is that a new computer system had failed to ensure that sufficient goods appear on the shelves. A fairly basic requirement of the retail computer system! The computer system designed to integrate all parts of the NHS is now said to be facing overrun problems both in terms of time and budget. The Ministry of Defence is notorious for 'delivering' sophisticated military hardware years late, grossly over budget and often unworkable!

Economic

The connection between the STEP headings becomes clear when we note that the globalisation of markets has been accelerated rapidly by the break up of the Soviet Union and the increasingly capitalist approach of 'communist' China.

In recent times, we have seen not only the movement of capital, and the outsourcing of

manufacturing, to areas such as South East Asia with their less expensive labour forces, but service industries, notably call centres, moving to English-speaking countries in Asia.

Governments and organisations need to watch their demography carefully and also the skills and cost of the workforce they require. A recent headline in the *Local Government Chronicle* (22 October 2004) indicates that the Employers Organisation sees almost 94 per cent of councils having difficulties in recruiting to one or more professional or managerial positions. Social care, teaching and environmental health are among fields with the most acute shortages. The Employers Organisation urges councils to proactively tackle the demographic deficit, which requires an increasing accent on bringing young people into organisations. As the Chief Executive of Hertfordshire County Council, formerly Director of Social Services, Caroline Tapster, put it: 'It is not just about salary, it's what makes you an organisation people want to be part of' (and this sense of a person-centred organisation will be dealt with in Part 3).

Political

Much of this has been inferred under the 'Social' heading, but clearly this is a world heavily influenced by the events of 11 September 2001, and the subsequent alliances and disagreements around the 'war on terror'.

Arguments still rage as to whether it is a clash of civilisations and faiths; a collision of faith versus secularism; a battle for scarce resources, especially oil, or as the BBC2 series *The Power of Nightmares* postulates, the manipulation of the majority by a small elite of ideologues inventing enemies to create a form of social cohesion, but one based on a fallacy of negativity, rather than inspiring hope.

What is clear is that technological change, international economic integration, the maturation of markets in developed countries, and the changing political climate has created a globalisation of markets and competition with both more hazards and more opportunities. Organisations of all types have no option but to respond. So it is important to emphasise again that in increasingly complex organisations, often straddling many continents, and in an increasingly turbulent world, management is required to provide sound, but not rigid, systems, and leadership is needed to engender that farsightedness and energy for change (see Figure 8).

Leadership Example 2: Jo Williams, Chief Executive of Royal Mencap

Having worked with Jo Williams over a number of years, a phrase that she uses resonates with me, 'it's the way I try to lead my life'. Jo who was Director of Social Services for Wigan from 1992 to 1997, and Cheshire County Council from 1997 to 2002, is now Chief Executive of Royal Mencap at a time when that organisation is coping with the major changes introduced by the Government White Paper, *Valuing People* (March 2001); the issues involved in being both a service user and carer organisation at a time of greater empowerment; and being a lobbying organisation as well as a provider of services.

Anybody who has worked with Jo Williams knows that she is a very driven individual, but that drivenness is understood and acknowledged through self-awareness (see Chapter 3), and she speaks of trying 'not to be seduced by power'. Part of that drive comes from her childhood, and a very strong inbuilt belief that 'every human being has equal worth', and everybody brings something different, unique and uniquely valuable to the table. Perhaps part of her drive, however, comes from an element of unfairness in a childhood where equity was an often-stated value. Her brother was sent to public school but she was sent to grammar school; and it is quite noticeable in effective leaders that, however well balanced they are, there is often a little grit in the oyster, usually from childhood which creates that pearl of achievement.

For Jo, social work was the career of choice, one where she could connect with people and work alongside them to assist them in gaining better opportunities. She feels that the values and strengths in social work, that bringing together of people and opportunities to create better lives, fitted her for a leadership role. She has used this insight to assist frontline managers use their skills as practitioners in management roles; as she says, 'you can't overplay the importance of interpersonal skills'.

Values and passion for a good service remain a constant, but Jo is clear that different situations require specific approaches. In Wigan, a unitary authority, intensive changes in the culture, e.g. bringing forward role models for women managers, in what had been a predominantly male environment, had a major effect. Moving to a county council, with a two-tier system of government and a whole plethora of partners, there is an emphasis more on being a 'boundary manager'. Moving to Mencap in 2002, Jo frankly states that it was a 'new world', and she experienced moments of uncertainty as she explored those new horizons. She had to hold back on her natural inclination to 'roll my sleeves up and get into action', and do much more initial observing and listening; but, she said, 'my values stood me in good stead', and 'people appreciated my passion'. These again are themes we explore at different points in this book, i.e. that different situations elicit varied approaches, but one's core values remain a constant.

In regard to Mencap, it is interesting to note from their corporate plan, that while there are new ways of working being promoted, the history and tradition is affirmed and celebrated. Leaders can be radical while, at the same time, valuing what has gone before.

The nature of organisations

'People are not human resources. They are living individuals with the right to be different. Organisations which are set up to exploit people are wrong' (Handy, 1989: 98). If you were going to lead an organisation, lead within it, or lead in partnership with it from another body, then you must understand the organisation you are dealing with. Gareth Morgan (1997: 3) author of one of the most persuasive books on organisations, writes that we have 'to become skilled' in 'the art of "reading" ' the situations appertaining to organisations.

Organisations can be understood in terms of:

- The roles they are set up to play, e.g. schools, the armed forces, commercial and industrial businesses, social welfare organisations, hospitals.

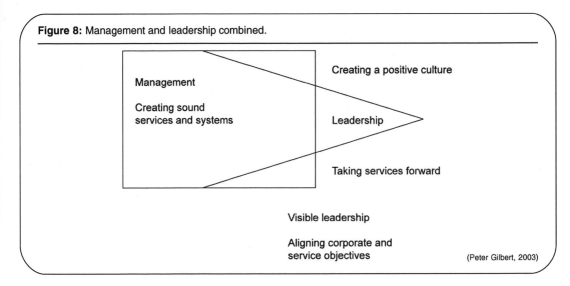

Figure 8: Management and leadership combined.

Management

Creating sound
services and systems

Creating a positive culture

Leadership

Taking services forward

Visible leadership

Aligning corporate and
service objectives

(Peter Gilbert, 2003)

- The changing nature of the roles that they have to take on, e.g. in current realpolitik, how quickly and effectively an armed force can turn itself from a body which wages war to one which keeps the peace.
- The kind of long-term organisational ethos they evince, and whether that changes under pressure.
- The way organisations model other societal phenomena e.g. do they feel like machines, organisms, networks etc?
- The state of integration, e.g. a unitary purpose, set up as a partnership, merged organisation (though it is said that there is no such thing as a merged organisation, only takeovers!).

In terms of role, this is an increasingly ephemeral concept, especially in public services where the thrust of the service is changing radically and rapidly (see Glasby and Peck, 2004, and Scott, 2000).

Jim Collins and Gerry Porras (2000: xiv) in their study of businesses with a long-term success rate, demonstrate that these are invariably responsive to external stimuli but tenacious regarding their core values. The authors put it like this:

Contrary to popular wisdom, the proper first response to a changing world is not to ask, 'how should we change?' but rather to ask, 'what do we stand for and why do we exist?' This should never change. And then feel free to change everything else. Put another way, visionary companies distinguish their timeless core values and enduring purpose (which should never change) from their operating practices and business strategies which should be changing constantly in response to a changing world.

This has to be the same for leaders, who have to be, as Niccolo Machiavelli (1961: 131) pointed out in 16th century Florence: 'The one who adapts his policy to the times'. But for long-term success, both staff, and the partners the organisation works with, need to see integrity as a central feature of the leader.

One of the most well-known thinkers on organisations is Charles Handy. In his *Gods of Management* (1979) and *Understanding Organisations* (1985) he provided a detailed insight into organisations and organisational behaviour. Partly intriguing because he linked the four organisational types he describes to Ancient Greek gods, Handy (1979, 1985) outlines the four as follows:

1. **The power culture** – frequently found in small entrepreneurial organisations. The system depends on a central power source (one person or a small coterie) 'with rays of power and influence spreading out from that central figure' (1985: 189).
2. **The role culture** – central and local government departments fit the description for Handy's role culture. Its strengths are its stability and predictability, but at a time of change, that is its weakness as well.

    It is noticeable that some public sector organisations today will set up small offshoots which are less role and perhaps more task orientated, which may refresh the staidness of the overall organisation.

3. **The task culture** – job or project orientated. The accent is on performance with a bringing together of the right people from any level in the organisation, with appropriate resources and setting them to get on with the task in hand.

4. **The person culture** – in this the individual is the central point. The structure exists only to serve and assist the individuals within it. Consultancies, barristers' chambers, architects' partnerships, and perhaps some GP general practices, fit the bill here.

Roger Harrison and Herb Stokes (1990) use a similar model but call them by slightly different names: power, role, achievement and support. Their *Handbook and Manual for Diagnosing Organisational Culture*, published by Roffey Park Management Institute, is an extremely useful way of understanding the organisation one is working in, and looking to harness some of the different and beneficial elements of each of Handy's organisational cultures. For example, it is not likely, or indeed sensible, for a large public sector organisation to move substantially away from the role type of organisation, but to engender elements of 'task' and 'person' within the role culture will be beneficial.

It is easy for people to confuse the power culture with leadership. In fact the former is very often the type of organisation that emanates from an energetic and visionary entrepreneur, who builds the business around their own persona. This may produce beneficial results for the company and those who work for it, although often casualties as well; but what is crystal clear is that when that entrepreneurial person steps down then the organisation has to rethink what type of organisation it fundamentally is.

In *Images of Organisation*, Gareth Morgan (1997) gives us one of the most developed dissections of modern organisational entities. Morgan points out that the origins of the word 'organisation' derives from the Greek 'organon', meaning a tool or an instrument; and therefore it is not surprising that many of our images of organisation are of the machine variety.

The generations of business models, as set out by Morgan and others (see Zohar and Marshall, 2000) can be seen as:

- The organisation as machine.
- Organisations as systems.
- Organisations as organisms (living systems).
- Organisations as emotional/social systems.
- Organisations as fully human systems.

Working in an organisation it is useful to listen to the words that people use to describe it. Are people 'driving' change, 'getting people on board', or 'planting seeds for the future'? The metaphors we use can be very illuminating both of our leadership style and the kind of organisations we work in and relate to.

In large organisations, especially those of Handy's role culture type, it is likely that there will be at least seven major elements, as set out in Figure 9.

It could be said that: structure, systems, and strategy are very much the 'hard' items required of management.

And the other four: shared values, style of leadership, staffing, and skills are more to do with leadership.

As I have stressed in Chapter 1, these issues are not exclusive. The modern organisation needs all seven to be attended to appropriately. If the head of the organisation or team is more comfortable with either the leadership or management role, then they must ensure that those items which they are least comfortable with are covered with as much or even more acuity than if they were attending to them personally. Eventually, as the leader comes to know themselves, their strengths and their weaknesses (as considered in Chapter 3), they must come to be able to challenge robustly the experts in fields other than those they are comfortable with. It has often been the case both in the private and public sectors that unchallenged specialists have overturned the whole organisational vessel.

Seeking meaning in the workplace

When it comes to attracting, keeping and making teams out of talented people, money alone won't do it. Talented people want to be part of something they can believe in, something that confers meaning on their work and their lives.
(John Seely Brown quoted in Holbeche and Springett, 2004: 5)

Picking up a broadsheet newspaper often one will find the invariable article about the 'long hours culture' prevalent in the United Kingdom and contrasting strongly with that appertaining in Europe.

With people spending such long hours in their workplace settings, it is not surprising that

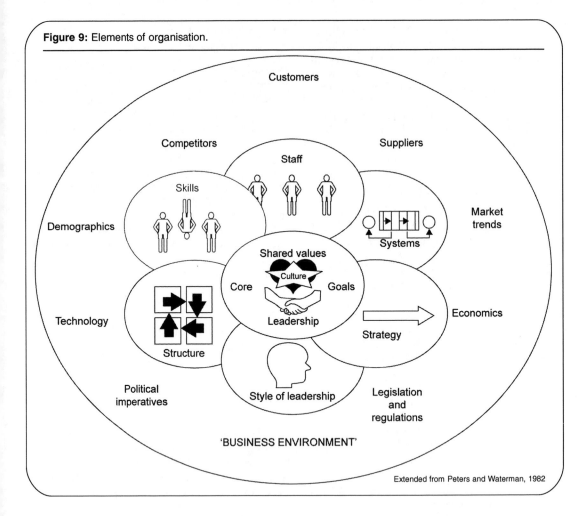

Figure 9: Elements of organisation.

Extended from Peters and Waterman, 1982

they want to find some form of 'meaning', especially as philosophers such as Viktor Frankl (1959) state that the search for meaning is humankind's primary quest.

Roffey Park Management Institute undertakes an annual Management Agenda survey of managers across the various sectors, and during the last four years, this theme which they have termed 'Quest for Meaning' has been a prevalent one. While, as Frankl suggests, this search for meaning is a part of our humanity, and one that has persisted since the dawn of time, there appear to be some specific reasons why it is so strong at this juncture. Holbeche and Springett (2004) suggest that a number of factors may be causing this:

- People generally spending longer at work than other parts of their lives.
- The pace of change and the ethic of aggression in many workplaces are making

relationships more transactional and mistrustful. People are feeling less 'connected'.
- The research indicates higher levels of employee cynicism. Corporate pronouncements around values, ethics, diversity policies etc., are greeted with scepticism (see also Mangham, 2004, on 'Leadership and Integrity').
- Changing value systems.
- A lack of trust in society's leaders (see also Onora O'Neil's Reith Lectures, 2002 on Trust).
- The search for spiritual fulfilment in therapeutic approaches, etc (see Holbeche and Springett, 2004: 3–4).

In their fascinating work, *Management Lives*, David Knights and Hugh Willmott use a number of novels e.g. David Lodge's *Nice Work*, in which the dynamic is between the male managing director of a firm, and a female academic. Vic, the MD says, sadly at one point: 'All I'm good for is work. It's the only thing I'm any good at.' When Robyn seeks to console him by responding that being good at work is something at least, Vic agrees but his unspoken thought is that in the small hours it did not seem enough (Lodge, 1989, quoted in Knights and Willmott, 1999: 37).

While it is true that the need for smart machines is increasing, the need for smart people is also gathering pace. It is increasingly recognised in business circles that the 'only real generic source of differentiation for western companies is 'knowledge'' (Scott, 2000: 6). But as Scott points out, the problem for business is that knowledge is often intangible, and is personalised – 'it tends to walk out of the building each night'! In the financial and related sectors, and in the public services, human interactions are key. Human knowledge and skill and their application are what make things work or not. The organisation which fails to speak to its employees desire for an organisation which recognises their humanity and provides meaning, will simply fail to recruit and retain those skilled people.

For those of my generation, one of the most compulsive television programmes was *The Prisoner* starring Patrick McGoohan as a captive who kept on repeating that he was a person and not a number. This is the cry of many employees today and we will return in Part 3 to a consideration of how this desire can be met.

CHAPTER 3

Leading Yourself

Know yourself.
The unconsidered life is not worth living.

(Attributed to Ancient Greek philosophers)

Trust and credibility come through everyone's observation of the manager's symbolic integrity, not his or her 'policy document'.

(Tom Peters, 1987: 149)

If the eyes are the window of the soul, you couldn't trust the man. I wasn't able to see anything in his eyes at all – he had gambler's eyes.

(staff member talking about a chief executive of a local authority)

'Wrong as living other people's lives for them?' she said. 'As a matter of fact, there's something even worse than that, which is living other people's lives for yourself'.

(Terry Pratchett, Maskerade, 1996: 320)

With the realisation of one's own potential and self-confidence in one's ability, one can build a better world.

(The Dalai Lama, 2001: 15)

Leadership is about winning hearts and minds. To do so requires first winning one's own.

(The Leadership Trust)

Introduction

We saw in Chapter 1 that people want to know what their manager stands for and whether they will stand by them when the going gets tough or will use them as a fall-guy.

Crucial to this is whether the leader has positive values, is aware of them, can nurture them and turn them into positive behaviours and actions. I say positive because an unthinking approach to leadership and cultural change can lead us to ignore the fact that many of the most evil leaders in world history had a great ability to articulate a vision, however depraved, and enculturate people to follow that dream – or nightmare! Iain Mangham's recent work on *Leadership and Integrity* (2004) and studies of the dictators of the 20th century (see, for example, Burleigh, 2001, and Evans, 2003) have demonstrated the dangers of being carried away on a tide of emotion.

Consciousness

The persons who are truly unaware of their values or warp them for their own ends are dangerous to those around them; and in the public sector, despite the United Kingdom's long tradition of civil leadership, there have been disturbing incidents of (public sector) managers being publicly scapegoated, or just simply disappearing. Some of the most notable have been the case of the Chief Executive in Lincolnshire (see Local Government Chronicle, 23 April 2004, and that of the NHS Chief Executive in Hertfordshire (Health Service Journal, 20 May 2004). Despite the checks and balances of life in the public sector, there are still too many instances of politicians or senior executives considering, not the good of the organisation, but purely their own ambition or interests. As one former Director of Social Services said to me recently, 'He (the Chief Executive) couldn't even speak to me face-to-face. He rang me to say, 'Things are getting difficult. It's either you or me – and it isn't going to be me'! In the event, while the CEO scapegoated the Director, the elected members sent him on his way, too!

A positive value-base in public service, especially around the innate value and dignity of each individual, is a corrective to the power of ideology and ambition. We tend to feel safer if we attach ourselves to an ideology and a model. The problem with this is that the

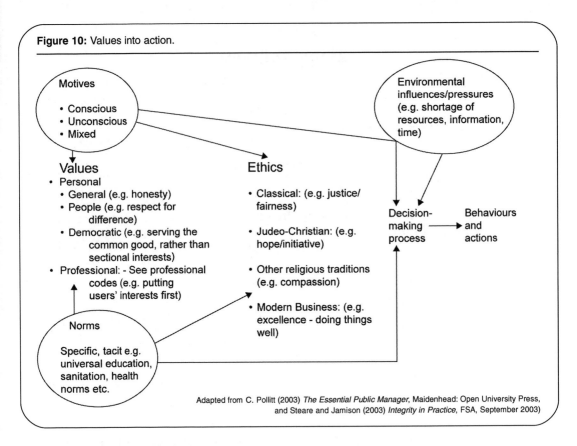

Figure 10: Values into action.

Motives
- Conscious
- Unconscious
- Mixed

Environmental influences/pressures (e.g. shortage of resources, information, time)

Values
- Personal
  - General (e.g. honesty)
  - People (e.g. respect for difference)
  - Democratic (e.g. serving the common good, rather than sectional interests)
- Professional: - See professional codes (e.g. putting users' interests first)

Ethics
- Classical: (e.g. justice/fairness)
- Judeo-Christian: (e.g. hope/initiative)
- Other religious traditions (e.g. compassion)
- Modern Business: (e.g. excellence - doing things well)

Decision-making process → Behaviours and actions

Norms

Specific, tacit e.g. universal education, sanitation, health norms etc.

Adapted from C. Pollitt (2003) *The Essential Public Manager*, Maidenhead: Open University Press, and Steare and Jamison (2003) *Integrity in Practice*, FSA, September 2003)

ideology can take over and provide a useful cloak in which to disguise personal ambition and acquisitiveness, and drive out the importance of individual human beings and humanity for the sake of a conceptual ideal. As Linus famously declared in Charles Schulz's *Peanuts* column: 'I love human kind, it's people I can't stand!'

Graham Greene (1955: 31) saw into the heart of this dilemma and described it in his novel, *The Quiet American*, which has considerable contemporary relevance. He has the Englishman, Fowler, challenging the American, Pyle: 'I hope to God you know what you are doing here. Oh, I know your motives are good, they always are . . . I wish sometimes you had a few bad motives, you might understand a little more about human beings. And that applies to your country too, Pyle'.

Motivation

We all have a motivation for being in the role we are in, forged throughout our lives: perhaps in childhood, with strong drivers often formed by parental attitudes, pushing us on to be

perfect, successful, good, assertive, etc. As Figure 10 shows, these meet with our assumptions regarding societal norms and are then put through the moulds of professional values and those dominant in society to create behaviours and actions which may or may not accord with our values.

Values

Increasingly, in a multi-cultural society, the values we engage with will be diverse, and leaders need to find ways of working with that while ensuring that their own core values remain constant or, if altered, are done so consciously, frankly and for the right reasons.

The Sainsbury Centre for Mental Health and the National Institute for Mental Health in England (NIMHE) have recently issued a pack for staff on the whole subject of values. The authors, Professor Bill Fulford and Kim Woodbridge (2004) have developed a tool which enables individuals and groups to work out, in a constructive way, how diverse values can be worked at to produce services which are value-based rather than value-less.

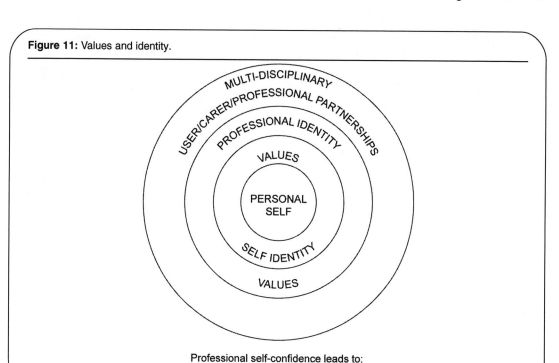

Figure 11: Values and identity.

MULTI-DISCIPLINARY
USER/CARER/PROFESSIONAL PARTNERSHIPS
PROFESSIONAL IDENTITY
VALUES
PERSONAL SELF
SELF IDENTITY
VALUES

Professional self-confidence leads to:
Confidence in professional identity in a multi-disciplinary setting

The Janki Foundation (2004) has also produced a training pack for staff to assist them in focusing on humane values, based partly on 'Eastern' concepts of compassion and valuing the individual human being, which aim to bring a humane approach back into the workplace. Both these products address one of the major tensions in human services today, namely how we can produce higher levels of performance, on a consistent basis, while keeping human services human! Weak leadership tends to focus too much on keeping the team happy, while bullying leadership generates short-term gains and long-term losses. As the doyens of public sector leadership, Beverley Alimo-Metcalfe, and John Alban-Metcalfe (2004: 174), put it: 'One of the real dangers of becoming driven by targets is that managers can become so target focused that they behave in ways that can destroy the motivation and morale of their staff, which of course, in turn deleteriously affects performance and leads to other costly outcomes.'

It is important not to be naïve about all this. While it is reassuring for professional workers to know that their senior managers have a professional qualification and have practised as professionals, this will not necessarily mean that they continue to hang on to their values as they move up the management ladder. Dana

> *Exercise 5: Value base*
>
> You are invited to set down your core personal values.
>
> What are the other values: professional, family, belief system, philosophy, which influence your leadership practice?

Weinberg (2003) in her study of acute hospitals in Boston, points to the importance of the choice of an experienced nurse leader at the Beth Israel Hospital in her twin roles as Vice President of Nursing and Clinical Nurse Manager for encouraging an appropriate, but not ghettoised professionalism for nurse practitioners. These were crucial in retaining and developing a professional and humane approach to patients. In my own experience, once as a senior manager I worked to an executive and an elected politician who were both professing Christians, an elected politician with no particular religious faith, and another senior executive who was a Christian. The first two I found personally untrustworthy and lacking in integrity, and they had a poor reputation both within and outside the organisation. The second two were perceived as people of integrity, who were prepared to take difficult decisions and stand by them in a way which exposed themselves to the difficulties of being challenged, and having to justify those decisions.

Again, speaking personally, I have always tried to manage in a humane and civilised way. I do not believe that this is in any sense a soft option, not only because of the point made by the Alimo-Metcalfes above, but because often the bullying approach is not only counter-productive in the long-term but may ironically be extremely ineffective in the short-term as well. Working as a service manager in London some years ago, I had responsibility, amongst other establishments, for an under-performing day service for people with learning disabilities. The Director was rightly unhappy with the way the service was operating. His aggressive style of tackling it, however, had simply led the manager and his deputy to dig their heels in. A much more effective approach was to spend some time getting to know the individuals; take the pressure off the deputy and invite him to think of his career in a more far-reaching way, which led to his early retirement, and doing something he enjoyed, rather than trudging on with a job which gave him and nobody else any satisfaction; and to give the manager more direction and support to turn the service round.

I have often been struck by the fact that a number of managers shout a great deal about what is required, but do not seem to have been able to convey this to the staff they manage. Staff who appear to be taking the service down the wrong road, and with whom I have sat down to examine their performance in the light of the service's mission and objectives, have often been taken aback that anybody should hold up a mirror to them of what they are meant to be achieving and what they are actually accomplishing.

Managing yourself and your career

Roffey Park Institute's Conference, *Women making the difference* (24 November 2004) featured amongst others Debra Veal, MBE, who became the youngest woman to row solo across the Atlantic. Readers will recall that it was meant to be a duo, but her husband, an experienced oarsman himself, left the boat after he developed an uncontrollable fear of the ocean. Debra recalls that she was an

underachiever at school and in many ways rather quiet and unassuming, but she has developed an 'immense self belief which I didn't have as a child', and it makes her 'want to reach out and achieve more and more'. During the voyage, she practised mental attitude and mental strength; 'I could easily have sat there and thought I'm lonely, I hurt, the food is dreadful, I've got months to go and there's 30 foot waves, sharks and super-tankers around the boat. There were so many negatives. But we all have a choice about the attitude we adopt' (Roffey Park Newsletter, Autumn 2004: 8). Now, in all situations, she visualises meetings, working with different people etc., so that she is always putting herself in a positive state.

Many of us spend a lot of time trying to understand others, but little time in attempting to understand ourselves! (see Thompson, 2005, forthcoming). Some of our common barriers to understanding are:

- We fail to understand our internal motivations, e.g. a desire to help, a drive to power etc.
- We do not grasp our power psychological make-up.
- We have not examined our personal values, and how these impact on professional/ managerial values, and our behaviours (see Figure 11).

Both Vivienne Martin (2003) and Jane Sturges (2004) invite us to look at our learning and leading. Sturges talks about the 'individualisation' of the career, where careers are no longer kept within the parameters of an organisation, but become boundary-less and portable (see Sturges, 2004: 256). This links strongly with the concepts of post-modernism and liquid modernity which we examined in Chapter 2. The modern manager is less likely to be climbing a vertical ladder, and much more likely to be scaling a complex cliff face, moving both up and across in the search for appropriate footholds and ledges.

Sturges identifies a number of ways in which people may define success:

- **The climber** – career success very much defined in terms of objective criteria, such as hierarchical position, promotion and reward.
- **The expert** – achieving a high level of competence in their role and gaining recognition and respect.

Pathological Leadership Example 2: Gustav III of Sweden

The historian, A.D. Harvey (2003: 15) calls Gustav III one of 'the great might-have-beens of history', but also the 18th century ruler 'who most strikingly anticipates the more disquieting features of 20th century politics'.

It is easy to forget that in the 17th century, Sweden had been a pivotal power in Western Europe, but by the time Gustav III came to the throne in 1771, the Swedish state had declined and become 'a byword for weak government, corruption and impotence'. The main parties in the Swedish parliament were, in effect, in the pay of foreign powers – respectively France and Russia, and it was Gustav, almost single-handedly, who faced down that corruption and began to use his power to place the state on a modernising path, along the lines of his fellow rulers in Austria, Prussia etc.

The downside of his character was that he never managed to fully inspire trust and respect, despite considerable physical courage in the face of adversity, partly because of the result of what Harvey describes as 'his obsessive deviousness and under-handedness'. As the British Minister at Stockholm reported,

'His confidants, are never entirely so, but he has a singular art in dividing the trust he reposes in each, and his whole life is a continual scene of intrigue and suspicion'. Bearing in mind the divided nature of the Swedish state and its instruments, such as the Armed Forces, Gustav needed all the loyalty he could gain, but unfortunately showed little gratitude for loyalty. When some of his ablest subordinates were scapegoated for problems that arose, loyalty inevitably was undermined.

Gustav used a number of strongarm tactics to cow his enemies, and it is in that that Harvey sees a prequel to some of the regimes of the dictators in modern times.

- **The influencer** – who can change, and be seen to change, aspects of the organisation's culture and performance, irrespective of their place in the hierarchy.
- **The self-realiser** – where career is governed very much by internal concepts, based on an internalised view of achievement which may mean little to other people (Sturges, 2004: 254–5).

It is vital to your and other's success and happiness that you examine your own real concept of career achievement.

Many practitioners remark that they find it difficult to see themselves assuming a management or leadership role, but in fact, the majority of effective practitioners are good managers through:

- The channelling of appropriate emotions (see Goleman et al., 2002).
- Keeping themselves 'in good shape' physically and mentally.
- Organising their life – I do not mean being obsessional – and their day so that they can make decisions and see them through.
- Communicating with those around them – many of us will have known brilliant individuals who sabotage a project simply by going their own sweet way without bringing people with them.

And effective leaders by:

- Developing their own narrative and vision for themselves and their work.
- Stretching themselves mentally, emotionally, physically and spiritually.
- Pushing forward the boundaries of practice.
- Developing others.

The main thrust of Eastern and Western philosophies can be enshrined in two words respectively: '**being**' and '**becoming**'. The ability to harness these two aspects of our lives is a vital ingredient in human development and therefore to becoming a truly effective leader.

Self-awareness

Howard Gardner, in his depiction of 10 modern leaders, in *Leading Minds – An Anatomy of Leadership* (1997: 14) quotes Charles Cooley as saying, 'all leadership takes place through the communication of ideas to the minds of others'.

The leaders Gardner brings into focus weave stories through how they live or what they do;

Leadership Example 3: Nelson Mandela

Mandela who opposed the apartheid regime in South Africa, was imprisoned for his beliefs, released in 1990, and was voted in as his country's first black President. He wrote about his experiences in *Long Walk to Freedom* (Mandela, 1994) when he said:

> I was not born with a hunger to be free. I was born free – free in every way that I could know . . . It was only when I began to learn that my boyhood freedom was an illusion, when I discovered as a young man that my freedom had already been taken from me, that I began to hunger for it. At first as a student, I wanted freedom only for myself . . . but then I slowly saw that not only was I not free, but my brothers and sisters were not free. I saw that it was not just my freedom that was curtailed, but the freedom of everyone who looked like I did . . . that is when . . . the hunger for my own freedom became the greater hunger for the freedom of my people . . . I am no more virtuous, self-sacrificing than the next man, but I found that I could not even enjoy the poor and limited freedoms I was allowed when I knew my people were not free. Freedom is indivisible; and the chains on any one of my people were the chains on all of them, the chains on all of my people were the chains on me (616).

Mandela's obvious qualities are:

- His *integrity* in holding firm to his beliefs; in *willingness* to sacrifice his personal happiness and comforts; and the *forgiveness* shown to his captors and political opponents.
- The *formation and articulation of the vision* for a new multi-racial South Africa. His political opponent, ex President de Klerk said of Mandela:

  The ordinary man would get to the top of the hill and sit down to admire the view. For Mandela there is always another peak to climb and another one after that. For the man of destiny the journey is never complete.

- The *energy* to take on the presidential role in his 70s and to tour other countries on behalf of South Africa.
- An extraordinary internal, personal process whereby justifiable anger is turned away from bitterness and into a search for *connectedness* over boundaries, and bring *courage* in sticking with the path he knew was right.
- His *commitment to peace and justice*, whereby Mandela uses his experience to urge other groups in conflict to find peace through justice.
- His ability to *live the vision* – for example, wearing the Springbok rugby jersey, with its Afrikaner connotations at the final of the Rugby World Cup, held in South Africa, and the mutual embrace with François Peinaar, the Afrikaner captain of the team.

---

they may extract stories from a group and rework them into a powerful motif; or they may create a new story – especially so for the nation-builder, company-founder etc (see leadership examples).

To weave stories or to transmit ideas, however, we have to have a narrative/concept within us to relate. Ursula Le Guin, in her novel *The Lathe of Heaven* (1971) tells of a progenitor of stories who is tricked by his therapist so that the latter takes over the dream-making. Because the therapist himself has no inherent values, however, the dreams that become reality are grey and lifeless and begin to suck dry reality itself.

As Shakespeare put it: 'The man [or woman] who has no music in himself is fit for treasons, stratagems and spoils' (*The Merchant of Venice*).

The music must come from within ourselves, and that can only be developed by an awareness of who we are; what our story is; how we relate to others; and how we can develop a narrative that is of mutual benefit to those we live in community with.

Without in any way advocating a long period of introspection – often almost as destructive as a blithe unawareness of self – it can be useful to consider the broad psychological types; how we perceive reality; and how/why we may feel threatened or insecure. People with major insecurities are probably the most difficult to work with, because they neither trust nor like themselves, and therefore, mistrust the motives of others, however well-intentioned.

Dorothy Rowe, writing in *The Successful Self*

(1998) describes two main psychological types in relation to the experience of existence:

• Those of us who experience our self as being a member of a group, as the relationship, the connection between our self and others, see the threat of the annihilation of the self as complete isolation, being left totally, utterly and forever alone, thus withering, fading away, disappearing into nothingness.
• Those of us who experience our self as the progressive development of our individuality in terms of clarity, achievement and authenticity see the threat of the annihilation of the self as losing control of your self and your life and falling apart, falling into chaos, fragmenting, crumbling to dust (12–28).

Just because I have been a social work practitioner for part of my career does not mean that I would recommend a long course of psychotherapy! Far from it, an over-investment in therapy, as opposed to the benefits of a more focused approach, can lead to too much introspection and a separation from colleagues and friends.

What is worth exploring is insights into your personality which assist you to:

• Ascertain your areas of strength and developmental needs.
• Explore issues around security and insecurity.
• Gain insight into how you learn and behave, and how to gain more from experience.
• Evaluate your interactions with others and how to become more effective.
• Promote a greater integration between aspects and areas of your life.

Models

1. The Belbin team matrix (Belbin, 1981, 1993) which assesses your aptitudes in a team context. This fairly straightforward approach can be a revelation in itself. If you individually, or your team as a whole, produce wonderfully creative ideas but no end products, then you/they may be a 'Plant (s)'. Changing the team structure so as to bring in 'Shapers' and 'Completer Finishers' may gain creativity and results together!
2. Briggs-Myers (1992) based on Jung's psychological insights, identifies where each individual is on a continuum of four poles:
   Extravert – Introvert
   Sensing – Intuitive
   Judging – Perceiving
   Feeling – Thinking
3. The Enneagram – which is compatible for use with Briggs-Myers – uses a nine point personality profile (see Palmer, 1995, and Hampson, 2005).
   This method provides valuable insights into your natural personality. It is much more complex than seeing yourself as one 'type' but also, crucially, in the work setting, it shows how one is likely to react under pressure; and how one can constructively interact with superiors, subordinates and other stakeholders, with differing personalities.
4. Neuro-linguistic programming – a way of looking at yourself and what drives you, and then using both conscious and unconscious thought processes in a positive way to influence attitude and behaviour (see O'Connor and Seymour, 1993).

These specific approaches, added to a continual reflexive practice, help us move along the continuum set out in Figure 12.

An holistic approach

*If you don't **believe** ... you can't solve these problems and you can't even survive them.*
(Harold Macmillan, former British Prime Minister, Horne, 1989: xiii, emphasis added)

Jagdish Parikh's masterly book, *Managing Yourself: Management by Detached Involvement* (1991), brings together the Western 'know yourself' with the Eastern 'become yourself' and places the manager in a situation where they have a realistic chance of bringing together in a congruent whole:

• self
• family and community
• the world of work
• the internal game
• mind, body, emotions, senses and spirit

This approach can lead to your becoming a more effective leader and a more complete person. It may also lead to a wholesale change of lifestyle. Some people decide that what they are being asked to do no longer accords with their values. Others, like Mike Grabner, CEO of Energis, decide to leave and start a new working lifestyle at 50 (*The Sunday Times*, 20 May 2001). As Professor Nigel Nicholson of the London Business School states in the same article:

CASE STUDY 4: SETTING UP A SPECIALIST CHILDREN'S DOMICILIARY CARE SERVICE IN OXFORDSHIRE

Contributed by Helen Ashmore, Registered Manager Children and Family Care Services, Oxfordshire Social Services.

'10 years ago I took on the management of a small, locally based service that had been providing carers with breaks from caring for about five years. The service was an innovative one and valued by the people using it. I had understood that the service was for carers of disabled adults, but soon established that there were about 40 parents of disabled children also using the service.

I had two main concerns about the service. The first was that the service was clearly valued but only carers in certain localities in the county were receiving help. The second was that staff were being recruited to work with adults but many found themselves also working with children.

After managing the service for about 18 months, I requested a meeting with the Assistant Director and my Service Manager. I felt that, at this point in time, I had a good understanding of the value of the service to its users and could give many examples of carers who had been supported to continue providing care to their relatives, which was clearly cost effective to the department. I wanted to ensure that the service was replicated throughout the county to prevent the 'postcode lottery' and ensure all carers had access to breaks from caring. I suggested a model at minimal additional cost for a county-wide service. The model was accepted and implemented gradually over the next 18 months until five locally based services were established.

I now had a peer group of managers to work with to develop the service further. I was then able to address my second concern: that there was no consistency in provision of services to children, nor were the training needs of care staff working with children or recruitment practices being addressed.

I was working closely with colleagues in Home Care services at this time and, after some research, discovered that they, too, had no consistency of service delivery to children. I proposed to senior managers that we consider establishing a specialist children's domiciliary care service. This was initially rejected as it was felt that the service would be too small and that specialising may pose problems in recruitment. I wrote a more detailed proposal about what I believed would be the benefits of a specialist children's service. These included: (a) developing appropriate recruitment practices and screening; (b) establishing a team of expert practitioners who were working with children because they wanted to; (c) bringing people into domiciliary care who may not have applied for posts to work with adults, thus increasing recruitment opportunities; (d) developing training which was child-focused; (e) managers developing expertise and knowledge of working with children; and (f) improved liaison with other child care practitioners.

A working group with Home Care colleagues and managers from children's services was established and we agreed to ring-fence money from existing resources to set up a small Specialist Children's Domiciliary Care service which integrated the Relief to Carers service and the Home Care services for children. The integration of the services provided continuity of care for families and a single point of contact for them. I was asked to manage the development of the service initially with a colleague from Home Care.

Six years later, the service provides care to about 240 families. It employs about 60 care assistants and 10 behaviour support workers who provide care to a range of severely disabled children and to families in need of support in the community due to illness or disability of a parent. The service also supports foster parents, and families where there are child protection concerns.

As a specialist service, it has developed good links with Community Children's Nurses, and through their training and support, is able to provide health care tasks to some of the more severely disabled children. It has also developed a specialist behavioural support service to care for disabled children with complex behavioural needs and, in conjunction with the Education Department, is now employing joint posts to support children in schools.

Recognising need and gaps in service provision, developing partnerships with service users and colleagues from other agencies, problem-solving, lateral thinking, motivating your staff team, having the courage and tenacity to take ideas forward and the enthusiasm to see them develop, are all essential qualities of good leadership.'

Figure 12: Emotional intelligence: Leadership competencies and connectiveness.

Self awareness	Self management	Self leadership	Social awareness	Relationship management
• Emotional self-awareness • Accurate self-assessment • Self-confidence • Integrity	• Self-control • Transparency • Adaptability • Trustworthyness	• Optimism • Initiative • Achievement • Iconic personhood	• Empathy • Organisational awareness • Serve to lead • Awareness of skills, strengths and deficits	• Inspiration • Influence • Intellectual stimulation • Individualised consideration • Developing others • Creating positive networks • Change catalyst • Conflict management • Teamwork and collaboration

Derived from D. Goleman et al. (2002), *The New Leaders: Transforming the Art of Leadership into the Science of Results*:
B. Bass and B. J. Avolio ed. (1994) *Improving Organisational Effectiveness Through Transformational Leadership*,
and S. Covey (1992) *Principle-CentredLeadership*.

People are looking at different lifestyles and values. It's an aftermath of the selfishness of the 1980s and 1990s and people have come to value a more balanced lifestyle ... and are working to live rather than living to work.

Working in Britain in recent years has tended to produce a very one-dimensional workaholic culture. Looking at ourselves holistically, we need to consider our:

- Social/emotional needs:
  - relationships: loving and being loved
  - security
  - acknowledgement and expression of feelings
  - kinship
  - friendships
  - community involvement
  - empathy
  - appreciation of creation
- Intellectual or cognitive needs:
  - opportunities for fresh thinking
  - reading, and reflection on the texts
  - planning ahead
  - creative writing
  - visualising positive futures
  - films and plays
- Spiritual needs:
  - recommitting to core values
  - meditation and contemplation
  - relaxation
  - exploration of 'being' and 'becoming'

- Physical needs:
  - a healthy diet
  - physical fitness
  - a sense of well-being and being better able to cope with the stresses of work
  - gaining a sleep and awake time balance
- Creative needs:
  - using our senses
  - exploring new ways of working/leisure
  - developing creative hobbies

These five elements interact. For example, the leisure firm, Cannons, recently undertook some partnership work with the mental health charity Mind. In a survey of the health club's members, 75 per cent used exercise to reduce stress; 67 per cent said they used exercise to maintain their mental health, such as in lifting 'low' moods; 64 per cent reported improved self-esteem; 64 per cent reported boosted energy levels; 58 per cent reported improved motivation and 35 per cent said their performance at work had also improved (see Gilbert, 2005).

Antony De Mello (1988) brings together Eastern and Western philosophy in his work on spirituality. He quotes the great German mystic, Meister Eckhart, as saying 'You should be less concerned about what you have to do and think much more about what you must be. For if your being is good, your work will be of great value (56).

Learning for the future as well as the present

As Scott (2000) has pointed out, knowledge is 'the only real generic source of differentiation for western companies', and knowledge 'is personalised. It tends to walk out of the building each night'! (6). As organisations transmute, restructure and transmigrate, bonds between firms and workers decay, and the 'savvy knowledge-worker is concerned about their own career, the development of their skills and their personal equity, independent of their immediate employer' (ibid).

Because the organisation (and therefore the corporate and individual role) of today is not that of tomorrow, public companies and private bodies need to appoint people adaptable enough to be competent in the job they have to perform immediately and the role they will have to fulfil in the near future. Managers, to survive and prosper, have to know themselves, their strengths and needs, how they learn, and what will increase their personal and employment proficiency.

In this climate, self-managed learning would appear to be an increasingly potent approach, as opposed to a blanket method, neatly encapsulated by the graffiti which Cunningham (1999: 3) quotes in his book on strategic self-managed learning: 'five hundred million lemmings can't be wrong'.

One way of integrating individual and group learning is through a learning set. Since 2003, for example, a learning set for directors of social care in mental health partnership trusts and care trusts has been running, initiated by Hari Sewell and Melanie Walker, and facilitated by myself. The mutual learning and support has been seen as invaluable, especially given the somewhat isolated nature of the role. A new set, for senior managers in social care in mental health organisations, commenced in February 2005, with support from SCIE (see Sewell and Gilbert, 2006: forthcoming).

Self-managed learning is about individuals managing their own learning – taking responsibility for decisions about:

- What they learn.
- How they learn.
- When they learn.
- Where they learn; and, most fundamentally.
- Why they learn (Cunningham et al., 2000).

The approach has its own seven 'S' model (see Figure 9) to match that of the rounded organisation (Bennett, 2000):

- Strategic – long-term with the big picture in mind.
- Syllabus-free – driven by the real needs of individuals and organisations.
- Self-managed – taking responsibility for own learning.
- Shared – integrating learning with others' and the organisations' needs.
- Supported – supporting people in achieving their goals.
- Structured – provides a clear structure for learning.
- Stretching – demands real, significant, learning.

As a rounded individual, working within an organisation, or working for yourself, you have to manage a number of roles in life and work, and a number of styles, depending on the people and the situation you are interacting with. Ultimately, you also need to be integrated within yourself because it is *you* you have to live with most!

CHAPTER 4

Theories of Leadership

Shakespeare does something . . . direct for modern managers. His plays portray leaders mobilising meanings to move people . . . He also demonstrates within his plays how his leaders, good and bad, use symbols and stories to provide a meaning that moves people in a certain direction.

(Corrigan, 1999: 24)

Level 5 leaders look out of the window to apportion credit to factors outside themselves when things go well . . . At the same time, they look in the mirror to apportion responsibility, never blaming bad luck when things go poorly.

(Collins, 2001: 35)

Whoever undertakes to set himself up as a judge in the field of truth and knowledge, is shipwrecked by the laughter of the gods.

(Albert Einstein, quoted in Bose, 2003: 39)

Leadership does not simply happen. It can be taught, learned, developed. Those who influenced me . . . all contributed valuable elements to my philosophy.

(Rudy Giuliani, 2002: xii)

Introduction

We have looked at leadership, in Chapter 1, as an overall concept, and then gone on to consider the world in which the practitioner and manager currently have to lead; a world environment which clearly has a considerable impact on what makes leadership effective. In Chapter 3, the necessity of leading oneself before attempting to lead others was examined, and ideas for self-awareness raising and continuous learning put forward.

In this chapter, we examine the theoretical constructs of leadership, because our practice in any field of life and work has to be both value-based and evidence-based. Many high-profile theories of leadership are built on an inadequate theoretical base, especially some studies from the USA which rely on a small, high-profile number of business leaders.

Theories of leadership

In the United Kingdom we have a besetting fault of going overboard on one paradigm, then throwing that out and going wholeheartedly for another one! As Alan Bryman (1996) puts it, in a very neat overview of the theoretical approaches: 'each of these stages [of leadership] signals a change of emphasis rather than the demise of the previous approaches'. For other succinct overviews see Storey (2004), Woodruffe

(2004) and Mullins (2002). For a valuable overview of leadership theory related to gender, see Wilson (2003, Chapter 5).

The singer, not the song: traits or qualities approach

In leadership theory, there is no greater controversy than that around the issue of traits and qualities; whether charismatic leadership is positive or pathological; and whether leaders are born or made.

Some of the first theories of leadership were predicated on the concept of the charismatic persona (see Smith and Peterson, 1988). It is easy to see the attraction of this idea and to concentrate on some of the well-known current and historical figures who appear to embody particular characteristics.

Keegan's (1987) study of Alexander the Great from a military standpoint, and Bose's (2003) recent profile from a business management perspective, shows a man of:

- Great strategic vision.
- Extraordinary energy.
- Personal (in fact sometimes reckless) courage.
- Excellent logistical sense – or at least the common sense to have a logistics expert close to him.
- Cultural sensitivity and enquiry.

- An ability and willingness to encourage talented subordinates.
- A demonstrative empathy with his soldiers.
- A talent at weaving stories to reinforce his vision.
- An extraordinary, though partial, ability to understand the constructs of cultural change, which would put the current USA administration to shame!

The historian, Arrian, tells us that after a battle, Alexander 'showed much concern about the wounded, visiting each, examining their wounds, asking how they were received, and encouraging each to recount and even boast of his exploits' (quoted in Keegan, 1987: 46). How many leaders in the public sector today would, after a personally bruising encounter for staff, take the trouble to visit them individually and in groups to assess the impact on them, and weave a narrative around that struggle?

At a time when cultural incomprehension and conflict is so stark (see Chapter 2), it is worth noting the views of both Partha Bose (2003) and the work of Professor Paul Cartledge. Cartledge (2004: 16) is of the opinion that, 'Alexander's apparently sincere notion of ethnic fusion, or at least co-operation, at the top of the administrative pyramid across cultural and political divides, is one surely to be welcomed – and maybe even initiated'.

Alexander, as we know, had his dark side, though this has to be placed within its cultural context; but it is interesting at a time when the charismatic approach to leadership theory is in decline, that Bose's fascinating work as well as, the novels by the Italian academic, Valerio Manfredi, and the Oliver Stone movie (2004), are reviving an interest in Alexander as a charismatic leader.

Edwards and Townsend (1965) discerned a number of qualities in successful business people:

- Strength of character and willingness to work hard.
- Perseverance and single-mindedness.
- Commercial flair.
- A willingness to take risks.
- An ability to inspire enthusiasm.

Argyris (1953), observing American executives, drew up a list of ten characteristics, though by no means all of these will be found in each individual:

- High tolerance of frustration.
- The ability to engage full participation from people.
- Self-questioning, without self-doubt (see Historical Leadership Example No. 3, Martin Luther King for a good example of this).
- An understanding of the 'laws of competitive warfare'.
- The ability to express negative feelings tactfully.
- The ability to accept victory with controlled emotions.
- Recovery from setbacks.
- An understanding of the need for bad news to be given.
- Identification with groups, and
- Realistic goal-setting.

Peter Drucker (1967: 18) was exceedingly sceptical about this approach. 'I soon learned,' he wrote, 'that there is no effective personality . . . all they (effective executives) have in common is the ability to get the right things done'. Drucker puts forward five elements of 'competency' which he believes anyone can attain and which lead to effectiveness:

- The management of time.
- A focus on results.
- An ability to build on strengths – their own and those of superiors, colleagues, subordinates and the situation overall.
- A concentration on a few major areas where superior performance will produce outstanding results; and
- Making effective decisions – taking the right steps in the right sequence.

The problem with the charismatic trait theory of leadership is that the emphasis tends to be on the individual, not the people who have to carry out the vision and tasks, or indeed the environment in which the organisation operates. It is too much 'I' and not enough 'we'.

The charismatic leader, often an entrepreneur in a business sense or a statesperson setting up a new nation state, may be excellent at starting something off, but hopeless at embedding an organisation/state in a way which can carry the vision forward.

Such people often do not know when to step aside, or believe themselves to be so much part of the country/company that they are irreplaceable. Alexander himself was able and willing to encourage talented subordinates, and

Historical Leadership Example 2: Florence Nightingale and Mary Seacole

At the height of her popularity, at the end of the Crimean War (1853–1856) Florence Nightingale was perceived by the British nation in highly visual, emotive and simplistic terms as: 'the lady with the lamp' (Longfellow, quoted in Small, 1998: 53) a comfort to injured and dying soldiers who had suffered immense hardship, not just at the hands of a resolute enemy and harsh climactic conditions, but through the incompetence and neglect of their own generals. Nightingale provided the human touch in a situation of great inhumanity, giving reassurance to people in a vulnerable state.

In the years following her death in 1910, however, her legacy became much more clouded and complex. Biographies began to fit her into a socio-historical pattern as: a career woman appropriate to an era (1910–20) looking forward to female emancipation; or a victim of family tensions, a 1950s preoccupation.

What Small's biography (Small, 1998) draws out is Nightingale's searing honesty and self-appraisal which caused her profound distress when she realised that her Crimean War Hospital at Scutari had caused huge numbers of unnecessary deaths because of the lack of attention to basic hygiene. That realisation incapacitated her and then drove her forward relentlessly.

Nightingale's early life is marked by her dreams of heroic action, and very strong personal beliefs and self-belief. In her youth she visioned scenarios in which she achieved her goals. She felt guilty about this but, of course, nowadays personal development and sports coaches see visioning as a powerful tool for growth and achievement. Later, she spoke of: 'Infinite wisdom . . . wills mankind to create mankind by their own experience' (14).

Bitterly frustrated at her role as a nineteenth century woman, she railed against her lot in life: 'Passion, intellect, moral activity, these three have never been satisfied in woman' (11).

She was delighted, therefore, to be appointed at the age of 32 as superintendent at a charitable hospital in Harley Street. Her ambition was wider, however, and she wished to be in a position to set up a nursing school in a large London teaching hospital, and advance nursing as a profession.

The commencement of the Crimean War, and *The Times* war correspondent's searing descriptions of an army betrayed by its 'leaders', led to the government sending Nightingale out to manage the nursing service.

Arriving at the converted barracks at Scutari, her 'towering optimism and confidence' (14) energy and administrative ability, coupled with an iron will, created an organised regime, but one which was fatally undermined by inadequate hygiene and battles with the medical staff.

Returning a national hero, Nightingale was honest enough to realise that the lack of basic hygiene precautions at her own hospital had naturally caused deaths which might have been prevented.

Minister, Sir Sidney Herbert, one of her main supporters in government, had set up a committee to raise money to establish a school of nursing at a major London teaching hospital. What is less well-known is that Nightingale became more and more convinced that environmental, rather than individual treatment, was the key to good health. In 2004, when the government has published a major White Paper on Public Health, it is interesting to speculate on what might have happened if Nightingale, at the highest point of her popularity and fame, had been placed in charge of Public Health – perhaps the health of the nation might be quite different today!

Relatively unknown compared to Florence Nightingale, Mary Seacole was recently voted 'the greatest black Briton'. Born in Kingston, Jamaica, the daughter of a Scottish Army Officer and a local Jamaican woman, she was brought up to recognise and respect both parts of her heritage. Following an upbringing which embraced both formal education, and imbibing her mother's talent for Creole medicine, she visited England on several occasions, where she married her husband. Having nursed in Jamaica during several epidemics which swept the island, she volunteered, at the outbreak of the Crimean War in 1854, to be a nurse with the British Army. The *Biographical Dictionary of Women* (1998) and Helen Rappaport (2005) opines that she was turned down on account of her colour but, undaunted, Seacole travelled to the Crimea at her own expense; set up a rehabilitation hostel; and went from this to nurse wounded soldiers on the battlefield, often under fire. She became known as 'Mother' or 'Auntie Seacole'. At the awards for the 'Greatest Black Briton', which she won, the President of the Royal College of Nursing stated that 'Mary Seacole stood against prejudices and discrimination against all the odds'.

give them independent commands; but as he never made plans for his succession, he simply left a large number of talented subordinates to fight over his empire when he died. Another more modern example would be Winston Churchill who hung onto power so long that he caused problems for his immediate successor (see Martin Gilbert, 1991). Nelson Mandela (see Leadership Example 3, Chapter 3) on the other hand, had the wisdom to know when to hand the baton on to his successor.

Separation from 'the followers' (citizens, employees, communities and so on) can lead to disintegration. Corrigan's study of Shakespeare's Roman general, Coriolanus, shows him as initially successful but isolating himself from all his followers. As one of his soldiers described him, 'he is himself alone' (Coriolanus, Act 1, Scene iv). By contrast, Benedict of Nursia, in his Rule which has endured for many centuries to build effective communities, urged that his chief executive, the Abbot, should call the *whole community* together when anything important was to be decided, because sometimes the most junior would have the best ideas (The Rule of St. Benedict, c. AD 540, English version, 1982). Followers are essential as Kelly (1988) argues. The leader who engages with and encourages good 'followership', and also demonstrates it in themselves, when appropriate, is likely to be hugely influential.

The direction of the charismatic leader may be one that leads to evil outcomes as easily as good ones. As Peter Senge (1990: 123) has pointed out, leaders 'must be able to help people understand the systemic forces that shape change. It is not enough to intuitively grasp these forces. Many 'visionary strategists' have rich intuitions about the cause of change, intuitions they cannot explain. They end up being 'authoritarian leaders'. This is a point reinforced recently by Iain Mangham (2004) in his study of *Leadership and Integrity* in the light of recent business disasters such as Enron.

The behavioural or style approach

Bryman shows that the emphasis on leadership began to move from a concentration on the personal characteristics of leaders, to their actual behaviour. One of the problems with the trait or qualities approach, especially when it is linked strongly with an extroverted charismatic

personality, is that most people think: 'while I can never be like X, I can't be a leader'.

Much of the research was carried out by the Ohio State University, and identified two main components of leader behaviour which could be called (see Bryman, 1996):

- Initiating or task-orientated – in which the leader defines clearly and closely what subordinates are meant to do, and actively performance-manages them.
- Consideration or person-orientated approach – in which staff are given a broad framework in which to work, and concern is expressed about them as people.

Not surprisingly, the research showed that the first approach led to higher performance and lower morale, with the reverse for the latter behavioural style.

In fact, at a time of considerable performance pressure within the public services, and a demographic deficit in terms of the available workforce, it is abundantly clear that leaders have to adopt a 'both and' rather than 'either or' approach.

Methodological problems with the Ohio research led onto the next theoretical stance.

Cometh the time, cometh the person; situational or contingency leadership

That canny Florentine, Niccolo Machiavelli, advises leaders to select the qualities and strategies they need to suit the situation they find themselves in. From the history of Ancient Rome, he suggests that a ruler in a time of instability would wish to select qualities from the Emperor Severus, soldier and statesman – who could be both 'lion and fox' to 'establish his state', and the attributes of Marcus Aurelius (philosopher and statesman), when skills are needed to maintain the state, 'after it has been established and made secure' (Machiavelli, 1514, Penguin edition 1961: 114).

In modern times, Richard Tannenbaum and Schmidt (quoted in Stewart, 1986) believe that managers should consider three interrelated factors:

- Their own character and qualities.
- Those of their subordinates.
- The situation at the time.

Managers' characteristics that are important in deciding how to manage include:

Table 3: Leadership styles appropriate for the various developmental levels

Developmental level of the individual	Required style of the leader
D1 Low competence • High commitment	S1 **Directing** Structure, control, and supervise
D2 Some competence • Low commitment	S2 **Coaching** Direct and support
D3 High competence • Variable commitment	S3 **Supporting** Praise, listen, and facilitate
D4 High competence • High commitment	S4 **Delegating** Turn over responsibility for day-to-day decision-making

(From Gilbert and Scragg, 1992, derived from Blanchard et al., 1986: 177)

- Their value system.
- The confidence they have or not in their subordinates.
- Their innate leadership style.
- Their ability to cope with ambiguity.

Flamholtz and Randle (1989) reinforce this in their book, *The Inner Game of Management*, when they say that the successful leader needs to be able to manage their own self-esteem so that they derive satisfaction from the things managers are supposed to do, and are enabling rather than doing; are able to manage their need for direct control over people and results; and can manage their need to be liked, so that it does not interfere with performing the managerial role.

The characteristics of followers include:

- Their dependence/independence.
- The ability to assume responsibility.
- Their tolerance of uncertainty – the need to be directed or their preference for greater choice in decision-making.
- Identification with the goals of the organisation.
- Experience and expertise.

The characteristics of the situation include:

- The type and culture of the organisation.
- The effectiveness of the teams.

- The scale and nature of the challenge.
- The amount of time available to make decisions.
- The external environment.

(Tannenbaum and Schmidt, 1958, quoted in Stewart, 1986)

Situational theory was further developed by Hersey (1984) and in Robert Blanchard's *One Minute Manager* series. In *Leadership and the One Minute Manager*, Blanchard et al. (1986) set out four basic leadership styles which can be used in different circumstances as staff develop and grow in confidence, and depending on the situation at the time (see Table 3).

In both the behaviours and the situational approach, it is worth bearing in mind the words of one of the most practical business leaders and advisers, John Harvey-Jones, former head of ICI, when he writes: 'Everything I have learned teaches me that it is only when you work with rather than against people that achievement and lasting success is possible' (Harvey-Jones, 1985).

Transactional and transformational leadership

Working with front-line and middle managers in a range of services for people with disabilities in St. Helen's MBC recently, we constructed what they called a Leadership Qualities

Table 4: St. Helens: leadership qualities framework (part only)

Quality	Behaviours	Actions (for further discussion)
1. Integrity (credibility)	• Responsibility to establish the facts of any situation. • Self-awareness and a commitment to self-development. • Respect for self and others. • Trusting others. • Openness. • Willingness to communicate both ways. Must be up and down the line and responses within a reasonable time.	• Clarity to users, carers, partners and staff as to the basis for actions. • Linked to appraisal. • Devolving budgets. • Using people's experience or expertise. • Communication strategy.
2. Honesty	• Learning from the past. • Admitting mistakes. • Mutual understanding of roles and constraints. • Knowing what you do not know.	• Sharing agenda and priorities. • Using experience to inform the present and future.
3. Change leadership skills	• Working up and down the line. • Using appropriate methods (see Table 3). • Recognise anxieties. • Use positives. • Support for managers undertaking direct changes. • Communicate up and down the line. • Anticipation of challenges.	• Collate and use practical examples. • Allocating roles and responsibilities and making expectations clear. • Developing a strategic plan and translating it into practical steps. • Specifically utilising individual and team skills from the appraisal system.

All qualities are necessary at **all** levels, but different emphasis depending on the role.

With my thanks to the St Helen's team

Framework, aimed at producing an agreed list of qualities and behaviours which provide common expectations across all management levels. This is, of course, very demanding of senior management. When we get onto Case Study 6 on Staffordshire County Council prior to the Pindown scandal, we will see that senior management had different expectations of front-line and middle management than they had of themselves, and this created a dysfunctional department which had to be effectively rebuilt. Modern business and public services will need to be competent at every level and this competence to be mirrored up to every layer of management. It is interesting to know that the initial research on Anglo-Saxon kingship demonstrates that it was based on an agreed conception with their people as to what leadership was. This point is very much reinforced by David Starkey in his recent series on *Monarchy* (Channel 4, 2004), where effective kings make a relationship of governance with the people they are governing.

The St. Helen's document demonstrates a desire for 'dispersed' or 'shared' leadership, which recognises and capitalises on the talent of a very experienced group of staff who are near to the users/clients/customers. (N.B. There are seven items in all: integrity, honesty, change leadership skills, approachability, courage and confidence, resilience, shared leadership, but only three are used here as an illustration.)

In the 1980s, what Bryman (1996) calls 'New Leadership' approaches appeared under the headings of 'Transformational Leadership', 'Charismatic Leadership', 'Visionary Leadership', and simply 'Leadership'.

Together, these labels revealed a conception of the leader as someone who defines organisational reality through the articulation of a vision which is a reflection of how he or she defines an organisation's mission and the values which will support it. Thus, the New Leadership approach is underpinned by a depiction of leaders as managers of meaning rather than in terms of influence process (280).

Kotter (1988, 1990, 1995, 1996) speaks of 'transactional' and 'transformational' leadership. In a sense, this is nothing new. General Bill Slim, one of World War II's most successful British commanders (see Historical Leadership Example 4) pointed out in the 1940s and 1950s that:

- Leadership was about people and strategy.
- Management was about resources and logistics.

In the same sense, Kotter talks about:

- Transformational leadership being about strategy and people.
- Transactional leadership being about systems and resources.

Kotter is quite clear that **both** are necessary in any organisation, though not necessarily combined in the same person.

An over-emphasis on transactional leadership can result in a team or organisation that runs smoothly but lacks capacity to cope with change which is an ever-increasing necessity.

On the other hand, transformational leadership can result in great ideas but founder on the practicalities. Both the Audit Commission and the Healthcare Commission have expressed concern that a target-driven culture may create unintended results: e.g. in distortions in patient care (*Health Service Journal*, 21 July 2005: 8); a lack of support for staff delivering the service (*Health Service Journal*, 24 March, 2005) and the end users being seen as some form of by-products of the targets themselves. As Simon Williams, Policy Director of the Patients Association put it: 'No organisation can survive if it ignores those it is here to serve. **Patients are not interruptions, they are the reason for the NHS**' (*Health Service Journal*, 21 July 2005: 8, my emphasis).

Bass and Avolio (1994) took some of these aspects further in defining transformational leadership as being made up of four components:

- **Charisma** – developing a vision, engendering pride, respect and trust.
- **Inspiration** – motivating by creating high expectations, modelling appropriate

behaviour, and using symbols to focus efforts (see Part 2 for discussion on organisational culture and change processes).
- **Individualised consideration** – giving personal attention to followers, giving them respect and responsibility.
- **Intellectual stimulation** – continually challenging followers with new ideas and approaches (see Bass and Avolio, 1993).

Too late the hero – post-transformational leadership approaches

Perhaps it is not surprising that in a post-modern world, there are considerable tensions in current leadership theory. While on the one hand, as businesses become more globalised and public sector organisations become geographically larger and more complex, staff often yearn for a more charismatic, communicative and approachable leader to relate to. Jack Welch (see Welch and Byrne, 2001) recently retired as CEO of General Electric, used to travel the world to carry the essential mission of the company to a disbursed workforce. But Jim Collins in probably the most thorough study of long-standing successful businesses, was 'surprised' to discover that the leaders who appeared to turn good companies into great ones, were 'self-effacing, quiet, reserved even shy – these leaders are a paradoxical blend of personal humility and professional will. They are more like Lincoln and Socrates than Patton or Caesar' (Collins, 2001: 12–13).

Box 1: Levels of leadership

Jim Collins's five levels of leadership.
Level 5 – Executive
Level 4 – Effective leader
Level 3 – Competent manager
Level 2 – Contributing team member
Level 1 – Highly capable individual
(From Collins, 2001: 20)

In the field of politics, at a time of great media exposure, it is not always the most thoughtful person who comes across most effectively to the public. The November 2004 United States election saw a decisive vote in favour of a president who to British and European eyes, seemed to be essentially proclaiming overly simplistic solutions to complex problems. In this context, the NHS Leadership Centre, has

CASE STUDY 5: THE ENGLISH RUGBY UNION TEAM

My maternal grandfather played fullback for Scotland at a time when Scottish teams used to win things! My mother thought soccer a vastly inferior sport, and I was therefore surprised to find her cheering vociferously for 'the auld enemy', England, during the 1966 soccer World Cup Final!

I suspect a number of people who are not naturally rugby fans will have watched England beat Australia by the margin of a last-minute drop-goal by Jonny Wilkinson, after a nail-biting final when England seemed, attempting by all means possible, to replicate our role as 'good losers' – even dropping the ball on the try line!

The most vocal critics of England coach, Clive Woodward, and there were many of them, would have to admit that beating the world champions in their own back yard, at the end of a gruelling season, was an immense opportunity, especially as they effectively out-played Australia. The next competitive games after the World Cup, however, saw a number of defeats, and accusations by some that Woodward's success had been built on the luck of having a number of outstanding players, including Captain Martin Johnson, available to him at that particular moment in history.

My own opinion is that this is mainly an inaccurate assessment; and as Woodward is very keen in his autobiography (Woodward, 2004) to consider the lessons he learned from his time as the proprietor of a small business, and from the business world in general, transferring that knowledge to sport. This is an interesting case study, and there are lessons to be transferred from sport to public or private sector business (see Case Examples in Gilbert and Thompson, 2002).

In a sense, Woodward's story as England coach ends as it began. When he resigned as England coach in September 2004, he berated the committee men of Twickenham as 'toothless' and 'apathetic', and 'compromising on potential greatness' (*The Independent*, 4 September 2004). Woodward's entry into the role in the summer of 1997 saw him with a coruscating view of the Rugby Union organisational culture he joined, despite an appreciation of the fact that some progress had been made.

Woodward's views on the management of English sport would be echoed by many (see Case Study 3), and there is no doubt that Woodward's own assessment is correct when he says that 'looking back, the one thing I'm most proud of has been creating a new culture in England Rugby and a shift in the very mindset of our players and coaching staff' (16).

What Woodward did was be prepared to think radically about every aspect of the English Rugby Union system, and to alter mindsets all the way down the line. While determined to learn from other rugby nations, he also sought to carve out a unique playing style, having watched England lose a previous Cup Final to Australia by changing their style for the final game, Woodward decided that attack and defence would be so interchangeable that strength would be consistent across the park.

Considering the diagrammatic representation of his process (417) we can see a picture which would not be that different from many non-sporting organisations: clarity of vision; a strong organisational culture, with a team involved in setting standards for themselves, which were probably tougher than those that would have been imposed from outside; a professional approach to everything; and what Woodward calls an 'elite team experience'; with vision, values and culture shot through a cycle of performance improvement which is always learning.

Unlike some soccer managers, Woodward is very clear that he is not going to criticise any individuals. Although he is critical of the old-fashioned culture at Twickenham, he is generous to those who strove to make changes. He is also critical of himself – especially in his 'errors in selection' during the 1999 World Cup, when England went out in the quarter-finals.

After Woodward stepped down, some players and rugby commentators believed that the factors which Woodward had used to induce success, had now become out of kilter, so that strengths were turning into weaknesses; specifically that Woodward had so professionalised the backup staff that the overall vision was becoming lost in detail

---

and, in the words of one commentator, 'the England team of two-and-a-half-hour training sessions and two-hour meetings' (*The Guardian*, 18 June 2004).

Whatever the reason for the dip in fortune after the World Cup Final, there is no doubt that the winning of the trophy itself was a supreme sporting achievement. Woodward took his squad training with the Royal Marines and they came away with a mental process they called 'jumping out of the helicopter', i.e. would you go into a difficult situation of any type (sport, battle, service operations, business, etc.) with this person, or are you feeling that you do not trust them?

The other point to make is the relationship between the coach and the captain. Martin Johnson, an iconic captain of few words, who describes himself, in great contrast to Woodward, as an unambitious person, somebody who does not set goals, but who simply aims to do the best he can in any situation. Perhaps the combination of Woodward's grand vision, with his detailed structure, and Johnson's focus on the immediate task in hand, was what lifted the cup.

NB. After the Lions defeat by the All Blacks in 2005, many of Woodwards critics felt justified in acusing him of putting details and structure ahead of vision and passion.

Leadership Example 4: Cardinal Basil Hume

The Rule of St. Benedict, written in the 6th century for communities attempting to light a beacon of civilisation to illuminate the 'Dark Ages' with love and learning, has recently come back into focus as a way of studying community leadership and living and achieving a sense of balance at a time of societal and personal stresses. (See Gilbert and Jolly, 2004)

Reading the Rule (Benedict of Nursia, circa AD 540) there are lessons for modern leaders in ethical governance. For instance, in Chapter 2 on the 'Qualities of the Abbot' (the monastic community's Chief Executive), St. Benedict states: 'To be worthy of the task of governing a monastery, the Abbot must always remember what his title signifies and act as a superior should' (Chapter 2, verse 1).

And again, 'The Abbot must always remember what he is and remember what he is called, aware that more will be expected of a man to whom more has been entrusted' (Chapter 2, verse 30).

Governance is set in the context of stewardship so that:

Once in office, the Abbot must keep constantly in mind the nature of the burden he has received, and remember to whom he will have to give an account of his stewardship (Luke 16:2). Let him recognise that his goal must be profit for the monks, not pre-eminence for himself. He ought, therefore, to be learned . . . so that he has a treasury of knowledge from

which he can bring out what is new and what is old (Chapter 64, verses 7–9 inclusive).

Ambition for oneself is not encouraged. Benedict describes the personality too often seen in authority: 'Excitable, anxious, extreme, obstinate, jealous or over suspicious he must not be. Such a man is never at rest'. On the contrary, 'he must so arrange everything that the strong have something to yearn for and the weak nothing to run from' (Chapter 64, verses 16 and 19).

Hume was head teacher of a Benedictine school and Abbot of Ampleforth before becoming Cardinal Archbishop of Westminster in 1976. As one of his obituarists wrote, 'The monk lived on in the Cardinal'.

As befits the spiritual leader of a faith that believes in a transcendent being, Hume always impressed people he met as someone who connected both vertically and with those around him. When John Crowley, Bishop of Middlesbrough, delivered the funeral homily on Hume, he declared:

For thirty-five years as a monk and for twenty-three years as Archbishop, Cardinal Hume centred himself on God. And from that store of wisdom he fed us. He addressed head-on the God-shaped emptiness which is within everyone. Without ever seeking it, he became a reassuring light for perhaps millions of people in this country and beyond (The Tablet, 3 July 1999).

Leadership Example 4: Continued

To talk about 'God' in a secular society is somewhat uncomfortable, but there is no doubt that this is an age when the search for some kind of 'spirituality' is a pilgrimage which many people embark on. Rolheiser (1998) writes of:

> *An unquenchable fire, a restlessness, a longing, a disquiet, an appetitiveness, a loneliness, a gnawing nostalgia, a wildness that cannot be tamed, a congenital all-embracing ache that lies at the centre of human experience and is the ultimate force that drives everything else. This dis-ease is universal. Desire gives no exemptions (4).*

It was this dis-ease which Basil Hume sought to identify, address and provide some consolation and answers for, which was the reason why he drew unto himself many people outside his own faith, or with no formal faith at all.

Allied to this vertical integration between human beings and the Other, Hume had an ability to relate to a wide range of people. John Crowley thought that this was partly because, 'that sense of the worth of the Other is strongly influenced by his conviction that every human being he meets is superior to him in some way' (Butler, 1999: 31) – the very antithesis of the narcissistic leadership model portrayed by some.

Hume's connectedness with a range of people from different cultures may have partly stemmed from his birth to an agnostic Scottish heart surgeon and a French mother. He had a good command of a number of European languages, and unusually in an English Archbishop led the convocation of European Catholic Bishops. The European and world dimensions are very evident from the contributors to Carolyn Butler's book (Butler, 1999) and there are contributions from Lord Jakobovitz, Sheikh Zaki Badawi and Cardinal Carlos Maria Martini.

In terms of his leadership, Hume was essentially an inclusive leader within an autocratic structure. The General Secretary to the Bishop's Conference recalls that his style of being chair promoted the 'discovery of the common mind'. Minority voices were always given a chance to speak, and a great deal of trouble was taken by Hume to discern the best direction before acting. Sometimes he was criticised for being too cautious, but he would often work deftly behind the scenes to produce change, and would attempt to find and steer a middle course between two extremes if that was right. Julian Filochowski, Director of CAFOD, recalls that it was Hume who was the only one to persuade Prime Minister Callaghan not to sell arms to a South American government which would have been used to oppress the civilian population. In 1996, the Catholic Church published 'The Common Good', a document on ethical, social issues, which true to the spirit of the rule of St. Benedict, looked back to the creative route of the past and forward into the future.

Cardinal Hume allied a sense of humour to a deep seriousness and dignity. Clifford Longley, a prominent Catholic commentator and journalist, wrote of Hume's significance:

> *Maybe the main part of it, was to be at the level of public image and perception rather than at the level of policy and strategy. That does not reduce its importance. Image and perception play a crucial role in chasing the relationship between a large historical organisation like the Catholic Church and the society within which it has to operate.*
>
> (Butler: 1992)

It has been pointed out that at a time when people demonstrate 'a great hunger for spirituality', a spiritual leader who 'embodies the long tradition of prayer of the Benedictine', and who is also able to speak to the concerns of present-day society, has much to offer (Butler, 1999: 78). (See also Howard, 2005.)

---

recently promoted a revival in 'servant leadership' (see Greenleaf, 1977) which links strongly with the Collins' research that shows the effectiveness of those who serve the needs of the organisation and its stakeholders rather than their own ambition. This links strongly with ancient truths, and a number of spiritual traditions (see, for example, Gilbert and Jolly, 2004) and why Leadership Example 4 considers Basil Hume's particular attributes in working

Figure 13: Developing and Redeveloping Theories of Leadership.

Traits or qualities approach
This is based on the assumption that leaders are born rather than made. Researchers examined a number of different traits which fall into three main groups: physical, abilities and personality characteristics.

Behavioural or style approach
Researchers identified two main styles: the consideration or people-orientated style; and the initiating or task-focused approach.

Although useful in some ways, this theoretical framework is too rigid at a time when people and situations change so rapidly that attention to both task and people is essential. (See Figure 4: Developing the concept of action-centred leadership)

Situational or contingent leadership
This approach is based on the commonsensical idea that there will be interactions in most situations between the leader's attitude and attitudes, the tasks to be undertaken, the strengths and weaknesses of the team, and the environment in which the leader and team have to operate.

Collins' recent research (2001) appears to indicate that the right leadership can transcend many of the situational elements in that Collins' research teams evaluated companies that were operating within very similar environments, yet gaining very different results. A successful leader coming into a new situation certainly needs to look at the situational issues. Success in one environment does not necessarily translate to another!

'New leadership'
Here, some of the themes from earlier research reappear, especially in the concept of 'charismatic leadership'. It is important to remember that the word 'charism' stems from the Greek for gifts. In the research studies, 'transactional' and 'transformational' leadership were examined and the characteristics identified.

It is worth reiterating that Kotter and others are clear that organisations need **both**.

Beyond transformational approaches
Concerns regarding companies that have strayed from the ethical compass under the leadership of individuals with powerful personalities, as in the case of ENRON, have led to an emphasis on a quieter, value-driven leadership where, as Collins puts it (Collins, 2001) 'professional will is seen alongside personal self-effacement'.

---

within complex settings, where influence and authoritativeness, rather than power are more effective. As Greenleaf puts it, servant leadership 'begins with the natural feeling that one wants to serve, to serve *first*. Then conscious choice brings one to aspire to lead. That person is sharply different from one who is *leader* first, perhaps because of the need to assuage an unusual power drive or to acquire material possessions' (Greenleaf, 1977: 13).

Combining a strategic vision, the ability to inspire, energise and empower individuals and groups, to create effective partnerships, and deliver performance in the long term without burning out one's workforce or disillusioning one's customers, is a tall order, and placing that on the shoulders of one person is even tougher.

The arrows show the movement of leadership theory, and the fact that older theories have often come back into fashion as time passes.

N.B. Some aspects of these theoretical frameworks are complementary and a number of themes recur. As we saw in Chapter 1, essentially, people want to be led by leaders they trust as persons of integrity, who know where they are going and can deliver what they say they are going to do.

It is often said of military leaders that they need 'an eye for the ground'. The Duke of Wellington, for example, was exceptional at choosing ground which would suit his tactical acumen. Leaders in the public and private sector, and in politics, also need to view the ground, see its heights and depths, and look across to new vistas and new paths. Perhaps one of the most telling remarks about Nelson Mandela came from F. W. de Klerk, who said of his sometime rival, and successor: 'Mr Mandela has walked a long road and now stands at the top of the hill. A traveller would sit down to admire the view, but the man of destiny knows that beyond this hill lies another and another – the journey is never complete' (quoted in Gilbert and Thompson, 2002: 284).

PART TWO

Integrating Theory and Practice

Many leaders and many peoples must do the building. It cannot be the work of one man, nor can the responsibility be laid upon his shoulders, and so, when the time comes for people to assume the burden more fully, he is given rest.

(Eleanor Roosevelt, upon the death of her husband,
President Franklin D. Roosevelt, quoted in Burns and Dunn, 2001: 501)

And that had led to all the trouble with How to Dynamically Manage People for Dynamic Results in a Caring Empowering Way in Quite a Short Time Dynamically *. . . Unfortunately, like many people who are instinctively bad at something, the Archchancellor prided himself on how good at it he was. Ridcully was to management what King Herod was to the Bethlehem Playgroup Association.*

His mental approach to it could be visualised as a sort of business flowchart with, at the top, a circle entitled 'Me, who does the telling' and, connected below it by a line a large circle entitled 'Everyone else'.

Until now this had worked quite well, because, although Ridcully was an impossible manager, the University was impossible to manage and so everything worked seamlessly.

(Pratchett, 1998: 24–25)

People talk about Sir Alex Ferguson's teams [Manchester United] but that effort epitomises it. How he keeps his teams motivated week in, week out; year in, year out; is just unbelievable.

(Alan Hansen, football commentator, Match of the Day, BBC1, 2004)

Introduction

In Part One we have seen a leadership thread running through the historical concepts of leadership, which stretch back well before our technological age; the specific need for leaders in a complex post-modern world; the essential requirement to manage and lead oneself before one attempts to lead others; and the theoretical approaches, which have changed over time, but still retain a number of common themes and factors.

In a world of extreme complexity and rapid change, professional and managerial leadership needs to be more sophisticated than ever without losing sight of the simple and essential characteristics of the concept. Leadership is essentially about path-finding.

Leaders must have, and demonstrate:

- Personal and professional integrity.
- Values that are constantly lived out in the workplace.
- A sound ethical base for decision-making.
- An ability to be self-aware and self-developing.

Leaders must act to:

- Set a clear, enticing and achievable vision for the future.
- Lay out the steps to achieve that vision.
- Align the mission, teams and individuals in order to achieve stated goals.
- Meet current objectives and build for the future.
- Manage change effectively.
- Inspire and empower people.

Leadership has an added impetus today at a time when organisations are often growing larger; in the public sector, across previous traditional boundaries; in the private sector, globalised corporations – but at the same time services are increasingly individualised, and therefore decision-making and the quality of service is at the front line. The NHS Leadership Centre's model of leadership (see Figure 14), contains these aspects under three main headings of: Personal Qualities, Setting Direction, and Delivering the Service. Reflecting this back to Chapter 4 and our consideration of theoretical frameworks, we can see in the NHS model that there are combined here the initiating and consideration styles, so that the modern leader has to be both task-focused and people-focused – it is not either or, it is both and.

Interestingly, while the NHS Leadership Centre's approach, and that of the National College for School Leadership (NCSL, 2004) are similar in their approach, the NCSL specifically places values and ethics in a prominent position, alongside personal awareness, managing self etc., but the NHSLC model does not. This may be partly due to the complexity of differing professional groupings, with their own professional ethics, within the field of health and social care, which makes a single value-base more difficult to articulate (see Fulford and Woodbridge, 2004).

CHAPTER 5

Who Leaders Are and What Leaders Do

It's not merely skills and techniques, but a subjective blend of personality and style. Leadership involves not only the body and mind, but the spirit and character as well: good leaders have the intuition, compassion, common sense and courage it takes to stand and lead.

(Graham, 1997: 11–12)

Vision without action is only a dream. Action without vision is a way of passing the time. Vision with action can change the world!

(Nelson Mandela)

Vision without action is hallucination.

(Beverley Malone, Chief Executive, Royal College of Nursing)

From knowledge into practice

When a practitioner moves into their first management role; an established manager moves up the career ladder; or a person steps into the most senior role in an organisation: managing a commercial company, school, NHS Trust, Social Services Department (and their successor organisations) PCT Connexions Service, voluntary organisation etc., they will be considering a number of aspects:

- What is my value base, and how does this value ethos fit with the organisation?
- Where is this organisation going? Are its vision, strategy, people and resources properly aligned to meet its imperatives and cope with the external environment?
- What do I bring to the table?
- What changes do I need to make to this organisation to improve all aspects of its performance?

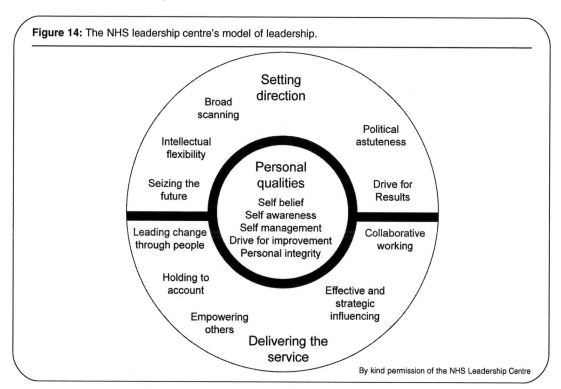

Figure 14: The NHS leadership centre's model of leadership.

By kind permission of the NHS Leadership Centre

- How do my previous knowledge and existing skills help me and the organisation achieve our mutual goals?
- What else to I need to learn?

When Stuart Rose took over as Chief Executive of the ailing high street retailer Marks and Spencer, he had worked for the company before and presumably had a shrewd idea of what he needed to do to turn it round. It is noticeable, however, that he did not simply rely on past knowledge, but got out to the high street stores themselves to converse with customers and staff, and consider the product lines and layout with fresh eyes.

The new Head of a failing school is likely to have a pretty clear view from OFSTED inspection reports as to the nature of the task. In some ways a harder task is to take over a school, or any other organisation, that is mid-pace, mid-stream, mid-ability – coasting along in the middle lane! In this instance, people will probably feel that they are doing o.k., and it may be difficult to generate sufficient energy to move the service up a gear without alienating those who are doing a reasonable but not outstanding job of work (see Chapter 8).

Creating a completely new organisation is a radically different challenge. In some ways it could be said to be easier, in that there is no detritus to be cleared first, it is a green field site. On the other hand, it involves a very high degree of strategic visioning and strategic planning (see Leadership Example 5).

Leadership Example 5: Professor Antony Sheehan and the creation of NIMHE

'We talk about patient expertise as if it's a newborn idea', said Sheehan on a visit to a voluntary organisation in South London for families with disabled children, 'well, visiting the people in Southwark – the phrase that rang out for me was the mum who said "I know my son inside and outside. When he had a stroke, I knew there was something wrong four days before the professionals assessed it as such." So there's that expertise; and if that's radical, well fine, I'm up for radical' (Brindle, 2004).

Antony Sheehan is one of those people who sheds light and brings hope. He is continually challenging everybody he meets to look at the whole person and the whole picture. This is not a soft message, it is perhaps the hardest message of all: challenging people to let go of their cherished boundaries, prejudices, myopia, habits and 'leylandii hedges', to focus on what really matters. I once asked a nurse who had worked for him what he was like as a senior nurse, 'like he is now', she replied, 'he listened as he led'.

Setting up the National Institute for Mental Health in England (NIMHE) in 2002 was an imaginative leap. Mental health has in many ways been the poor relation within the NHS, and social services have often seen it as a health specialty/responsibility, and under-funded it. The cost to the nation of poor mental health has been estimated at £30 billion, and is a major issue at a time when Western European countries depend for their future, economic strength and general well-being on mental well-being and creativity of their citizens (see Gilbert, 2003b). NIMHE was set up to:

- Turn policy into reality on the ground.
- Improve the quality of life for people of all ages who experience mental distress.
- Work in partnership beyond the NHS.
- Develop services.
- Support staff to put policy into practice.
- Resolve local challenges in developing services (NIMHE, 2002).

What was new about NIMHE was that it provided a strong developmental focus on mental health. As the Prime Minister wrote in the foreword to the Strategy, 'For too long people with mental health problems have been stigmatised by society . . . they have not always received the support and services they needed . . . the National Institute . . . will be an important vehicle for delivering these changes, providing a gateway to learning and development'. A number of previous policy approaches had seen a yo-yoing of focus between preventative services and those for people with severe and enduring mental illness. The NIMHE approach was to encompass the whole range, all ages, and ensure that those with dual diagnosis were not neglected. User participation was placed 'at the heart' of all NIMHE's work. There was a major accent on partnerships, both to break down

Leadership Example 5: Continued

boundaries and bureaucracy, but also to add value at every stage. Speaking as a student of history, one of the aspects which struck me most profoundly was the fact that the national, regional and local scenes were to be connected, both through the structure and the focus of NIMHE. British history is littered with conflict between these three tiers of national life, to the detriment of citizens.

Antony Sheehan is seen as a visionary leader, with a whole person and whole systems approach, which he now has to carry forward as Director of Care Services for the Department of Health, with responsibility for all services for adults, and liaising across with the Education Ministry for Children's Services. Through visiting a range of services on the ground (not just statutory services), and supporting, when he was CEO of NIMHE, the regional partnership conferences, Sheehan has linked a vision for a valued lifestyle, and service delivery, with individual people, with values at the heart of the process. He is a natural partnership-maker, and a lateral thinker who is always looking to maximise the value that can be gained by situations. Joining the NIMHE Core Group setting up NIMHE in September 2001, I was struck by the contrast in values between that management group and the one I had recently left in local government, in terms of authenticity and values.

Professor Sheehan would describe himself more as a leader than a manager. His awareness that he is likely to be planting beacons ahead for people to reach to, has led

him to bring in to his teams those who can add a structural framework.

NIMHE is organised around:
- A small central hub, providing leadership and co-ordination.
- Eight regional development centres, based (except in one instance) around the local government regional boundaries – which is significant in terms of the whole systems approach.
- A research network.
- National programmes and projects. Also Fellowships around specific themes, usually in partnership with other organisations, e.g. the Social Care Institute for Excellence (SCIE).

Work on specific areas such as acute care, is also balanced with cross-cutting issues such as stigma, work with black and minority ethnic groups, spirituality, social inclusion, gender issues, etc.

NIMHE, along with a number of other governmental organisations, such as the Valuing People Support Team, will be moving into a new cross-cutting care services organisation (CSIP), with the aim of joining up those parts of real life where people live and work.

Philip Larkin, the poet, once said, 'they give me medals for negative thinking, I'm not stopping now!' Antony Sheehan may not have got any medals, but he is by nature and by record a positive thinker with an accent on outcomes for people. 'There may be many reasons why I fail in this job, but it won't be for lack of talking with people, networking with people. I don't think I could do this job from behind a desk' (*The Guardian*, op. cit.).

Creating a newly integrated organisation, e.g. a Children's Trust; a Local Authority Children's Directorate; a Care Trust; a Connexions Service (see Case Study 7) or a Mental Health Partnership Trust, is an amalgam of the above. In these cases, there are existing organisations which need to be brought together and a new culture (see Chapter 7) created and embedded.

Of course, the nature of the organisation/team you are leading, and your place in the whole scheme of things, will determine your room for manoeuvre in terms of

strategic position. This should not, however, prevent you from undertaking a strategic exercise and creating as much elbow room for manoeuvre as possible. Jean, a Team Manager in Case Study 1, working as a local government frontline manager within the constraints of local government aims and structures, could easily have stuck simply to delivering on caseload imperatives. She certainly did that, but at the same time, encouraged all team members to have liaison roles with GP surgeries, schools, special schools etc., which greatly enhanced the working relationships within the area to the benefit of all concerned. The Head of a residential or nursing home for older people (whether public, private or voluntary sector) who creates links with local schools and colleges, at a time of a shortage of care workers, is thinking strategically.

Setting the strategic direction

Henry Mintzberg (1994) talks about making a clear distinction between strategic thinking and strategic planning. Strategic thinking is not only analysing the environment in a consideration of existing strategies, but utilising intuition and creativity to think new thoughts. Strategic planning is taking that analysis and thought processes into an over-arching plan for the future.

Johnson and Scholes (1989) consider five steps towards gaining a strategic position:

- Audit of environmental influences.
- Assessing the nature of the environment.
- Identifying key environmental forces through structural analysis.
- Identifying the competitive position.
- Identifying key opportunities and threats.

They talk about three main strategic periods: strategic analysis, strategic choice and strategy implementation.

This very rational approach is set out in clear terms in Richard Lynch's *Corporate Strategy* (2000: 66–74) in what he calls 'the prescriptive strategic process'. While this has value, it can induce the delusion that the world stops while we strategically plan in our own little corner of the world! Collins and Porras (2000) have pointed out that many of the great firms: Hewlett Packard, Sony, Wal-Mart and others, did not start with a grand plan. As Bill Hewlett put it:

> When I talk to business schools occasionally, the professor of management is devastated when I say that we didn't have any plans when we started – we were just opportunistic.
>
> (quoted in Collins and Porras, 2000: 24)

So, while in the public sector, strategic planning is essential, leaders need to stay light on their feet, to take advantage of the opportunities offered. One of the worst tasks I was handed as a middle manager was to chair a group mainly composed of people who were senior to me ('you don't need the formal position', my

director said to me optimistically, 'you've got the right expertise and that's all that matters'!): senior managers in health and social care, where the senior NHS manager wanted to produce a ten-year strategic plan with no room for opportunistic deviations; while the social care manager wished to have maximum opportunism and minimum strategic planning!

Box 2: Strategic decisions

Strategic decisions are concerned with:
- The scope of an organisation's activities.
- The matching of an organisation's activities to its environment.
- The matching of activities of an organisation to its resource capability.
- The allocation and re-allocation of major resources in an organisation.
- The values, expectations and goals of those influencing strategy.
- The direction an organisation will move in the long term.
- Implications for change throughout the organisation.

(Johnson and Scholes, 1989: 8)

Although some cynicism is expressed about vision statements and corporate mission, if we think about it, there is nothing more important than establishing the direction and the values of the organisation or team. The new leader who fails to spot the complacency within the group, or conversely the individual wedded to their own pet solution, thus changing direction unnecessarily, will affect the whole success or otherwise of the operation. Recent research on global leadership identifies the need for a high measure of interpersonal skills and cultural sensitivity – something that is required by leaders at all levels in an increasingly multicultural society in Britain (Sinclair and Agyeman, 2004).

We have already spoken of the need for positive values, but it is worth reiterating here as recent corporate corruption cases (see Holbeche and Springett, 2004: 11) have 'shaken consumer and investor confidence'. The recent report by the Chartered Management Institute, in conjunction with the Department of Trade and Industry, in its survey of public and private sector managers, found that 62 per cent thought their managing director or chief executive was 'out of touch', and 90 per cent of respondents felt that in return their boss did not trust them (CMI/DTI, 2004). Managers wanted to see in their leaders a genuine shared vision, real confidence and trust in teams, and respect for employees, colleagues and customers. Warren Bennis, one of America's foremost management thinkers, has argued that one of the main reasons why corporate leadership was so vulnerable in the lead-up to and wake of recent scandals, was a long-term failure in creating a climate and culture of candour. Bennis asserts: 'It is not easy to welcome criticism, however honest and tactful. But a willingness to do so is one of the indispensable qualities of authentic leaders . . . People know what is wrong, even know how to fix it, but are afraid to speak out for fear of reprisals . . . Most CEOs say they want honest input but the company's truth-tellers are marginalised, if not driven out' (quoted in Sinclair and Agyeman, 2004: 19).

Perhaps one of the most difficult aspects for leaders coming into a new situation is that their cherished ambitions for the way they want to do things may be properly challenged by a variety of internal and external stakeholders. A new chief executive of a Primary Care Trust (PCT) or Strategic Health Authority might feel that their financial challenges could be solved by the closure of community hospitals. Local communities, politicians, and social care organisations, might put a counter argument that community hospitals provide not only a better quality of life, but take the pressure off the acute hospitals. How the new person leads through conflicting points of view and decision-making processes, will be the making both of the resolution of this challenge and future challenges to come.

Vision and values must be stated clearly and publicly. Arriving in Staffordshire County Council Social Services as Operations Director for Adult Services, in May 1992, I found that there were almost no strategies, policies or procedures extant, because the previous directorate had not wished ever to be held accountable to anything that was written down! This translated itself into strategic approaches where preparation for the implementation of the NHS and Community Care Act, 1990 (to be implemented on 1 April 1993) was dependent on pilot studies in care management, which were due to report in June 1993, two months after the legislation became operational! (see Case Study 6, Chapter 6).

From strategy to performance

One of the main challenges facing the sectors this book is aimed at, is how to increase performance effectiveness while keeping stakeholders on board – not least the staff who have to deliver human services to people in a humane manner.

There are often complaints by managers about the practical application of the performance measures. There is little disagreement, however, that there should be a performance framework. In the public sector, and in the private sector with whom statutory agencies contract, there should be clarity about what is delivered to whom and how. Arriving in Staffordshire in 1992, I found that in one third of the county (with an overall population of a million people), the mental health services had become so skewed by GP fund-holding, and other related primary care initiatives, that they no longer had a vision of service for those who had the most severe mental health problems. When the Health Trust and I surveyed the service, we discovered that the most seriously ill and disadvantaged people were being worked with by those who were most junior and least qualified amongst the whole staff group. Social workers had got into a counselling role, which had moved them drastically away from the effective delivery of social work in the round (see Gilbert, 2003b). Conversely, a metropolitan area I worked with recently, had invested too little in primary care mental health services, so that now referrals were inappropriately coming through into secondary services, reinforcing an illness rather than a wellness model.

So, leaders have to be hard-nosed about performance and effectiveness. They need to know what they are delivering, to whom, and how they are going to do it. They then need to monitor and evaluate that service delivery. Even the governmental evaluators, however, have expressed concern recently that, to quote James Strachan, the new Chair of the Audit Commission:

Too many people are beginning to see the perform- ance indicator as an end in itself. They lose sight of what that performance indicator is supposed to be an emblem for, and once you have done that, frankly you have lost the plot.

(quoted in the *Health Service Journal*, 14 November 2002: 19)

The current President of the ADSS, Tony Hunter, believes that:

Social care needs leaders who focus on people's experiences and outcomes.

(quoted in *Community Care*, 21–27 October 2004: 32)

And in another article specifically on performance indicators ('Stars in Their Eyes', *Care and Health*, 16–29 October 2002), Hunter talks about 'knowing your story', where the narrative of what is happening in one authority, because of its own particular circumstances, is candidly compared with those of other authorities in a spirit of challenge.

Recent surveys of the NHS have concluded that many of the key indicators did not appear particularly relevant to patients or users themselves: 'Patients' opinions of individual acute trusts are much more influenced by how well they feel they were looked after . . . There is a very strong correlation between the extent to which patients feel they are treated with dignity and respect and their overall perception of a hospital' ('What they really, really want', *Health Service Journal*, 8 April 2004: 16–19).

As well as external indicators, organisations may well be operating their own performance management system based on, for example:

- The Excellence Model, launched in 1991 by the European Foundation for Quality Management (EFQM) (see Moullin, 2002, Chapter 4).
- The Balanced Score Card (see Kaplan and Norton, 1996).
- Quasi-Governmental frameworks (e.g. Audit Commission, 2001).

Mark C. Scott identifies 'seven waves of reinvention' from 1985 to 1999, which have squeezed the inefficiencies out of many private and public sector organisations (Scott, 2000).

All these movements have achieved cost efficiencies in both private and public sectors, but with decreasing returns in terms of cost benefits, and an increasing alienation of employees. As one annual audit of employee attitudes put it: 'It is disturbing to report such an erosion of loyalty amongst internal customers (i.e. staff) when most firms are so avowedly pursuing loyalty campaigns with their external customers!' (quoted in Scott, 2000: 8).

Motivation

Executives need to be clear about how they see the factors which motivate or demotivate those who work for them. It was the American social scientist, Douglas McGregor (McGregor, 1960), who worked up his theory X and theory Y, based on a pessimistic/optimistic dichotomy, depending on how we view human nature. In theory X people are seen as naturally lazy and needing a stick and carrot approach; in theory Y workers are seen as basically self-motivated but requiring a favourable environment in which to work. In the 1980s the work of Peters and Waterman (1982) and William Ouchi (1981) was instrumental in trying to puzzle out why companies in the 'Tiger Economies' of the Far East were more successful than their US and UK counterparts. Ouchi came up with Theory Z (see Table 5).

The work of Herzberg (1960) is very useful in pulling these theories together. When he interviewed workers in the United States, his survey groups identified two sets of factors: hygiene or maintenance factors, which would cause dissatisfaction if they were absent, and motivators which gave a positive incentive. The hygiene or maintenance factors were company policy, administration, supervision, interpersonal relations, status, a salary, security and the impact of the job on personal life. The motivators were achievement, recognition, responsibility, advancement, interesting work, and the possibility of personal growth.

Clearly many of these interlock and it is the responsibility of managers to look at individual and small group methods rather than the blanket approach that proved so unsuccessful as incentives in the old Soviet Union economy or the British car industry of the 1980s.

There is often very little room for manoeuvre in the public sector which has over-relied in the past on 'job satisfaction'. Here an even more imaginative approach must be used with recognition, career structures for advanced practice, opportunities for personal growth and the building of effective teams which enjoy working and possibly recreating together. The administrative burden needs to be lifted as far as possible within the constraints of public accountability, and employees need much greater feedback that the work they are doing day by day is having a positive effect and changing people's lives. Kent SSD is a good example of creating a radically improved career

Table 5: Motivational theories

Theory X	Theory Y	Theory Z
People dislike work and try to avoid it.	People see work as fulfilling part of their psychological need to find value and meaning.	People identify with a corporate vision, value system and presentation which is accurate and explicit.
People work only if you use a 'carrot and stick' approach.	Most people can be motivated if given a realistic and noble goal to aim for.	Workers respond to clear and achievable organisational goals.
People avoid responsibility at all costs.	Self-discipline is far more effective than that imposed from outside. People enjoy the challenge of responsibility if given guidance and support.	Teamwork and intensive socialisation have worked well for Japanese firms in Europe, the USA and Japan.
Money and fear make things happen!	The desire to realise our full potential is even more powerful.	Individualised performance-related pay is a motivator. Each individual should feel a hero or heroine in trying to improve own performance.
People are only creative when it's a case of trying to buck the system.	There is a great deal of untapped creativity waiting to be released.	Creativity exists but organisations have the responsibility to ensure that knowledge and skills are made available to workers so as to translate motivation into performance.

(Gilbert and Scragg, 1992: 141, derived from McGregor, 1960, and Ouchi, 1981)

structure in social work, which brings in consultant practitioners to develop high standards of practice.

Alan Fowler, considering the issues from a public sector perspective, makes eight key points:

- How well people work is influenced as much by attitude and motivation as by competence.
- Motivation is affected by an amalgam of influences – personal, job related, environmental and managerial.
- Managers need to understand each employee is a unique individual.
- Jobs need to be meaningful and interesting, and people need feedback on their performance.
- Work needs to be seen as partially a social process, and motivation is affected by group attitudes.
- In organisations, general culture has a strong motivational influence.
- Motivation can be stimulated by effective systems of recognition and reward.
- Managerial leadership is vital: qualities such as consistency, commitment, fairness, decisiveness and communication are common factors.

Fowler stresses that, 'For managers, the requirement is to know each employee well and

so understand the individual characteristics which are likely to influence each person's motivation' (Fowler, 1988: 64).

For the manager tempted to delude themselves that frontline workers will be fooled by facile motivators, a good corrective is to read Scott Adams' books featuring the archetypal employee, Dilbert. One of the most famous cartoons has the managing director saying 'I've been saying for years that employees are our most valuable asset. It turns out that I was wrong. Money is our most valuable asset. Employees are ninth' (Adams, 1997: 53). One of the employees replies, 'I'm afraid to ask what came in eighth?' to which the managing director responds, 'carbon paper!'

Wheatley (1999) in her recent text, *Leadership and the New Science*, poses the enduring questions: 'How do we create structures that are flexible and adaptive, that enable rather than constrain? How do we simplify things without losing what we value about complexity? How do we resolve personal needs for autonomy and growth with organisational needs for prediction and accountability?' (79).

Action-centred leadership

We recall from previous chapters that transformational leadership is different from the

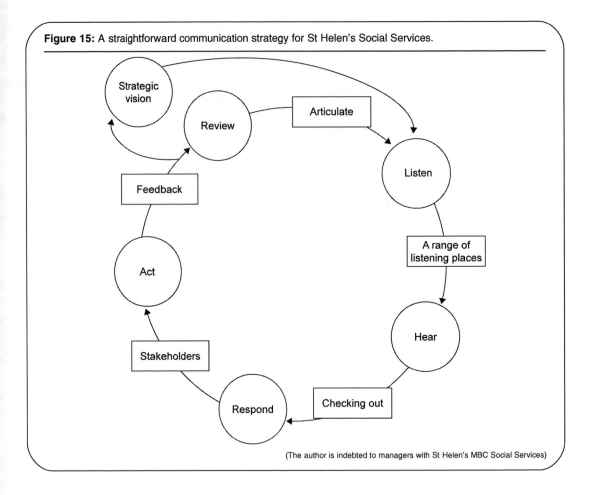

Figure 15: A straightforward communication strategy for St Helen's Social Services.

Strategic vision

Review

Articulate

Listen

Feedback

A range of listening places

Act

Hear

Stakeholders

Respond

Checking out

(The author is indebted to managers with St Helen's MBC Social Services)

transactional approach, but that organisations need both. Leaders who, through self-awareness (see Chapter 2), realise that they concentrate on vision and people (see Figure 9), must ensure that they develop transactional skills, or have those within their management team. Leaders who temperamentally incline to more of a transactional approach, need to ensure that the vision for the organisation is firmly in their mind (and heart!), and that they are attending to the people issues.

Jane Cranwell-Ward et al. (2002), in their write-up of the round the world yacht race (103–146), demonstrate through intensive observation of the skippers and their crews, that the most successful had a blend of:

- **Personal attributes**, e.g. inner purpose, personal goals, integrity, values, personal standards, self-belief and self-motivation, self-development, openness, presence, emotional intelligence.

- **Management skills**, e.g. agreed goals and values, preparation and planning, sound management procedures, resource management, communication, conflict management, continuous improvement.
- **Leadership attributes**, e.g. purpose, vision and values, support and trust, recognition, belief, performance focus, motivation, communication, shared leadership, humour and fun.

Effective communication is one of the keys to success. Staff may not like the message, but they will usually respect and go with a leadership approach which is up front, honest and responsive. Working with the managers responsible for services to vulnerable adults in St. Helen's MBC recently, we came up with a straightforward model of communication which, if followed, would resolve a lot of the standard problems of staff hearing only part of the message, or hearing it from the wrong people and not having any means of

---

Historical Leadership Example 3: Martin Luther King

We cannot walk alone. And as we walk, we must make the pledge that we shall always march ahead. We cannot turn back. There are those who are asking the devotees of Civil Rights, 'when will you be satisfied?' We can never be satisfied as long as the Negro is a victim of the unspeakable horrors of police brutality . . . We cannot be satisfied as long as a Negro in Mississippi cannot vote and a Negro in New York believes he has nothing for which to vote. No, no, we are not satisfied, and we will not be satisfied until justice rolls down like waters and righteousness like a mighty stream.

Those are just some of the lines from Martin Luther King's momentous 'I have a dream' speech on the 28 August 1963, from the steps of the Lincoln Memorial. They still send a tingle down the spine today, because they represent the cry of the oppressed and dispossessed of any race, creed or nation, and they carry with them the foundation of King's commitment to non-violence, 'let us not seek', stated King on that day, 'to satisfy our thirst for freedom by drinking from the cup of bitterness and hatred'.

Howard Gardner (1997: 219) writes that 'King wedded a strong, effective visionary message with the embodiment of that message'. He was very much a man of original community, within the southern black, church groups. Professor Adam Fairclough (1990: 6) writes that, 'deep roots, a strong sense of identity, and a love of the black church placed him at the heart of Atlanta's black community'. Unlike many driven people, King does not seem to have been battling inner demons, but found himself, initially reluctantly, the right person at the right place; and he found himself able to articulate in words and embody in deeds the often disparate, inchoate and unspoken feelings and impulses of those he worked with. Like Gandhi, who was one of the greatest influences on him, especially in his approach to non-violence, King was an iconic figure, often simply opening doors through the fact that everybody knew what he stood for. He was also able to embrace 'a broad inclusionary vision that was friendly to a variety of intellectual and cultural strands. He was comfortable with ideas and individuals from the Islamic, Catholic, Jewish and Eastern religious traditions', (see Gardner, op. cit.: 209).

Fairclough's succinct, dissecting and at times moving biography portrays all the complexities that King faced, including criticism and rifts within his own community and movement, especially over his stance on non-violence. It also shows how difficult this was to effect in American society, which often seemed bemused by King's self-sacrifice and his willingness to put himself at physical risk – even death.

One can be quizzical as to how much King actually achieved in America. Clearly progress has been made, and blacks at all levels in society are far more prominent. On the other hand, the blatant vote-rigging against blacks in Florida in the 2000 Presidential election was a huge scar on the face of America. But King's influence was not confined solely to America, there is no doubt that, in one of these strange cycles of fate, Gandhi who started his life of political protest in South Africa before moving to India, who influenced King so much, was a progenitor of King's influence on the freedom movement in South Africa.

Perhaps some of the lessons for us from King are that he was rooted in a particular community and value-system; he was, as Fairclough writes, 'more than a figurehead. He inspired not only by the word but also by the deed' (136) and he was continually prey to self-doubt, though that never stopped him from undertaking the actions he thought were right. 'I'm still searching myself', he confessed. 'I don't have all the answers and I certainly have no pretence to omniscience' (quoted in Fairclough: 139).

---

contributing to the direction in which the whole organisation is travelling.

Principles

Listen – Hear – Respond – Act

– timeliness
– clarity
– appropriate spacing
– responsiveness and respect

Figure 16: Action-Centred Leadership.

Key Actions		Task	Team	Individual
Define objectives		Identify tasks and constraints	Hold team meetings Share commitment	Clarify objectives Gain acceptance
Plan	Gather information	Consider options Check resources	Consult Develop suggestions	Encourage ideas Assess skills
	Decide	Priorities Timescales Standards	Structure	Allocate jobs Delegate Set targets
Brief		Clarify objectives Describe plan	Explain decisions Listen Answer questions Enthuse Check understanding	
Monitor support		Assess progress Maintain standards	Co-ordinate Reconcile conflict Recognise effort	Advise/Praise Assist/Reassure Counsel/Discipline
Evaluate		Summarise Review objectives Replan if necessary	Recognise and gain from success Learn from mistakes	Appraise performance
			Guide and train Give praise	

(The Industrial Society)

John Adair, in his model of action-centred leadership (Adair, 1983) sets out a number of defined tasks:

1. **Planning.** Planning can be done at any level, from the strategy of organisations to the work of small teams and groups. Every team, however small, requires a sense of direction and a plan of action. In more complex situations, specific project planning will be essential. As in the case of Staffordshire's implementation of Community Care, mentioned previously, there is no point in having pilots which report after you have to implement the whole policy. (For more detail, see Martin, 2002.)
2. **Briefing.** As we have seen, communication is vital, and the communication strategy must ensure that **all** members of the team are on board. When I used to meet residential or day care teams, I would always watch to see whether the cooks, cleaners, drivers and other ancillary staff were involved in the team meetings. If not, I would ask why not! If the night staff were not able to be at a day

time meeting, I would question how they were going to be involved in the decision-making and briefed on the plan.
3. **Monitor and support.** Inevitably plans will not go smoothly. It is worth reflecting on Field Marshall Erwin Rommel's dictum that 'No plan survives contact' (Fraser, 1993: 418). The bureaucratic manager may well be at a loss when that brilliantly created plan hits practical problems from lack of productive capacity, market demand, shareholder confidence and so on. The leader is likely to have the ability to rethink and plan anew. Peter Drucker (Drucker, 1967: 111) recalls that the American President, Franklin D. Roosevelt, who masterminded the American recovery from economic recession and their success in World War 2, found that on becoming President in 1933, his plan for economic recovery was upset by changed circumstances. Roosevelt immediately substituted a political objective for his former economic one. He switched from recovery to reform. He knew that he had to change his plans radically to have any hope of success

(Drucker, 1967, see also Gilbert and Thompson, 2002).

When Worcestershire externalised (contracted out to the not-for-profit housing and care organisation) the majority of its homes for older people in the late 1990s (not least because the previous management had allowed the buildings to deteriorate to an alarming degree) and invested in a number of strategically placed homes around rehabilitation and respite, while members eventually accepted the necessity for making the change, staff quite rightly needed ongoing encouragement, information and support as local stakeholders raised issues.

4. **Evaluate.** One of the major problems in the public sector is that the learning loop of evaluation and reformulation is often left out. Inevitably there are lessons to be learned from both successes and failures. In fact, it is often harder to learn from success than to learn from failure, where the lessons are more obvious.

Finally, it is important to celebrate success so that people feel that their, often exceptional, efforts have been recognised.

As David Blakey, former Chief Constable for West Mercia, and latterly HMI, put it:

There is a time when leadership is about being there and being visible. It's about caring about people, and not just disappearing into the ether with no connection with the people doing their job.
(conversation with the author, August 2004)

CHAPTER 6

Organisational Culture

Oscar Wilde defined a cynic as one who knows the price of everything, but the value of nothing – reminding us that value inheres in those things (love, loyalty, altruism, faithfulness) that are not marketable; that are earned, not bought; part of who we are, not what we own. A culture in which everything can be bought is one that has de-valued value and institutionalised cynicism.

(Sacks, 2002: 76–77)

We are all fighting for our careers. If we are not in the premiership at the end of the season, the money simply won't be there. The club [Northampton Rugby Union Club] has been rocked by massive changes and, to be perfectly honest, we lost our identity.

(Steve Thompson, incoming Captain, *Daily Mail*, 2 December 2004, my emphasis)

At Tesco, we look after our people so they take care of our customers. This simple, but effective equation is at the heart of our success. It is through our people that we have become the UK's leading retailer and this investment in them is helping us become a global player. Underpinning the success of the Tesco Team are core values, which ensure our people stay motivated and committed. Our One Team continues to be number one for customers. We value our staff through trust and respect, make their work more satisfying and enable them to progress and share in our success.

(Sir Terry Leahy, CEO, Tesco Stores (quoted in Cranwell-Ward et al., 2002: 147)

He had been far too busy becoming himself to give a moment's thought to who he actually was.

(Dibdin, 2003: 18)

Introduction

Walking into a Tesco store eight years ago, to get some last minute shopping, I found myself unfavourably impressed compared to my local Sainsbury's. The shelves were haphazardly stacked with poorly presented goods, which looked far from appetising. The staff were lacking in courtesy and did not seem to know where anything was. Eight years on, Tesco is transformed as the UK's foremost food retailer, and the organisation's valuing of its staff has transformed the way its stores operate. Customers are valued by staff who are valued, and as Hampden-Turner points out in his book on corporate culture: 'Those who cared best were best cared-for by their supervisors. The culture was one in which people passed on to others the quality of the care they received' (Hampden-Turner, 1990: 89).

What is true of Tesco is true of public services at many points. When we go into a residential home or a day centre, are visitors greeted, and how? What is the technical quality of care? What is the human quality of care? Are people listened to, or are the staff talking to each other

and ignoring the users of the service? Is the culture working with, or doing to? Is the shift pattern for the benefit of the users, or of the staff? The questions go on and on, but it is with these questions that we build up a sense of the culture of the organisation.

What is culture?

Edgar Schein, a leading figure in the study of organisational culture, defines it as:

> ... a pattern of basic assumptions – invented, discovered, or developed by a given group as it learns to cope with its problems of external adaptation and internal integration – that has worked well enough to be considered valid and, therefore, to be taught to new members as the correct way to perceive, think, and feel in relation to those problems.

(Schein, 1985: 9)

Much simpler versions are: 'how we do things around here' (Ouchi, 1981) and 'a hidden, yet unifying theme, that provides meaning, direction and mobilisation' (Kilmann et al., 1985 – both quoted in Newman, 1996: 14).

Newman (1996), in her comprehensive and eminently readable work on shaping organisational cultures, identifies two major themes in the literature:

- The **corporate culture approach** (Hampden-Turner, 1990), which sees culture as a variable that can be managed in the same way as structures and systems can be: 'It is something which an organisation *has*, rather than an organisation *is*' (Newman, 1996: 15).
- The **interpretive approach** (for example, Sackmann, 1991), where a culture is actively created by organisation members through their social interactions.

One formulation which links closely with Bass and Avolio's approach (see Chapter 4), where communication, both corporately and individually, is so important, is that when culture 'represents a web of understanding that we need in order to make sense of and cope with the complexity and confusion of organisational life. This web then gives shape to what we do and the ways in which we do it' (McLean and Marshall, 1988: 11).

The transformational leader understands, and is able to cope effectively with, the 'web of understanding' so that they have a chance in turning around a malevolent culture, energising a moribund one, or harnessing the potential of one that is able to deliver value-based leadership in its fullest sense (see Nicholls, 1999).

Culture is complex

Organisational culture is likely to have the following features:

1. It will manifest itself at various levels and in different ways. Schein's (1985) model shows three distinct layers, some easily visible and some less so:
   Artefacts and creations – visible but not often decipherable:
   - technology
   - art
   - visible and audible behaviour patterns
   Values – greater level of awareness:
   - testable in the physical environment
   - testable only by social consensus
   Basic assumptions – taken for granted and invisible:
   - relationship to environment
   - nature of reality, time and space
   - nature of human nature

   - nature of human activity
   - nature of human relationships
2. It will be embedded in the informal organisation, demonstrable in the cartoons on the notice board, and the jokes around the coffee-maker and so on.
3. It will be taken for granted, and therefore needs to be identified as soon as possible by the leader before they have an opportunity to be sucked into it.
4. Through the culture of a corporate body, or specific team, events are given meaning within a particular worldview.
5. Culture is learned. It is passed on from individual to individual or group to group:
   > *Culture is like language: we inherit it, learn it, pass it on to others, but in the process we invent new words and expressions – it evolves over time.*
   >
   > (Newman, 1996: 17)

   Usually it evolves, but sometimes it can get stuck for decades. The branch bank at Little Barset-on-the-Hill (if not closed by now in a branch restructuring programme!) will probably have had the same office culture, for good or ill, for many years, along the lines of: 'it's the way we do things here'.

   It is a building society which Johnson and Scholes utilise in their exploration of strategy formation as a cultural process (Johnson and Scholes, 1989). They believe that a strategy is likely to fail unless the 'recipe' of the culture is understood and taken into account. This 'recipe' is made up of:
   - symbols
   - rituals and myths
   - power structures
   - organisational structure
   - control systems
   - routines

   Each 'ingredient' is likely to be mutually reinforcing, except at times of change, when one or more components will begin to act to change the 'recipe'.
6. It is unrealistic to talk about a single organisational culture in a large entity. Even with a strong corporate identity, individual sections will be likely to operate in ways which make the overall culture complex and multi-layered. This is especially true in professional areas, such as health, social care and education. In the 1990s, for example, the new NHS Trusts attempted to create organisational coherence, but always struggled because each area of physical

CASE STUDY 6: STAFFORDSHIRE SOCIAL SERVICES

In early 1991, on my way to an interview for the role of Operations Director for Adult Services for Staffordshire Social Services, I read the report of the Staffordshire Childcare Inquiry, 1990, by Allan Levy QC and Barbara Kahan. Reading the report was a shocking experience. The first blow was that the 'Pindown' regime was such an abuse of vulnerable children who had been placed in the care of the County Council, ostensibly to gain a better standard of parenting than they would have received if they had remained in their own homes. Levy and Kahan (1991) stated clearly in their conclusions that in their view, Pindown 'is likely to have stemmed initially from an ill-digested understanding of behavioural psychology; the regime had no theoretical framework and no safeguards', and again, 'Pindown, in our view, falls decisively outside anything that could properly be considered as good childcare practice. It was in all its manifestations intrinsically unethical, unprofessional and unacceptable' (167).

The second shock was, in fact, that it appeared the whole of the Department had been abused. Para 17.5 (page 151) is a perfect illustration of a dysfunctional organisation:

> *We found that there were many staff at all levels who worked extremely hard, in some cases much harder than was desirable for them or for the people they were serving.* Vision, leadership, commitment to quality services, and a recognition for the need for adequate knowledge, training and skill in the care of children were all seriously lacking.
>
> (151, my emphasis)

As I visited all parts of the department and had contact with all client groups, in my initial role as Operations Director for Adult Services, and then later as Director of Operations for all client groups, and in charge of the Policy and Planning Unit, I believe Levy and Kahan's opinion to be judicious and entirely justified. Because of what I read, I spent the evening prior to taking up my role, visiting a couple of residential homes, to give the specific and explicit message that the interface between frontline staff and those they served was the crucial relationship, and the frontline staff deserved the support of senior management. In my visits to services during my first year, I came across the very sad sight of experienced managers being very nervous at the sight of a deputy chief officer arriving on their doorstep. Managers described the previous regime as 'seagull management', i.e. the only time you saw senior managers was when something was perceived to have gone wrong and they flew in, dumped all over you and flew out again! (see para 17.6 of the report).

One of the basic problems was simply the level of trust between different layers of the department, with the previous director blaming middle management for blocking his communication with the frontline, and frontline managers having made formal complaints that they had no confidence in the department. To win trust you cannot rely on the authority of your role, nor the use of personal or positional power. It has to be hard won. There is no other way than to take the knocks, which are quite often to do with people's past experiences, not the present, and hold the situation while you put things right, keep things going and do new things (see Figure 2). What was abundantly clear, was that there were some enormously talented and committed people, who had been treated in an unacceptable manner, and the new senior management had to get alongside them, and get them alongside us.

Levy and Kahan identified a number of problems with Staffordshire:

- Political turbulence.
- Inadequate funding for the department over many years.
- Inadequate change management of the absorption of Stoke-on-Trent and Burton-on-Trent into Staffordshire as part of local government reorganisation in 1974.
- 'No formal participative management', and 'minimal joint planning with Health Authorities'.
- A management structure which was shaped not by strategy or service delivery, but 'largely as a response to requirements for cuts in services' (13).
- Users and carers fitted into services, rather than services produced to fit need. A

CASE STUDY 6: Continued

philosophy of 'containment rather than care'.

- An absence of written policies, procedures and joint strategies.
- A remote senior management, which was partly a result of style, and partly because there were six vertical layers of management separating heads of residential establishments from the director!
- A lack of vision and values.
- Confused management arrangements; allied to a system of over-reliance on internal promotions.
- An inward-looking culture.
- Inadequate commitment to the education and training of staff with qualified staff looked on as being troublesome because they would demand good practice!

Interestingly, many of those points were made to the inquiry team by the outgoing Director of Social Services, who had been appointed in 1985. He had formerly been the Deputy to the first Director of Social Services, and had been in the department since the mid-1970s. As he had been in post as Director for four years before Pindown became a public issue, one of the questions is, why did he do nothing about it? Levy and Kahan were much less interested in finding scapegoats than they were in identifying, forensically, the pathology of the department, and making sensible recommendations. They do not finger any particular politicians, though they do not excuse the political leadership for allowing the department to get in the state that it had. Interestingly, there appears to be no criticism of the Chief Executive, who had also been with Staffordshire for a long time, and should have known, if not the detail of what was going on in the department, then at least the culture of it, especially as he had been the committee clerk for social services. Until Lord Laming put the Chief Executive for Haringey Council on the spot, during the inquiry into the death of Victoria Climbié (see Snell, 2002: 28–29) chief executives seem to have been a breed who could take all the credit and none of the accountability!

The new management team's approach was to:

- Set a vision for what the department could be.
- Enunciate explicit values in respect of good practice with users and carers, and also with staff – and a diagrammatic representation of that in what we called the Vision and Values Constellation.
- Challenge the 'inward-looking culture' (para 3.21), by opening the department up, and by proper recruitment processes. We were also careful not to denigrate the many good things that had happened in Staffordshire, which tended to get overwhelmed by the shame of the Pindown experience.

People will recognise the syndrome of a new Chief Officer or Chief Executive coming in, making coruscating comments about what they find, recruiting people from their own authority, and lauding that authority to the skies in unrealistic terms. Having come from Kent, which was acknowledged to be the leading council on the interaction of the reforms under the NHS and Community Care Act, 1990, I had to be very clear about what I did and did not want to change about Staffordshire's approaches to Adult Services, some of which, especially those for older people being of very good quality, even if somewhat traditional. There were new approaches to involving users, carers and advocates put in place, to the extent that a number of initiatives gained national attention in the forthcoming years.

- Consult staff on what were the three main issues they would like changed (one was, understandably, an approach to staff care). In these three issues, a middle manager was chosen to lead on the subject, mentored and supported by a member of the departmental management team, and a wide range of staff and the unions were brought in as participants. Again, the staff care scheme, when implemented, received national attention (Gilbert and Farrier-Ray, 1995).
- Develop partnerships with health and other agencies.
- Create specific links with the two universities within the county, with

---

professorships in childcare and adult care part sponsored.

- Make major investments in training across the board.
- Draw up policies and procedures, especially on vital issues, such as supervision, which Levy and Kahan have been so concerned about (see e.g. Figure 20).
- Introduce business planning approaches alongside good care practice (see Gilbert and Palmer, 1995).

The major underpinning change was cultural. This ranged from making sure that elected members kept the lessons of the past, and the needs of the future firmly in mind, and challenging the prevailing and pervasive machismo culture amongst some members; to getting across the message that in a personal service, **every single person had a value which needed to be recognised**.

A lot of the work fits into what Goffee and Jones (2000) describe as 'tough empathy'. All this cultural change had to take place at a time when there was less than a year to implement the 1990 NHS and Community Care Act (full implementation, 1 April 1993), and no infrastructure and planning on which to build it. In fact the two care management pilots were due to report in June 1993 – three months after the whole system had to be implemented! There were also major joint-service issues such as when a number

of tragic deaths at Starlington Hall Hospital for people with learning disabilities broke as a national scandal in the mid-1990s, and with no learning disability expertise within the Health Authority (this lack of capacity in learning disability and mental health is still with us in 2004), it fell on social services to take much of the lead. We also had to play a certain amount of brinkmanship with our health colleagues by insisting that the funding for each individual coming out of the hospital should be 'in perpetuity', because I had seen the disastrous effects of inadequate funding within the South-West Thames region, as a junior manager. Some very inadequate responses had to be challenged, as for example when the Chief Executive of the lead health authority said to me, 'why do we need to fund care managers within the new system? We are giving these people life plans, what do they need care managers for?'! My response to this was to ask an ambitious man how he would like somebody to give him 'a life plan' for his career?!

As we can see from Chapter 8, and the work by John Kotter, one of the main elements of positive change is to anchor that change within the culture of the organisation. Tough empathy involves saying to people, 'we are changing – **I mean it!**' and seeing that it takes place.

---

activity within, for example, an acute hospital, is likely to create its own distinct culture.

In the commercial/industrial world, some companies may consciously strive for variable cultures – for example, a very tight, homogeneous corporate HQ, with work bases (for example, in an IT conglomerate) having quite a different feel from the HQ and each other, precisely because of their different requirements.

Diagnosing and creating organisational culture at a time of mergers and acquisitions can be particularly convoluted. Merging an acute and community NHS Trust with strongly antipathetic management mores is an exercise requiring considerable effort and involvement:

Achieving cultural change is a complex journey requiring constant revival and review. It also demands unyielding commitment from the Trust Board.

(Spreckley and Hart, 2001: 28–9)

Challenging institutional oppression

Institutional oppression has always existed within the governance and practice of organisations, and this has always been predicated upon an abuse of power, non-existent or corrupt values and the human need to feel secure by creating an 'out group'. Perhaps one of the most obvious examples is that of the Metropolitan Police, who, more than 20 years after Lord Scarman's report into the

Brixton riots and five years after the Met stood accused of 'institutional racism' in the wake of the Stephen Lawrence murder inquiry, is still seen as having 'ice in the heart' as regards race issues.

While there is no doubt that the Metropolitan Police force has attempted to combat racism within its ranks, a recent report by Sir David Calvert-Smith, a former Director of Public Prosecutions and High Court Judge, found that while the police force was 'thawing at the top, it was still frozen solid at the core' (*The Guardian*, 9 March 2005: 5). In many ways, the Met is facing the worst of both worlds: its staff from ethnic minorities are still feeling discriminated against, while many white Caucasian staff appear to see the move towards diversity as 'political correctness'. In the NHS the Department of Health has recently responded to the inquiry into the death of David 'Rocky' Bennett (Blofeld, 2003). The response (Department of Health, 2005) did not accept the label of 'institutional racism' as the government felt that rather than assisting progress, it could lead to paralysis. Instead, the response focuses on a framework of reducing and eliminating ethnic inequalities in mental health service experience and outcome; developing the cultural capability of mental health services; and engaging the community and building capacity through new types of community development workers.

It is significant that the department uses the word 'equality' and Peter Ferns in his recent work for the Social Perspectives Network (Tew, 2005) makes it clear that, 'it is essential that equality is not just replaced with the politically less contentious issue of 'cultural diversity' or even worse still 'cultural awareness'. Awareness does not guarantee any change or action, and diversity does not guarantee structural change or any meaningful political analysis of the realities' (Chapter 7).

Ferns points to the need to change the vicious circle of abuse of power and authority added to stereotyping, leading to negative values and norms and subsequently to oppression and discrimination; changing to an ethos of protective authority and/or co-operative power plus diversity leading to positive values and norms and subsequently to equality.

The role of the leader in challenging negative and discriminatory power in institutions (whether described as 'institutional racism' or not) is crucial. Leaders must set a vision and

practice of valuing individuals and groups by their own actions, which is why mentoring, and leadership action through including personal 'stretch' targets on race equality plus senior leaders is a major item in the Mental Health Race Equality document (DoH, 2005: 17). Changing the culture of organisations positively must start at the top. As we have seen with the Metropolitan Police, however, thawing the senior strata is simply not enough. Nor is relying on a 'trickle down effect', because this just usually leads to muddy water! Leaders need to be reaching down through all the levels in the organisation in both a personal, systematic and systemic way to ensure the culture changes at every level, and a virtuous circle begins to operate. The recent Department of Health document on mental health lists ten actions: strategic direction, aligning incentives, development, communications, partnerships, mentoring, leadership action, expanding training development and career opportunities, systematic tracking, and celebrating achievements (16–17).

Gaining a proper valuing of diversity for those who use services and those who provide them, is a long journey, and it requires to say what they mean, and mean what they say. If staff feel that this is just 'another fad', then they won't go with it. It has got to be at the heart of leadership.

Culture in changing organisations

As we shall see in Chapter 7, one of the major issues in public services at the present time is the extent and pace of structural change. This may come from mergers of components of health and social care into new organisations; the de-merger of social services departments as the new Children's Departments and Children's Trusts are formed; and the creation of new forms of organisation e.g. Sure Start and Connexions, etc. In all of these new organisational forms, culture will be factor. As we see in Case Study 7, Connexions was formed partly out of the old Careers' Service, and took a great deal of transformational leadership and the management of cultural change to bring it all together.

We have seen in Chapter 2 that the modern manager spends a great deal of time at work, and desires to gain meaning from their working experience (e.g. see Holbeche and Springett, 2004). Deal and Kennedy point out that 'we need to remember that people make businesses work. And we need to re-learn old lessons about how culture ties people together and gives meaning and purpose to their day-to-day lives' (1988: 4–5).

The Health Education Authority, in its document on supporting staff through mergers and beyond (HEA, 1999), stresses the need for attention to cultural influences. There needs to be honesty about whether a merger is really a merger at all, or really a takeover. Again, to use another example from retailing, when Morrisons took over Safeway, Mr Morrison was asked what the prevailing culture in the new merged organisation would be. His response was short and sharp. 'It will be Morrisons, no question about that!' But, if a merger really is meant to be a merger then the imposition of one culture on another, without proper explanation and communication, will result in tension, mistrust and annoyance – and even sabotage! (HEA, 1999: 7).

In their study of Somerset's mental health services, which we will return to in Chapter 7, Peck et al. (2001) flag up some of the problems with organisational change and forming a new culture, even in a county with a history of positive joint working. As they write:

> *There is an apparent ambiguity in Somerset in the outcome being sought in relation to cultural change. Is the desired result one entirely new culture, albeit comprised of elements taken from all the current professional cultures – the 'melting pot' approach to culture? Or is the desired result the enhancement of the current professional cultures by the addition of mutual understanding and respect – the 'orange juice with added Vitamin C' approach to culture? These are very different, and the methods adopted for achieving one or the other might also be very different. To date, this study in Somerset seems to demonstrate that the creation of a combined trust is not in itself a sufficient condition to create either. Indeed, in the short-term at least, structural change may have served to strengthen attachment to existing professional culture. This is an important message for ministers anticipating 'big cultural change'.*
> (325)

Integration should provide a great opportunity to bring together different traditions and expertise to the benefit of service users and carers. While there is considerable argument as

to whether culture can be managed by leaders (see Peck and Crawford, 2002), my own view is that the lessons from business, albeit that many businesses do not have the complexity of professional groupings, as occurs in many public services, are that a focus of culture around common tasks and outcomes can produce results. Working recently with a group of professionals who had worked from very different geographical and professional bases for many years, and were coming together in a multi-disciplinary team, my first exercise with them was to ask what service users and carers would want from them as a team. This elicited a very positive and perceptive response, which showed a great deal of unanimity across the diverse professional boundaries.

The leader's role

'The only thing of real importance that leaders do', writes Schein (1985: 2) 'is to create and manage culture'. He goes on to say: 'and that unique talent of leaders is to create and manage culture'. Culture and leadership, Schein believes, are two sides of the same coin. Leaders, therefore, must:

1. Identify the cultural recipe and how malleable it is.
2. Diagnose its features and its layers (see Handy, 1978; Harrison and Stokes, 1990).
3. Ascertain how appropriate the recipe is for the desired strategy.
4. Use transformational values and skills to mould the culture, by acting on ingredients within the recipe. For example, managers going 'back to the floor' and working with staff, will not only inspire by example (walk-the-talk) and learn a great deal, they will also begin a weaving of stories and relationships which create a powerful force for positive development.

Inspirational and influencing leadership will mean using oneself in:

- Living the value and the vision.
- Creating meaning for people.
- Coping creatively with ambiguity and paradox.
- Being aware of the symbolic nature of our actions. As Peters (1989: 1) wrote, 'managing at any time, but more than ever today, is a symbolic activity'.
- Changing language and behaviour to model values and goals.

- Conceiving a sense of path-finding as a team. As one follower said of their leader, who had led them through a series of gruelling challenges, he was a leader 'we followed because he had ideas and because, for a brief moment in our lives, he made us bigger than ourselves, (Hickey, 1992: 120).

CHAPTER 7

Leading in New Organisations

We need to concentrate more on services and then the right structures to deliver those services will emerge organically. If we concentrate on providing appropriate and high quality services, rather than obsessing about structural 'solutions' then we will gain more credibility with users and carers.
(an experienced Chief Executive, NHS, talking to the author)

I think I've had a remarkably successful first year as PM.
Indubitably, you have, Prime Minister.
But I want to find ways of improving that record of achievement.
Have you thought of 'masterly inactivity', Prime Minister?
(Prime Minister Jim Hacker and Sir Humphrey Appleby in *Yes, Prime Minister*)

All movements start with prophets and end with policemen.

(anon)

It's not the voices I hear when I'm ill that's the problem, it's the voices I don't hear when I'm well.
(service user)

Many in the Anglo-American elites glorify change and novelty for its own sake. Nothing is good unless it is 'innovative'. Bureaucrats gaily reorganise the public services, oblivious of how each reorganisation destroys a major channel of personal security and trust.
(Richard Layard, LSE (2005: 164–165) adviser to government on economics and society)

Structural change and integration

Some years ago, before I became a social worker, I was an Army officer, training in mountain warfare. One day I found myself as a middle climber of a group of three, roped up and traversing a difficult ledge. As I moved on to the ledge it gave way, leaving me dangling in mid-air and looking at the jagged rocks 800 feet below me. As an example of organisational health, it has remained with me as a lesson, because although the systems and structures were important in preventing my death: the rope held, the harnesses were secure, etc.; more important than the systems and structures were the people and relationships. Despite the multi-culturalism of the group, we had trained together, worked together and trusted each other, so that in the end I relied for my life on their integrity and expertise. All of us have probably worked for someone who would have been more inclined to cut the rope than to hold it! (see Gilbert, 2004a).

One of the current problems with the debate around integration, whether it be for children or for adults, is the preoccupation with structure as an end in itself. In fact, structures are means to an end, they are never the destination. Structure,

as the word suggests, is a framework for delivery, but not the embodiment of delivery. A prime example of this is the recent scandal over care given, or rather not given, at Rowan Ward for elderly people with mental health needs, within the Manchester Care Trust. Stephen Ladyman, the Minister of Health, speaking at the 2004 Summit on Mental Health and Older People, commented that, in his opinion, having read the report on Rowan Ward, Manchester had attempted to resolve problems with relationships, through a structural 'solution', which left the vital issues around relationships and services unattended to – thus resulting in poor standards for very vulnerable people.

Clearly there are times when structural change is absolutely necessary. The prime example is the range of new structures and services brought into being in the 1940s, in the post-war Welfare Settlement, where it was believed that a People's War should result in a People's Peace. Major organisational change used to take place about every 15 to 20 years. Now it is annual, or even quicker, with new agencies set up and dismantled with bewildering regularity. It is noticeable that many senior professionals and managers still refer to organisations by their old name or initials several months after a name change, and one wonders how the public are meant to recognise which agency is accountable for what! In fact, there is little doubt that the extent and rapidity of organisational change is now having a dysfunctional effect on the delivery of public services. Leaders have to be even more skilled at managing and delivering effective performance through the turbulence of major organisational change. For those with integrity, as opposed to 'job-hoppers' who are serving their own ambition first, it is essential that they are skilled enough at organisational politics to keep their jobs, whilst at the same time continuing to focus on the end-user and the end-product.

Most delivery systems are either composed of multiple partners, or the incorporation of a number of different strands of professional groupings. Again, therefore, the leader has to be particularly skilled at achieving two objectives which may be mutually antagonistic, namely forging a single direction, while at the same time keeping all the partners on board. General Dwight D. Eisenhower is one of the obvious examples from history, in that he had not only to mastermind the Second World War on the Western Front, but also to keep on board a number of ego-centred generals, such as Montgomery and Patten; while at the same time remaining on good political terms with Prime Minister Churchill and President Roosevelt. Interestingly on the evening of the invasion of Normandy on the 6 June 1944, Eisenhower made a decision which betokened his integrity, in that he wrote a note which he would read out to the Press should the invasion fail, stating that, 'If any blame or fault attaches to the attempt, it is mine alone' (see Gilbert, 2004b).

In the last few years we have seen a remarkable transformation of public services, including:

- An evolving structure for the NHS as a whole, which seeks to create some kind of equipoise between National Frameworks and local delivery; a Primary Care-led NHS and the power of acute hospitals; between commissioning and performance management; between health-only objectives and partnership.
- The setting up of Mental Health Partnership Trusts and Care Trusts in Mental Health.
- New configurations of Children's Services, and also Children's Trusts, in the wake of the Government Green Paper *Every Child Matters* (2003), and its resultant legislation in 2004. (See Hudson, 2005), and Singleton, 2005.
- The setting up of new organisations and partnership organisations, e.g. Sure Start, Connexions, Youth Offending Teams, etc.
- New formations of Adult Services within local authorities, and partnerships with Primary Care Trusts (PCTs), as Children's Services are separated out.
- The outsourcing of provision: in local authorities following the NHS and Community Care Act, 1990 (fully implemented 1 April 1993), and latterly, and more controversially, within the NHS.

Essentially, the question is about how a government with limited resources, and declining person power, can gain the best health outcomes for its citizens at a reasonable cost. Related to this is a more political one, namely, how can national politicians, whom the public see as ultimately accountable, devolve decision-making in a way which does not lead to every mistake or shortfall being routed back to the Ministry? This is especially true as Britain is the most centralised country in all of those in the old European Community (see Jenkins, 1995). Britain, in health as in so many other areas, is caught ideologically between the United States of America and much of Western Europe. In terms of health, the USA delivers very high-quality healthcare to a relative few, leaving many people uninsured, and even for those who are, the managed care system often produces very standardised and often rather inhuman care (see Weinberg, 2003). Visitors to France often speak of clean, well-run hospitals with short waiting times and efficient treatment. But the French health system, as in other aspects of the Welfare State, is facing hard financial choices.

The British Government approach in the Thatcher era was to produce an uneasy synthesis of centralised management and a pseudo-market economy (see Jenkins, 1995, Chapter 4, and Webster, 2002). The Labour Government, in 1997, pledged to do away with the market and engage in partnership approaches. Inevitably there were some pros and cons: many GP fund-holders felt that they had engendered substantial cultural, attitudinal and service changes through their purchasing power, especially in gaining better quality attention from consultants, and highlighting inefficiencies, especially in the acute sector. Overall, however, there were both huge inequalities, and a mammoth expansion in paper and the bureaucrats to feed it, much of it completely useless, as ultimately neither politicians nor managers were willing in the main to stick to the logical conclusions of their commissioning assessments and policies. It has to be said, that competition in social care worked in a radically different way. The impact of the NHS and Community Care Act, 1990, and some of the financial incentives and disincentives that went with it, meant that many previous local authority monopolies, especially in the area of residential care, were opened up to strong competition. In many cases this has produced a much better quality of life for people, and the opportunity for commissioners to exercise genuine choice. Weak commissioning has, however, led to the government recently expressing alarm at the number of adults with learning disabilities ending up in private institutions; and it is acknowledged that the Thatcher Government's refusal to regulate the domiciliary care market exposed vulnerable people to abuse.

Partnership working

Partnership certainly sounded like a more effective and ethical approach than competition, especially a competitive framework which did not actually operate as such. The essential issue for partnership, of course, is that it is based on relationships, both personal, professional and organisational. To gain partnership outcomes you have to work as partners – a simple truth which unfortunately escapes many people! In too many places across the UK the title of the partnership novel is much more 'Pride and Prejudice' than 'Sense and Sensibility'! Hardy et al. (1992) set out a number of barriers to effective partnership working:

- Structural (the fragmentation of service responsibilities across and within agency boundaries).
- Procedural (differences in planning and budget cycles).
- Financial (differences in funding mechanisms and resource flows).
- Professional (differences in ideologies, values and professional interest).
- Perceived threats to status, autonomy and legitimacy.
        (Quoted in Glasby and Peck, 2004: 19)

As the Labour Government got into its stride, it introduced the 'flexibilities' contained in Section 31 of The Health Act, 1999, removing some of the formal barriers that had been seen to obstruct a closer working between the NHS and local authorities. While progress on these flexibilities and their partnership outcomes was being researched by people like Bob Hudson from the Nuffield Institute (see Glasby and Peck, 2004, Chapters 2 and 7), the government was already beginning to lose patience with the tensions between the NHS and local authorities, perhaps without recognising its own need to create a nationwide framework which would reconcile competing priorities and performance measures. As the Chief Officer responsible for setting up a new Youth Offending Team (YOT) across Worcestershire and Herefordshire (one police service, one county council, one unitary county council, six district councils, two health authorities, four PCTs, one probation service, etc.), one of the skills was to persuade a variety of partners, with their own pressures, to back, both morally and financially, a new service which was a government priority, but was not necessarily one of the named priorities for their specific service.

In its NHS plan of 2000, the Department of Health stated clearly that:

> *If patients are to receive the best care, then the old divisions between Health and Social Care need to be overcome ... the division between Health and Social Services can often be a source of confusion for people. Fundamental reforms are needed to tackle these problems.*
>
> (DoH, 2000: 70)

Following this, there was a push towards new forms of organisation, called Care Trusts (essential reading on all of this issue of partnership working and structural change is Glasby and Peck, 2004, Part 2). At the same time continued change was taking place in the NHS itself. GP fund-holding had given way to Primary Care Groups, undertaking Primary Care Commissioning, often across the same geographical boundaries as district councils. The example of Primary Care Groups (PCGs) exposes one of the dilemmas of health structures overall. In my own experience in Worcestershire, the PCGs undertook innovative work on health promotion with their geographical partners, involving user and carer and voluntary groups, as well as local government, in a way that had not been seen before. Unfortunately, they were also too small to be effective commissioners. PCGs gave way to Primary Care Trusts (PCTs), now spanning several district council boundaries in shire counties, and losing their local focus. Health authorities, which had often spanned a shire county or unitary local authority, had given way to strategic health authorities, designed to manage performance, but unfortunately having no geographical congruence with anything at all! Most people, especially the general public, have almost no idea what areas these authorities cover. PCTs lost their local coherence but were, in many cases, still too small to be effective commissioners across all groups – mental health and learning disability being especially poorly served. Anybody reading the *Health Service Journal* will be aware that complaints about the ineffectiveness of PCT commissioning are heard in almost every issue.

So in effect, we have a high level of structural change, which has caused considerable concern. Research by Birmingham University's Health Services Management Centre and others, has recently stated that:

> *Primary Care-led commissioning organisations have often struggled to engage patients and the public in their work. Constant reorganisation has produced a highly unstable environment that has inhibited development and made it hard for Primary Care-led commissioning to prove its worth.*
> (Smith, 2004)

James Strachan, Chair of The Audit Commission, has also raised concern about endemic structural change:

> *The fundamental thing is about behaviour change; what will really change the world for people using services are things like strong leadership, motivated, empowered and capable staff and the ability to work in partnership.*
> (2004)

But there clearly are advantages of integration, and those commonly acknowledged in, for example, the mental health setting, are that:

- Management and service delivery are more cohesive and congruent.
- The organisation is easier for users and carers and potential referrers to understand – one door of entry to services.
- There is greater specialist expertise – knowing 'the business'.

And also:

- A co-ordinated approach to staff development, skill-mix and skill-sharing.
- The encouragement of appropriate specialisms within an overall framework.
- Economies of scale.
- A recognised centre of specialist expertise.
- The management 'clout' to get things done.
- And for social care, integration with health bringing it into an organisation which has a better track record for professional development than the local authorities.
                (see ADSS/NIMHE, 2003)

The disadvantages of structural change, however, are not only evident in the public sector, but in the private sector as well. Field and Peck (2003: 742–755) in their research in the private sector, highlight the following challenges:

- Most private sector mergers only partially achieve their stated objectives.
- They usually do not save the money that was anticipated.
- There is a reduction in morale and productivity, while people take their eye 'off the ball' of business objectives, and look internally.
- There is either a struggle to reconcile two very different cultures, or there is a cultural takeover which leaves those who have been taken over feeling demoralised. Development is often stalled for up to 18 months. As the authors put it: 'To a significant extent, the focus of the implementation became the creation of the merged organisation, with other objectives being overlooked'.

While a member of an Area Management Team in Kent in the early 1990's, I was involved in the merger, in effect the takeover, by our area of a neighbouring area that had run into difficulties. Our management team had resolved a very serious financial crisis when we had first come into post, and was now making substantial service improvements. The absorption of the second area, though in effect not a new organisation but part of an existing social services department, meant that service development slowed appreciably for six months while we got the new people on board.

An interesting example from the academic world, demonstrates that partnership working can be effective with minimal structural change. Oxford University (Kenny, 2004: 12–14) has been fraught from the beginning with tensions between the University and the Colleges. The former Vice-Chancellor, Sir Colin Lucas, however has overseen major progress in governance reform, while at the same time creating major investment and service improvements. As Kenny puts it: 'Lucas has presided with great skill over the interlocking network of conflicts of interest that is Oxford's preferred system of governance'.

Essentially, it is vital to look at the outcomes to be expected of organisational change. In the case of integration, the ADSS/NIMHE *Briefing on Integration in Mental Health* (see ADSS/NIMHE (Gilbert and Joannides, 2003) sets out the following outcomes:

- An organisation which achieves effective outcomes for its stakeholders in a way which maximises participation and partnership.
- Service users and carers at the heart of the service.
- Service models which focus on the whole person in the context in which they live, and which can bring an effective 'whole systems' approach to bear.
- A value-driven organisation which has all staff and partner agencies working to common values and goals.
- A recognition of a valuing of diversity.
- Sound governance arrangements which value openness, learning and innovation, and links to the wider community governance.
- A workforce which has the right skill-mix to achieve its objectives, is supported, developed and empowered.
- Combining service effectiveness with cost-effectiveness;
- Proper attention to dual diagnosis.
- Integration of mental health and public health, so that the service is not simply a 'mental illness' service.

Linking structural change with cultural change (see Chapter 6) it is essential to ascertain whether there can be a 'both/and', rather than 'either/or' approach. As new children's services departments are set up with an integration of education and social care cultures; and in integrated older persons' services or mental health services, with an integration of social care and health cultures, there is an opportunity to take the best of these and meld something new. This of course is not easy. In learning disabilities services, it has been noticeable that, because the vast majority of staff share a common philosophy based on valuing people and

person-centred approaches, there is an increased opportunity to bring together the skills of different professionals to a common aim.

Crude depictions of stereotypical social workers, teachers, doctors, etc. are not helpful, but it is vital to tease out the fundamental issues. A recent article in *Care and Health* (Reed, 2004) quotes a culture and values continuum which polarises health and social care services sectors. It depicts health services as focusing on ill-health, while social care focuses on well-being. Poorly handled, this kind of extreme dichotomy could raise hackles, though on the other hand some doctors in public health have been heard to describe the NHS as 'an ill-health service', so such an extreme description might gain some agreement as well as some dissent. What is perhaps more helpful, is examining some of the ways that can bring these different aspects together, and I set out below one such chart produced by a colleague:

The leadership role

Professor Beverly Alimo-Metcalfe, in her work on Public Sector Management is clear that modern leadership has to be effective working across boundaries with different people, professions, organisations, inspectorates, performance models, each with their own motives, drivers, objectives, etc. As she puts it

Figure 17: Leaders pulling people and agendas together: the parallel worlds of partnership in mental heath.

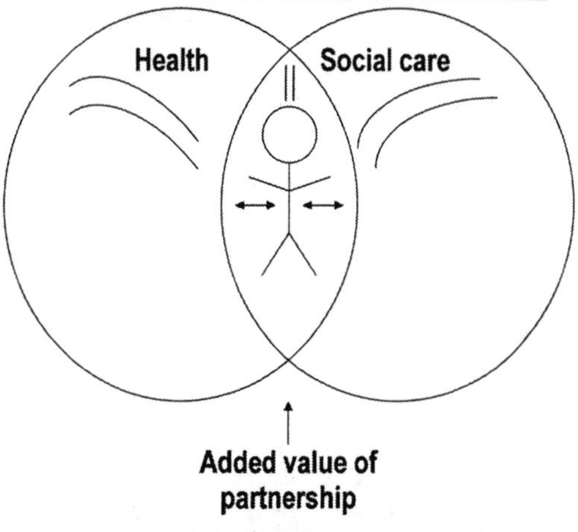

Health   Social care

Added value of partnership

(I am indebted to Philip Douglas, Northamptonshire Partnership Trust, and members of the Directors of Social Care National Learning Set for Figure 17)

Table 6: The parallel worlds of partnership in mental health

Health care	Added value	Social care
NHS Service Mental Health Trust	Better outcomes for service users from an integrated service provided by partnership trust	Local authority social services
Medical model Nursing model Psychological model OT, physio rehab model	Whole systems approach Bio-psycho-social model Spirituality	Social care model Self-actualisation
Medication Rehabilitation Treatment Therapy In-patient/out-patient Ward round	Recovery approach/social inclusion CPA Alternatives to hospital admission Alternatives to continuing care in hospital (intermediate care)	Accommodation Employment Adult education Social networks
Health centre Medical centre Day hospital Walk-in-centre	Integrated locality Centre which public are accustomed to access	Local office Referral teams
NHS plan Dept of Health Government funding for modernised NHS	Pooled budget enabling new services to be funded and duplication of services to be reduced	Local authority funding streams Specific grants Supporting people
NPfIT programme	Integrated information systems Integrated mental health Electronic record	Care management IT systems
Patient public partnerships PALS	User and carer empowerment	User and care support Involvement with BME Communities
Community health councils Patient forums	Patient/service user representation at the centre of all integrated services	Voluntary sector/independent sector networks and funding
Training and professional registration of doctors, nurses, therapists, psychologists	Integrated training programme and joint post qualification certification	Training and professional registration of social workers
CPN, OT	Approved Mental Health Professional under new MHA	ASW training and authorisation
Trust boards NHS governance	Care trusts Local authority health scrutiny committee	Local authority members Local government Legislation
Free at point of delivery	Mixed economy	Charging for services
Improving working lives	Integrated workforce Development strategy	Investors in people

(Alimo-Metcalfe website, 9 December 2003), 'Leadership is not about being a wonder-man or wonder-woman. It is about being someone who values the individuality of their staff, who encourages individuals to challenge the *status quo* and who has integrity and humility. *It is about removing barriers between individuals, teams,* *functions and other organisations to work towards the achievement of a joint vision'.* (My emphasis.)

Peck et al., in their study of Somerset Mental Health Partnership Trust (see Glasby and Peck, 2004, Chapter 3), highlights that much of the progress was made by excellent working relationships at a senior level. Service users' satisfaction with services was positive, and they believed that integration had led to a better co-ordination of those services. Staff morale, however, was more problematic, with issues around organisational identity, role clarity and inter-disciplinary working; and management development. This demonstrates not only the cultural change at a strategic level, but the need for leadership at all levels. Professor Steve Onyett (2003) focuses in detail on the way the teams need to be designed around task, team and individuals, with an outside focus on the needs of users and carers to create the effective response and a culture which encourages individual and group development.

Exercise 6: Attributes

We have seen from a number of sources how personal attributes, management attributes and leadership attributes have to fit together to create synergy.

What do you see as your personal attributes?

Management attributes?

Leadership attributes?

Too often, teams are engaged in so much internal conflict that they are not focusing on what they are meant to be delivering.

Ultimately, we will have to wait to ascertain whether the new Children's Services can both deliver academic performance standards, protect and nurture abused and disadvantaged children, and outreach to the community. Bob Hudson, in an incisive article on the feasibility of the new agenda for Children's Services, points to the fact that a number of key policy drivers appear to be pushing in different directions. As he counsels: 'The wave of a legal wand does not remove generations of cultural separatism. The rational solutions . . . will not in themselves be sufficient to overcome the cultural resistance to change that will almost certainly be encountered' (Hudson, 2005: 9–10). We will also have to see whether Mental Health Trusts use their potential to promote well-being, as well as serving those who are most severely mentally ill, or whether they become a kind of community institution that was so pertinently described by social commentators and historians like Goffman and Jones (see Gilbert, 2003b). As Professor Anne Davis puts it, 'The evidence from the growing body of research based on Service User experiences . . . suggests that integration is not just about providing a single door or seamless service, it is about working with Service Users in ways that build respect, understanding, self-esteem and confidence in Service Users as well as workers' (Davis, 2004: 22–23).

CASE STUDY 7: SETTING UP A CONNEXIONS SERVICE

The Connexions Service was set up in England during 2001/2 with the aim of co-ordinating support for young people aged 13–19 years by allocating them a personal adviser (PA). It involved bringing together services such as Careers in a new approach that was intended to be a universal service for that age group, but targeting especially young people aged 16 and 17 who are not in, or at risk of, disengaging with education, employment or training (Rowntree, 2004). There has been some criticism as to whether Connexions has achieved the right balance in its service provision, nationally; and now that the government has published its green paper

Youth Matters (*Community Care*, 4–10 August 2005: 30–1) there is further turbulence in store for this service, which increases the relevance of this case study, as central government has a tendency to set up and then dismantle/reconfigure services with bewildering rapidity!

One Chief Executive of a new Connexions Service has previously led the establishment of another multi-agency, multi-professional partnership – a Youth Offending Team (YOT). The CEO believes that his 'very mixed professional background' (conversations with the author, 2004): residential social work, probation, social services, multi-agency partnership working,

CASE STUDY 7: Continued

has left him without any particular strong allegiance to any specific professional group of methodology. This, he believes, 'undoubtedly helped me to work with organisations where we have brought in staff from a range of disciplines and achieved effective joint working which builds on individual strengths without homogenising the workforce'.

A common feature of the organisations has been the need to bring together different professionals in multi-disciplinary teams and produce effective integrated practice. The CEO is clear that this cannot simply be achieved through co-location and common purpose (see Glasby and Peck, 2004). It 'requires strong team leadership with explicit ongoing opportunities for staff to explore and build on different professional experiences and perspectives'.

This particular CEO is a driven and energetic leader, who effected fast and substantial change in his previous role in youth justice, and therefore it is interesting to note that he regards the timescale for these partnership projects as unrealistic. He believes that building a new and effective customer focused public service organisation is a long-term task. Unfortunately, public service policy requires evidence of delivery within much tighter timescales than this might suggest. Because of the complexity of the changes; the speed of the policy imperative; and the need to create a new organisation, with radically different accountabilities; and because a number of the incoming staff were at different points with regard to their readiness to accept the proposed changes, the CEO describes his leadership style as requiring 'an acute balancing of autocratic/conflict-orientated style on the one hand, while seeking to develop a culture of learning/listening and inclusivity on the other'.

From the outset, the CEO set out to give a clear and unambiguous message about the scale and nature of pending organisational change, and as we can see from Chapter 8, radical change can be effected positively if leaders are clear about the change and are supportive to staff. The Connexions CEO talks about: 'creating the balance between clarity of vision and outcomes; and holding people, acknowledging that change takes time and there is a need to grieve'.

Perhaps his approach could be described as 'tough empathy', as set out by Goffee and Jones (2000). New partnerships – either within new structures, or new networks, are going to be increasingly common. There will be a need for leaders to articulate a vision which transcends, but at the same time integrates, professional identity and skills. This leader's experience, and his clarity about never being 'prepared to compromise in areas where I have control and accountability for achieving results, as this would be compromising young people's right to a quality service', is an experience which leaders will increasingly go through. In these situations, support for the leader (see my change process outlined in Chapter 8) is essential. As the CEO puts it, 'sitting on top of an organisation is a lonely place' and 'in my experience it is compounded when leading intense organisational change and building new services'. Leaders have an individual responsibility, but so do organisations to support those leaders, especially in setting up new organisations with complex boundaries and highly visible performance targets.

CHAPTER 8

Leading and Managing Change

Nothing is more difficult to handle, more doubtful of success and more dangerous to carry through than initiating changes . . . The innovator makes enemies of all those who prospered under the old order, and only lukewarm support is forthcoming from those who would prosper under the new.

(Niccolo Machiavelli, 1514, Penguin Edition, 1981: 51)

'The wise man does not see enlightenment, he waits for it. So while I was waiting it occurred to me that seeking perplexity might be more fun,' said Lu-tze, 'after all, enlightenment begins where perplexity ends. And I found perplexity.'

(Pratchett, 2001: 93–94)

Leaders achieve their effectiveness chiefly through the stories they relate.

(Gardner, 1997: 9)

The role of the corporate leader is to manage conflicting needs in a synergistic way, creating an environment in which opposing forces can be reconciled to create rapid and strong growth.

(Hampden-Turner, 1990: 11)

What worries me about this organisation is that as I visit services, nobody tells me stories. There is no narrative.

(newly appointed NHS chief executive to the author, 2004)

Introduction

A common perception is that change in the modern world is endemic, and change processes are occurring at a faster and faster rate. For most managers, even at very senior level, change is often something that is done to one; nevertheless the real leader has to mark the change process with their values, skills and personality for them to be a true leader. Research done by the Chartered Institute of Personnel and Development (CIPD, 2003) found that, though change is a major challenge for people, a proper change strategy, sound project management, managing the human factors, and effective leadership led to better outcomes.

In the case of mergers, and this is not simply for services, but has recently affected Inspectorates as well, with the National Care Standards Commission only lasting 17 days, before a ministerial announcement proclaimed a wider structural change and the creation of the Commission for Social Care Inspection (CSCI), massive cultural change is the order of the day. Glasby, Peck and Davis (2005: 4) in their analysis of possible structural models for the future, comment that 'the impact of almost constant re-organisation in the NHS damages local relationships and makes partnership working that much harder'.

The helpful Health Education Authority booklet *Supporting Staff Through Mergers and Beyond* (HEA, 1999) likens mergers to selecting a life partner, including:

- Initial optimism.
- Blindness to any undesirable qualities in the other partner.
- An over-confident belief that any differences will be resolved as one partner adapts to the other post-combination.

(Cartwright and Cooper, 1994, quoted in HEA, 1999: 6)

As we saw in the previous chapter, there are plenty of lessons from the private sector of change processes in major companies which have not fulfilled their promise (see, for example, the article on the merger of Daimler and Chrysler in *Business Week*, 29 September 2003: 44–49).

Change is endemic, but that must not lead us to be careless about change and its processes. In the party political conference season of the autumn of 2004, many senior players in health and social care made strong statements about the need for change processes to lead to positive outcomes. For example: 'We should also be looking at solving the needs of [service users] in employment, housing and social networks', from Niall Dixon, Chief Executive of the King's Fund, and warning that 'structural reorganisation is easier than cultural change, but it achieves far less', from the Chief Executive of the New Health Network, Margaret Mythen (*Health Service Journal*, 20 September 2004: 14). In their Annual Management Survey across the public and private sector in the UK, Roffey Park Institute found that while managers felt confident of managing through change processes, they were experiencing change for change's sake, with the majority not feeling that their organisation had become high performing as a result of change (Glynn and Holbeche, 2001). Recently, Denise Platt, Chair of the Commission for Social Care Inspection (CSCI), rebuked Ealing Council in London for engaging in a 'modernisation' of its services which the inspectors felt left vulnerable children and adults more vulnerable. 'Change is a fact of life in Social Services', stated Platt, 'because the whole point is to make people's lives better, but it has to be done right. Change through chaos is not helpful if staff want to do their jobs properly' (quoted in *Care and Health*, 23–29 November 2004: 7).

In terms of recent lessons, perhaps none is more pertinent than that of the railways. Simon Jenkins (1995) is clear that in his opinion, Margaret Thatcher would never have privatised the railways, because her political nose would have warned her against it. Under John Major, privatisation went at a faster, rather than slower pace, not because he was more orientated towards free market economics, but that he was too weak a Prime Minister to lead change processes effectively and know what would work and what would not. While it may have made sense to privatise the train companies, it never made sense to privatise the track, and investigations into major crashes and issues of maintenance, have shown lack of clarity concerning accountability, and a fundamental lack of professional and managerial expertise. In a remark which could very similarly be levelled at the case study in this chapter of CAFCAS (Case Study No. 9) the rail regulator accused Railtrack of getting rid of most practical experts, the engineers, who could monitor and control the contractors (see *The Observer*, 27 July 2003: 13).

For change to be effective in creating better outcomes requires vision, attention to processes, a constant learning cycle and an emphasis on relationships with all stakeholders. In his recent seminar with NHS leaders, Sir Nigel Crisp, as the Chief Executive of the NHS, focused on the essential relationships between different groupings as the organisational wheels changed. It is, he stated, 'about how we all behave' (*Health Service Journal*, 24 June 2004).

Why transformation efforts fail

John P. Kotter (Kotter, 1996) sets out a number of reasons why transformation processes so often change, leaving managers, as in the Roffey Park Survey quoted above, feeling that change has caused disruption with little positive to show for it. His reasons are as follows:

- Allowing too much complacency – the dissatisfaction with the status quo is not identified, and insufficient urgency and pressure is built up for change.
- Failing to create a sufficiently powerful guiding coalition – this is both within the organisation and with stakeholders outside of it (see, for example, Pathological Leadership Example 1, Chapter 1).
- Underestimating the power of vision – staff and other stakeholders need to understand and sign up to the vision, and be developed in order that they can achieve the stated goals (see Figure 18).
- Under-communicating the vision by a factor of 10 (or 100, or even 1,000). Leaders such as Jack Welch or Antony Sheehan (see Leadership Example 5) get out to meet with and listen to those at the frontline, to test out the vision, reinforce it and weave a continuous thread of narrative (Welch and Byrne, 2001).
- Permitting obstacles to block the new vision – when I took over Worcestershire Social Services as Director in 1997, I discovered a reorganisation of the Home Care Service which had disastrously stalled under previous directors. Middle managers were perfectly capable of producing the change, but they simply did not believe that the change was really going to happen, because of the previous failures. We set about unblocking those obstacles all the way down the line.
- Failure to create short-term wins. People need to see and touch some measure of success. Field Marshall William (Bill) Slim (see Historical Leadership Example No. 4) was a prime example of this following the disastrous failures of the Burma Campaign in the Second World War.

Figure 18: Changing services.

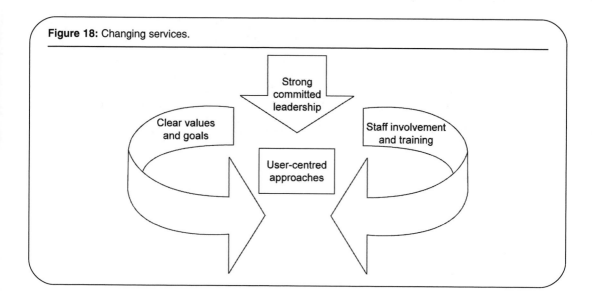

- Declaring victory too soon – as we have seen from Chapter 6, cultural change is incredibly complex. Partha Bose's study of Alexander the Great (see Bose, 2004) demonstrates Alexander's remarkable attempts at cultural change, which were partly undermined by his failure to appreciate the effects on his original supporters amongst the Macedonians.
- Neglecting to anchor changes firmly in the corporate culture – as Kotter says, 'in the final analysis, change sticks only when it becomes 'the way we do things around here' when it seeps into the very bloodstream of the work unit or corporate body' (Kotter, 1996: 14).

These common errors lead to new strategies not being implemented well, acquisitions and mergers which fail to achieve the expected synergies; re-engineering taking too long and costing too much; morale plummeting; outcomes not delivering the hoped-for results.

Achieving results

Terry Scragg (Scragg, 2001: 102) in a work which we commissioned in Worcestershire to aid the development of frontline managers, writes that, 'all large-scale change means stepping into the unknown to some extent and staff will need to trust you as their frontline manager if you are to work effectively in the change agent' role. As Kotter demonstrates from his work in mainly private sector companies, the first error is not to understand the change processes and build up a head of steam for positive change. The Chartered Institute of Personnel Development,

in its 2003 study quotes the reorganisation of Du Pont, the chemical company, which was followed by a 12 per cent increase in stock price, but also Proctor and Gamble who launched a new globally integrated structure in 1999, which a year later was seen as a failure, with the Chief Executive on his way out (CIPD, 2003).

Scragg suggests using a 'force field analysis' (Scragg, 2001: 102–105) which considers a number of factors: personal, inter-personal, group, inter-group, organisational and environmental; under the two major headings of forces promoting change, and forces resisting change; and how those press on to the present condition, and move towards the desired condition. An understanding of these pressures can ensure that major change processes achieve their results, sometimes in a surprisingly ameliorative fashion.

When Worcestershire County Council realised that it needed to externalise the vast majority of its homes for older people, because of past lack of investment, current condition, market forces and investment imperatives and conditions; suspicion from the unions was anticipated – in fact they would have been failing in their role if they had not challenged the council. But because we involved the unions and other stakeholders, with a special emphasis on residents and their carers, right from the start and they could see that the status quo was unsustainable, and a better future was possible with properly managed change, we were able to get all stakeholders on side. In the tendering process, there were imaginative ways of testing

CASE STUDY 8: LEUKAEMIA CARE

Managing in the not-for-profit sector

The not-for-profit sector has changed significantly over the last decade and has shaken off some of the unprofessional image that it has unduly attracted. Managing a fast-developing not-for-profit organisation is not that dissimilar to management in a private company. The business and management principals and disciplines needed are the same, although the balance is often different. Within the voluntary sector, there is greater focus on meeting the aims and public benefit of the organisation as there are a significantly greater number of stakeholders involved, from beneficiaries and volunteers to funders and partners.

Initially at Leukaemia CARE there was an increased focus on governance and compliance issues. Specifically, the relationship between the Chief Executive and Chair created the backbone to the organisation and provided the critical link between the Board and employees. Through this relationship, there were clear and defined responsibilities for the individuals involved, both as employees and volunteer Trustees. This resulted in the Chair and Board taking the responsibility for developing the strategy and the Chief Executive the implementation.

The most significant discipline that was undertaken was the development, and subsequent implementation, of a strategic plan for the organisation. This focused the organisation clearly on the objectives and ensured that everyone in the charity worked towards, and understood, clearly defined aims and goals. This was created from the heart of the organisation and took into consideration all stakeholders and ensured the charity fulfils its aims and meets public benefit.

At the forefront of this strategy was the delivery of services and this provided the benchmark for the charity. It was though, difficult to measure the impact as many of the services are not tangible and the work of the volunteers is not recorded stringently. There are some tangible services that were measured although due to the nature of the organisation, the true public benefit that the organisation provides is more difficult to quantify and monitor.

Emphasis on the management of people, whether employed or voluntary, was also critical to the business. The organisation undertook a complete review of the personnel and implemented enhanced personnel contracts, policies and working practices. Through the support, co-operation and commitment of the employees, the organisation encountered significantly less problems. This succeeded in the development of a very strong team that assisted the management and positioned the organisation to undertake schemes such as the Disability Symbol and Investors in People.

Specific attention was made to ensure increased accountability to maximise charitable expenditure whilst controlling the cost base. Financial management became more focused and full accounting procedures were installed to budget, account for and review the financial position of the organisation on a regular basis. This was paramount as the income streams are not secure, therefore making it more difficult to commit financial expenditure.

Through the implementation of key strategic and business principals, Leukaemia CARE tripled in terms of income and resource levels in a three-year period. The more focused provision of care and support significantly increased both the quality and quantity of service to patients and carers and positioned the charity as the leading national patient group for people affected by leukaemia.

(Contributed by Marc Stowell, former CEO of Leukaemia CARE)

Historical Leadership Example 4: Field Marshal William ('Uncle Bill') Slim

Slim's Fourteenth Army in Burma was sometimes referred to as 'the forgotten army'. William Slim might also have been referred to as the forgotten general in the years immediately after the war: an unfashionable early career with the Gurkha Rifles, and an unspectacular start to the war, it was Slim who had halted the Japanese invasion at the gates of India, in the desperately fought battles of Kohima and Imphal, and then, having rebuilt an army, he launched it against the Japanese in a campaign that took the allies back through Burma. It was apt that Slim's own account of the campaign should have been called *Defeat into Victory*. Both sides in the war used a great deal of propaganda, and it is useful to get behind that to see the man beneath the general's hat. As the author, George MacDonald Fraser wrote in his autobiography of life as a private soldier in the Burma Campaign: *Quartered Safe Out Here* (1992):

> *By rights each official work should have a companion volume in which the lowliest actor gives his version (like Sydenham Pointz for the Thirty Years War or Rifleman Harris in the Peninsula); it would at least give posterity a sense of perspective.*

(xi)

And this should be so for frontline workers in the health and welfare fields as well!

Lord Louis Mountbatten, Supreme Commander, south-east Asia, stated firmly that 'Slim was the finest general the second world war produced' (Fraser, 1992: 31), but perhaps the frontline soldier's perspective is even more crucial, especially in fighting that often became hand-to-hand combat:

> *The biggest boost to morale was the burly man who came to talk to the assembled battalion by the lake shore – I'm not sure when, but it was unforgettable. Slim was like that: the only man I've ever seen who had a force that came out of him, a strength of personality that I have puzzled over since, for there was no apparent reason for it . . . His appearance was plain enough: large, heavily built, grim faced . . . the rakish Gurkha hat that was at odds with the slung carbine . . . he might have been a yard foreman who had become a managing director . . . nor was he an orator.*

(Fraser, op. cit.)

- Slim had that ability to be 'Uncle Bill', the soldier's trusted uncle, while at no time there being any doubt who was in command.

- Duncan Anderson who wrote the chapter on Slim in Keegan's edited work says that Field Marshal Slim 'revealed a natural talent as a manager of men' (1991, p. 302). Bill Slim would often pick out people who seemed to be rogues or misfits and bring out the best of them. At his time with the Gurkhas, he learned the languages and customs of the people of north India. The Fourteenth Army, in Hickey's (1992) opinion was possibly the most multiracial army since those of the ancient world, and he brought the best out of a potentially complex and difficult command.

- Because of the particular problems in Burma, Slim never forgot the importance of good logistics and took great care to see that his staff officers knew that their contribution had a vital role to play in success at the front line.

- 'Slim was both a good student and a good teacher' (Anderson, 1991: 303). He could absorb both quantity and quality of information and impart it well.

- Slim always accepted responsibility. The retreat from Burma was handled with great determination and skill.

- Because of the massive defeat the army had suffered and its heterogeneous nature, Slim decided not only to train his troops but to motivate them by personal contact.

- 'From past experience, Slim had learned that the best approach was the most simple and direct – to talk to as many troops as he could, man to man, cutting through the traditional barriers of military hierarchy' (Anderson, 1991: 313 – a method which Fraser describes so graphically).

- Some generals are characterised, sometimes unfairly, as either good at defence or offence. Slim was a master of both, and Anderson believes that he ranks with Guderian, Manstein and Patton as an offensive commander.

(Anderson, 1991: 319)

It was a desperately hard campaign and there still remains the memorial to the defence at Kohima and Imphal:

> *When you go home, tell them of us and say*
> *For your tomorrow we gave our today*

(quoted in Hickey, 1992: 263)

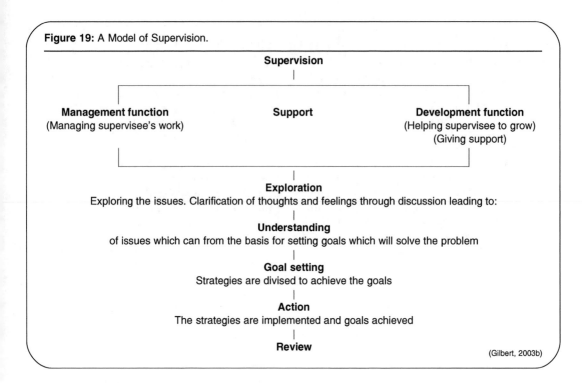

Figure 19: A Model of Supervision.

Supervision

Management function	Support	Development function
(Managing supervisee's work)		(Helping supervisee to grow)
		(Giving support)

Exploration
Exploring the issues. Clarification of thoughts and feelings through discussion leading to:

Understanding
of issues which can from the basis for setting goals which will solve the problem

Goal setting
Strategies are divised to achieve the goals

Action
The strategies are implemented and goals achieved

Review

(Gilbert, 2003b)

out those organisations which were long-listed and then short-listed for the final contract, so that there was unanimity with the conclusions.

Such involvement is not some kind of soft option, it is an essential part of the process. If staff and unions had not been assured that we were acting in the interests of the service as a whole, what kind of messages would there have been going to residents and carers – hardly positive ones! This was especially true after the previous partial externalisation of homes had created considerable disruption and distrust for only marginal benefit to the council.

As we can see from Scragg's force field approach and Figure 18, enabling staff to work with change, in line with organisational vision and processes is essential. The new Leadership Pack by TOPSS (TOPSS, 2004) looks at aligning vision, organisation and individual. In public sector services, a great deal of this will be done through 'supervision' (see Gilbert and Thompson, 2002).

It is important to remember that supervision, so prevalent in social work, is not always recognised in the health service, for example, and not always inculcated in social care as a whole. Colleagues in the human services, who have come across supervision as a process, have commented positively on its merits.

One of the best studies of change in human service organisations is that by Rebecca Ann Proehl (Proehl, 2001). Although the examples are American, they are largely transferable to a British welfare situation. Proehl quotes extensively from Galpin's work on *The Human Factors in Change*, and provides useful models for working through the change process with groups of people who lack knowledge, and need communication and involvement; those who lack skills and attributes, and require emotional support, education and training; and those who have dug their heels in and require a skilful approach including building alliances, setting goals, coaching and recognition with reward (Proehl, 2001: 158–168). In Chapter 7, Proehl considers five of the most well recognised change models, including Kotter's, which have laid out specific steps ranging from five to nine. Proehl suggests an eight-step change management model, but in British public services, even that I think is liable to miss out some vital steps for successful change leadership and management.

In this context, it is useful to consider the work on partnership by Harrison et al. (2003). My proposal for a change process model should at least ensure that some of the major pitfalls are avoided and the process undertaken which encourages maximum learning so as to gain maximum effectiveness.

Exercise 7: Force field analysis

The Force Field Analysis enables you to identify a number of factors which are likely to help in the change process and those which are likely to hinder it. Once you have identified those issues, you can consider a strategy for increasing the positives and reducing the negatives. You are invited to set down those forces which are (i) promoting change, and (ii) resisting change, in a change process you are currently engaged on, under the headings of:
- personal
- inter-personal
- group
- inter-group
- organisational
- environmental

Box 3: Social care in England by numbers

- **1.6 million:** people using social care services in England at any one time.
- **8,000:** children in children's homes.
- **371,238:** older people in care homes.
- **12,994:** care homes for older people.
- **8 million:** carers providing informal care for relatives and friends.
- **1.4 million:** people working in the social care sector (more than the NHS).
- **150:** local authorities in England giving social care.
- **2,500:** people who are working for the Commission for Social Care Inspection (CSCI).
- **17 days:** the length of time the CSCI's predecessor, the National Care Standards Commission, was in existence.

These steps are subject to changing circumstances and to resistance, so that steps may need to be revisited and revisited. Human beings and human services do not always follow a rational path!

1. **Determining the need for change**
   - Evaluating the present state.
   - What is the dissatisfaction with the status quo?
   - Testing out the need for change.
   - Gaining 'hard' and 'soft data'.
   - Identifying what potential 'allies' and 'rivals' are doing.
2. **Establishing a sense of urgency**
   - Examining the market and competitive realities.
   - Identifying and discussing crises, potential crises, or major opportunities.
   - Influencing people.
3. **Creating the guiding coalition**
   - Putting together a group with enough power to lead the change at all levels.
   - Ensuring that change is user/consumer-driven.
   - Getting the group(s) to work together like a team(s).
   - Working with key stakeholders (NB Political dimensions, especially in local government, and 'political' factors – the organisational politics in any organisation).
   - 'Engage the Heart'.
4. **Developing a vision and strategy**
   - Creating a vision to help direct the change effort – define the desired future state.
   - Developing strategies for achieving that vision.
   - Identifying required resources.
5. **Communicating the change vision**
   - Using every vehicle possible to constantly communicate the new vision and strategies.
   - Demonstrating you are listening – and hearing!
   - Having the guiding coalition role model the behaviour expected of employees.
   - Listen – Hear – Respond – Act.
6. **Working with the human factors**
   - Getting everybody on board.
   - Appropriately integrate the past with the present and future. 'Rites of Passage' as a way of building bridges.
   - Strategies to deal with resistance.
   - Build in the new attitudes and skills to cope with and 'grow' the change process.
7. **Empowering broad-based action**
   - Getting rid of obstacles.
   - Changing systems or structures that undermine the change vision.
   - Encouraging risk taking and non-traditional ideas, activities, and actions.
   - Budget implementation resources.

8. **Generating short-term wins**
   - Planning for visible improvements in performance, or 'wins'.
   - Creating those wins.
   - Visibly recognising (and rewarding) people who made the wins possible.
9. **Evaluating and consolidating gains, and producing more, purposeful change**
   - Using increased credibility to change all systems, structures, and policies that do not fit together and do not fit the transformation vision.
   - Evaluating the process so far and instituting 'double-loop' learning, where actions are reflected upon, evaluated, and the results are used to improve individual and organisational performance next time round (see Gilbert and Thompson, 2002, Part 2, and Martin, 2003, Chapter 1).
   - Adjusting the change process to take account of the lessons learned.
   - Building in measures of the current situation *and* where you want to get to.
   - Hiring, promoting, and developing people who can implement the change vision.
   - Reinvigorating the process with new projects, themes, and change agents. But in a way which *does not distract* from the main purpose/thrust of change.
10. **Anchoring new approaches in the culture**
    - Creating better performance through customer and productivity-oriented behaviour, more and better leadership, and more effective management.
    - Ensuring stakeholder (inc. political) acceptance and ownership.

- Articulating the connections between new behaviours and organisational success.
- Developing means to ensure leadership development and succession.
- Celebrate successes.

Major themes
- Accent on leadership.
- Keep the vision firmly in view.
- Remember that change is not a linear process. You will probably need to revisit a number of stages to accomplish successful change which sticks.
- Don't panic!
- Communicate, communicate and keep communicating!
- Listen – Hear – Respond – Act.
- Positive thinking and talking – using narrative.
- Ensure you make a positive difference.
- Make sure **you** have support during the change process.

Change in the public services is in many senses more complex than that in the private sector, not least because the stakeholders are more diverse, and their relationships more complex, and because there is usually less money to invest in a positive process of change. It is instructive to learn from research that many well-resourced change processes have foundered, or run into the sand, and much of this is due to factors that we have always known about such as creating the right momentum, and getting and keeping people on board. As Richard Beckard once put it, 'people do not resist change; people resist being changed'! (quoted in Proehl, 2001: 144).

CASE STUDY NO. 9: CAFCASS

Positive change processes
'There is no idea of these managers having an understanding of children. They were just obsessed with targets and with constant change'. So spoke an experienced social work guardian in a radio interview with Fergal Keane (2 March 2004, BBC Radio 4).

CAFCASS (The Children and Family Court Advisory and Support Service) was set up in 2001 by the Department for Constitutional Affairs to represent, safeguard and promote the welfare of children involved in Family Court Proceedings in England and Wales, as part

of the government's restructuring of how the judicial system and welfare agencies interacted. One of its primary goals was to reduce the time a child had to wait for a court decision while ensuring that such a decision was the right one.

By 2003, however, a House of Commons Select Committee was censorious in its criticism: 'no effective overseeing organisation', it stated, 'should have allowed such a serious breakdown in the performance of the key functions for which it is responsible' (quoted in 'A Tragedy of Errors', *Society Guardian*, 22 October 2003: 2).

CASE STUDY NO. 9: Continued

Before CAFCASS was set up, 95 per cent of public law cases were allocated within 24 hours. At its lowest point, CAFCASS had a target of allocating just 85 per cent of cases within 7 days, and according to the service's own figures, more than 1,100 public and private child custody cases did not have a CAFCASS guardian allocated.

Its first chief executive was sacked, its chair was also later removed, and the whole board was asked to resign. The service has now transferred to the Department for Education and Skills, as part of the Children's Ministers remit; with a new Chair in Baroness Jill Pitkeathley and a new Chief Executive in Anthony Douglas, who has considerable social care management experience and, crucially, in the words of the Chair of the Guardian's organisation, Nagalro, 'a great depth of understanding of child care issues'.

When you look at the initial vision of striving to create a new unified service, it is difficult to fault it. But the implementation of this complex merger was profoundly flawed in that:

- It had a shorter timescale than was needed to properly integrate the organisations it would replace.
- There was insufficient attention to the cultural change processes, especially one involving very experienced professionals, who had a prime, professional duty to serve the interests of children first.
- The organisational shaping was undertaken by civil servants, not managers and professionals with detailed knowledge of the environmental context.
- There was an element of force majeure, especially when management attempted to force traditionally self-employed guardians to join the payroll, which the latter felt would result in less flexibility in their work with children and poorer working conditions for them.
- There seemed to be a lack of understanding about the respective roles of the Chair and the Board, the management, and the Chancellor's department. Alan Beith, MP, Chair of the Constitutional Affairs Select Committee which held the enquiry, criticised the Lord Chancellor's department for 'giving instructions to staff members rather than it being run by its own management board'.

(*Guardian*, ibid.)

With a new Chair and Chief Executive, there is a good chance of CAFCASS delivering what everybody wants and 'pursuing the same goal – better outcomes for children; and working effectively to that end with partners' ('Back from the Brink', *Care and Health*, 1–7 June 2004).

PART THREE

Creating Person-centred Services

His (Shakespeare's Richard III) method of gaining power simultaneously creates its own fear that the same method can be used to take it from him. This is the most straightforward lesson Shakespeare teaches. You know that if you have lied and cheated your way to the top others can lie and cheat their way to the top, and there is nothing you can do or say about it. The moral activity in gaining power brings its own anxiety, since you know what is possible for others to do to you.

(Paul Corrigan, 1999: 144)

CHAPTER 9

Power and Authority

I have never worked in a Council where officers at all levels openly show so much contempt for those in power. Putting loyalty and friendship above integrity leads to the chaos and shambles we have before us now.

(Former Lincolnshire Chief Executive, David Bowles, to elected Members quoted in *The Local Government Chronicle*, 10 September 2004)

He has risen without trace.

(standard saying of those with ambition but little integrity)

Political government doesn't use management techniques. No Prime Minister ever gave me a ministerial role and told me what was expected of me!

(Former minister Michael Portillo, *Radio Five Live*, 12 September 2004)

If one candidate is trying to scare you, and the other candidate is trying to get you to think; if one is appealing to your fears, and the other is appealing to your hopes; you better vote for the one who wants you to think and hope.

(Former President Bill Clinton, 24 October 2004 – the American people did not follow his advice!)

Tell me what you're thinking, Susan.
Do you really want to know, Sir?
Only if it suits me!

(conversation between a police superintendent and his detective sergeant in *Murder City*, ITV)

Introduction

In the week beginning 20 December 2004, USA Secretary of State for Defence, Donald Rumsfeld, was heavily criticised by members of his own Republican Party, when it transpired that the condolence letters from his department, sent to those bereaved by the death of American soldiers in Iraq, were not personally signed by Rumsfeld himself, but were done by rubber stamp (one of the cultural relics of the old Staffordshire regime – see Case Study 6, Chapter 6, was that the previous director had in use a rubber stamp for his signature. This was discontinued forthwith.) This highly emotionally charged issue, was laid alongside the wider factor of the inadequacy of the numbers of troops and equipment to undertake the work willed by politicians in the White House. Again, the accusation from Rumsfeld's own supporters was that he did not listen sufficiently to his 'uniformed advisers'. This takes us very starkly back to one of the original points of this book that, however much power an individual is seen to have, they must be seen to act with integrity. The leader in a professional area: education, healthcare, social care, the police, fire service, army, etc., must weigh up the advice given them by their professional advisers, and decide when professional paradigms hold sway within a wider context.

It is a most uncomfortable truth for professionals that Britain's worst serial killer, Harold Shipman, was that apparently most reassuring of figures, a family GP. In her summing up of her inquiry, Dame Janet Smith criticised the professional registration and inspection body, saying:

I have found that the GMC has not safeguarded patients as it should have done. The culture within the GMC has been such that it focused too much on being fair to doctors and not sufficiently on the need to protect patients.

(quoted in *The Guardian*, 10 December 2004)

We tend to use the word 'power' a great deal. In fact, I worked for one CEO for whom 'powerful' appeared to be his only verbal adjective! It might be said that we use the word, because we have very little explicit power that we can use, and often in frustration use what we have in ways that are pathological.

Perhaps a more appropriate word is 'authority', because we carry authority through how people view us as an individual; through our personal attributes; our professional or trade skills; our relevant experience; and the role we are asked to fulfil. We say that people are authoritative when we can see in them the personal and professional/managerial attributes which we wish to follow. One of those attributes may well be the ability of the 'leader' also to play a role in a number of circumstances as a 'follower', so that the leader is listening and learning.

Abuses of power

Abuse of power can clearly take place at different levels and in different ways:

- **National:** The most obvious example is still that of Hitler's Germany. We tend to distance ourselves from the Hitler phenomenon, but we need to remember that Germany was a western democracy, the home of Beethoven and Goethe, and yet the whole nation, in effect, with a few notable and heroic exceptions, signed up to this bizarre apocalyptic vision (see Burleigh, 2001 and Evans 2003). As Burleigh (2001: 3) puts it, 'Ground down by defeat and endemic crises, many Germans looked at his [Adolf Hitler's] carefully selected range of poses, and saw their own desired self-image reflected'.
  For those in the health, education, and social care professions, it is of course the Nazis' programme of euthanasia for those with mental health problems, or a physical or learning disability, which is perhaps most pertinent, especially as it followed the Weimar Republic's social welfare reforms. As Burleigh puts it:
    Social Darwinism fused with a pseudo-Nietzschean contempt for humanitarian succour of the weak. In line with many advocates of eugenic sterilisation and euthanasia at the time, Hitler believed that anyone not fit for life should perish, and that the state could give nature a helping hand.
                                                    (2001: 99)
  The power of Hitler's corrupt and corrupting message, was all the more potent because it tapped into human beings' desire for meaning and narrative (e.g. see Holloway, 2004).

Those tempted to feel complacent that 'it would never happen here', should watch the disgraceful depiction of the care of frail, elderly people in a Brighton District General Hospital, shown on BBC1's *Panorama* on 20 July 2005. It is worth reminding ourselves that the German Weimar Republic, which was replaced by the Nazis, had a civilised welfare state, whose philosophy was deliberately undermined by propaganda denigrating the lives and value of vulnerable people (see Gilbert and Scragg, 1992, Chapter 1).

- **Organisational:** Collins and Porras (2000) suggest that organisations need to have a kind of cult-like culture to succeed. We know the potential of a positive organisational culture, but also how recent corporate disasters such as Enron, WorldCom and Parmalat (see Storey, 2004) have resulted in huge disruption for the staff and clients of these firms, and a loss of confidence in corporate business overall.
  In December 2004 there were two major new stories about organisational discrimination. In the first a captain of a Navy frigate was ordered home, after a number of his crew members had complained of bullying. In an instance in a London employment tribunal, a senior woman banker lost her case of sex discrimination against Merrill Lynch, but the ruling was critical of the banking firm:
    We note ... the culture of secrecy and opaqueness regarding pay, the subjective approach to bonuses, coupled with the litigation history ... It also criticised *the degree of hostility, personal attack and denigration disproportionate to the claimant's perceived shortcomings.*
                        (employment tribunal ruling,
                                22 December 2004)

- **Professional:** The stated design of professionalism is to ensure a regulatory framework, ethics and education, which can attest to the public and other professionals of the profession's probity.
  As we can see from the criticism of the medical profession's approach to Harold Shipman, quoted above, regulation of professionals by their own profession often delivers less than expected. There has been considerable criticism from patients and patient groups in recent years of the perceived arrogance of medical professionals. This does not mean that the public wish doctors to be self-effacing. In effect, they wish for authoritativeness, but not control and

autocracy. Media commentator and patients' advocate, Claire Rayner, on a recent radio phone-in, stated that she did not want to be 'empowered', she wanted doctors who knew what they were doing, and were able to put that across in a communicative, empathetic and caring manner. Harry Cayton (2004), National Director for Patients and the Public, quoted Bernard Shaw's definition of professionalism (*Health Service Journal*, 9 December 2004: 17) in a *Doctor's Dilemma*: 'All professions are a conspiracy against the laity'. Cayton points out that patients want 'confidence in expertise from their doctor, and confidentiality, but they are also increasingly concerned about the manner in which they are treated, wanting respect and courtesy, as well as kindness, good communication, and assistance in giving informed consent to a range of choices'.

Cayton's answer is partly that regulatory bodies of professions should move from self-regulation, through profession-led regulation, to shared regulation.

- **Individual:** Alistair Mant in his book *Leaders We Deserve* (1984), talks about two types of leaders: 'binary' (or 'raiders') and 'ternary' (or 'builders'). The binary leaders are often obsessed with their own ambition. The ternary individual fits with Jim Collins' description of the Level 5 leader (Collins, 2001) who is driven by wider values and ideals towards the common good, not simply the satisfaction of their own desires. The ternary mind can cope with paradox and grapples with questions of meaning and morality.

Paul Corrigan, in his commentary on Shakespeare's *Coriolanus* (Corrigan, 1999, Chapter 8) shows how the Roman general has not only separated himself from those he leads, whom he treats purely as instruments to his own ambition, but is divorced from himself as well. As a soldier describes him 'He is himself alone' (*Coriolanus*, Act I, Sc. 4, l. 50). Good leaders have a strong sense of who they are and what they should be doing, and how that is brought together congruently into effective leadership – see Figure 20.

Coriolanus is a bully, but we have become rather obsessed with bullying as a dysfunctional way of managing. There can be many other ways of misusing power, e.g. through political/political

manipulation; undermining, or simply ignoring your staff's positive performance; engaging staff in intensive consultation and improvement exercises and then not implementing them. This latter is an excellent way of demotivating people; in Case Study 9, that of CAFCASS, staff reported that intensive work with taskforce teams and stakeholder groups resulted in management using very little of what had been elicited from front-line staff ('So What Went Wrong?', *Community Care*, 17–23 July 2003: 33–34). Stopping the abuse of power is clearly difficult to achieve. At the level of a national state, the importance of 'checks and balances' is essential. In the British Constitution there is a balance between different branches of the Executive: Prime Minister and Cabinet and House of Commons; and between the Executive and the Legislature. Recently, the Law Lords ruled against the government on the detention without charge of suspects held under terrorism law. David Starkey, the historian, in his recent overview of monarchy in these isles, continually picks out the issue of a contractual relationship between the monarch and their people, and the importance of this, even at a time of rule through power. Continually, those kings who wish to be effective place themselves, through their pronouncements and their laws, on the side of the people (Starkey, 2004).

In the realm of organisations regulation is often sought as the means of control, but in the city, while regulation has increased, financial probity has not. As an attempt to introduce an ethical framework alongside the regulatory one, the former head of the Financial Services Authority (FSA), Sir Howard Davies brought in a number of people (including a Benedictine abbot), to construct an ethical framework (see Steare and Jamison, 2003). Their work brings together the classical virtues, core values, and the ways in which virtues can become vices if taken to extremes.

In the last century and this we have been surprised and shocked by the fact that increased scientific discovery, technological advance, and the spread of apparent democratic government, has not lessened the abuse of power. Indeed, the worst tyrannies have occurred in the 20th century. The increasing individualisation and atomisation of society (see Chapter 2) and the spread of media outlets, has made people more vulnerable to manipulation. That pertinent observer of societies, Alexis de Tocqueville, moved from commenting on the *Ancien Régime*

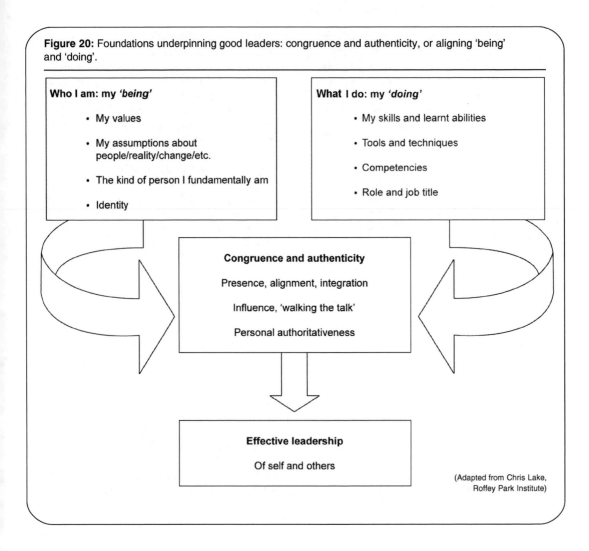

Figure 20: Foundations underpinning good leaders: congruence and authenticity, or aligning 'being' and 'doing'.

Who I am: my *'being'*

- My values
- My assumptions about people/reality/change/etc.
- The kind of person I fundamentally am
- Identity

What I do: my *'doing'*

- My skills and learnt abilities
- Tools and techniques
- Competencies
- Role and job title

Congruence and authenticity

Presence, alignment, integration

Influence, 'walking the talk'

Personal authoritativeness

Effective leadership

Of self and others

(Adapted from Chris Lake, Roffey Park Institute)

and the Revolution in France, to democracy in America, and saw new forms of oppression arising (de Tocqueville, 1864).

Pathological leaders cannot allow themselves to be followers at any time. They are the ultimate control freaks. Charles Hampden-Turner (1992: 8) notes that: 'the whole notion of leaders and followers is increasingly out of date'. As he states: leaders may have to spend considerable time 'following' what their subordinates with specific skills are telling them. Rebecca Proehl (2001: 104) believes the employees of the future must be people who:

- Own their work – rather than seeing it being owned by others.
- Are self-initiating, self-correcting and self-evaluating.

- Are clear about their own values and vision for the future.
- Are responsible for what happens.
- See the organisation from the outside in – from the customer's/patient's/user's perspective.

Finally, no reflection on power and its abuse would be complete without a reference to the myth-makers of our age, and their disquisition on power: Tolkien, Philip Pullman, J.K. Rowling and Ursula LeGuin. All of these writers speak eloquently about the pathology of power and the need to challenge it without falling into power's own trap. Paul Kocher (1974) says that Tolkien's Sauron is destroyed because he cannot envisage that his enemies will deny themselves the use of the ultimate weapon, which he covets. 'Lacking imaginative sympathy', writes Kocher,

---

Leadership Example 6: Andrew Bright

I have been delighted to see more people with learning disabilities become leaders and campaigners. This has encouraged me to speak up, not just for myself but also on behalf of the many people that need to know about direct payments and person-centred planning. This awareness raising is something I think is very important. It helps to get things started by encouraging people to think about what they could do and what they want.

For me, nothing beats seeing people with learning disabilities take on the challenge of leadership. Some like Andrew Lee at 'People First' have led the way in encouraging self-advocacy. I like the idea of a 'role-model' – someone that can show you it can be done. Setting an example and showing how to make a difference, has really helped me to develop new training for direct payments.

Leaders that did not have a learning disability have also influenced me. These are people that had knowledge; experience and commitment that they used to help people with learning disabilities get better lives. In particular the late Ken Simons was always teaching and explaining. Ken had great ideas about how the Government could really improve things. He really understood the discrimination experienced by people with learning disabilities. Ken took time to listen and was always ready to explain and discuss ideas he was putting forward. Ken is one of many people I have met that have really tried to get people interested in new ideas.

Leaders are not just people that introduce new ideas at conferences. Leaders have helped people with learning disabilities to get the support they need so that they are full citizens. For my part, I have been designing new training. This increases the awareness of self-advocates and family carers to use person-centred planning and direct payments. As a leader I want to go beyond teaching people this. I want people to go on and get direct payments and new lives. I don't just want to be a trainer – I want to train more people with learning disabilities to become trainers. I hope then they will train self-advocates and professionals like social workers. It is very important that the people that provide services recognise that people with learning disabilities can be leaders!

Andrew Bright is Director of Participation at the National Development Team, a national, not-for-profit organisation assisting the development of valued lifestyles for people with learning disabilities and people with mental health needs.

'an evil intelligence cannot by understanding penetrate a good one, which does have that power in reverse. *The former is too involved in self* (57, my emphasis). Sauron's subordinates become mere imitations of him, often having no name of their own (and therefore no identity). Gandalf, on the other hand, refuses to use the Ring and understands that 'the way of the Ring, to my heart is by pity, pity for weakness and the desire of strength to do good', but knows that it will corrupt him because, as Kocher describes: 'Good objectives turn bad when achieved by the absolute power over others' wills which the Ring confers' (58).

The abusers of power drain all life and colour and energy from the world around them to feed their own ambition and empty dreams. The American Taoist, Ursula Le Guin, is perhaps one of the best depicters of this manifestation, and in *The Farthest Shore* (1973) she has her hero Ged, confronting a man who insists on clinging on to existence, to an extent now that, as Ged puts it: 'You have no self. You have given everything for nothing.' Ged goes on to say:

And so now you seek to draw the world to you, all that light and life you lost, to fill up your nothingness. But it cannot be filled. Not all the songs of Earth, nor all the stars of Heaven, could fill your emptiness.

(463)

CHAPTER 10

Making the Difference

Effective leadership requires diversity as it brings richness and a breadth of knowledge, skills and experience.

(Annette Sinclair and Barbara Agyeman, 2004)

It is the motivation for change that is most likely to separate Black and Minority Ethnic leadership from 'White' leadership. People from BME groups are more likely than others to be driven by the awareness of injustice, based on race, because of their personal experiences.

(Hari Sewell, Director of Social Care, Camden and Islington Care Trust)

We live in the conscious presence of difference . . . that can be experienced as a profound threat to identity. One of the great transformations from the 20th to the 21st centuries is that whereas the former was dominated by the politics of ideology, we are now entering an age of the politics of identity.

(Jonathan Sacks, 2002: 10)

Despite the myth of the 'Black Superwoman' busy outstripping her male counterparts, if you are young, female and black in Britain, chances are slim that you will find a job to reflect your academic ability or potential.

(H.S. Mirza, 1992)

I've given twelve years of my life to this and no-one gives a damn.

(Dr David Kelly, *The Government Inspector*, Channel 4 drama documentary, 17 March 2005)

Introduction

In Chapters 1 and 4 particularly, concern was expressed at the dominance of leadership research and models from the USA, and the tendency for white men to be promoted as role models. Organisations can have a tendency to become very one-dimensional, with boardroom strife at Ford being described recently as, 'Tsarist Russia looks tame by comparison [with Ford]' (*Detroit News* – quoted in *The Guardian*, 15 November 2004). This very straight-jacketed approach can lead, for example in the education sector, to the demand for specialist faith schools, because the generic education sector is not seen to fulfil those needs.

As organisations have to become more globally orientated, and through a multi-cultural society in Britain, the world comes to us, a celebration rather than a denial of diversity is what is required.

The Challenge

Until recently, cross-cultural aspects of leadership were relatively neglected. The work of Geert Hofstede (e.g. Hofstede 1980, 1992),

taken forward by Hampden-Turner and Trompenaars (1993), has opened up whole areas of meaning within corporate life and leadership. Linstead et al. (2004: 353) quote Akio Morita, the former President of the Sony Corporation, as saying that 'US and Japanese management are 95 per cent the same, and differ in all important respects'. If one of the prime aspects of leadership is managing culture (see Chapter 6), then that 5 per cent is crucial. We can see this in all aspects from the macro-international to the micro-local. When General Sir Mike Jackson remarked on the methods of peacekeeping in Iraq in 2004, and mused that, 'We work with the Americans, not as the Americans', he was flagging up a crucial cultural difference in the way that the two armies, though allies, worked with the local population. If you are a human services executive working with partners in other countries, or an academic working across international boundaries, an understanding of culture is essential. If you are commissioning or providing services anywhere in the UK, especially in the major cities, where a wide variety of different cultures are now embedded, cultural sensitivity is imperative. As Yoni Ejo points out in her work on managing practice in black and minority ethnic organisations, not only have a growing number of organisations been set up and run by people from minority groups because of dissatisfaction with the *status quo*, but there are often elements of suspicion and inadequate knowledge from commissioning organisations (Ejo, 2004).

Roffey Park, in its recent work on *Strategies For Success In Global Leadership* (Sinclair and Agyeman, 2004) sets out a number of characteristics, attitudes and approaches which global organisations and their leaders need, and these could be transferred to managing within a multi-cultural society: knowledge; recognising the influence of culture; seeking, not simply celebrating diversity; encouraging creative thinking from the workforce; cultivating positive relationships with stakeholders; managing and uniting a diverse workforce; developing capacity to build and sustain trust.

When we look at the report into the Metropolitan Police by Sir William (Bill) Morris, (December 2004) it demonstrates that the Met had, in effect, alienated much of its black and minority ethnic workforce and its white workforce, despite considerable investment in diversity training. Morris concluded: 'There is no common understanding of diversity within the organisation . . . it remains at worst, a source of fear and anxiety and, at best, a process of ticking boxes'.

In our rigid, Western-centric models of leadership, organisations risk stultifying the creativity which they need to succeed. The Audit Commission's Report following the first round of comprehensive performance assessments (CPA) of local government, pick out recruitment and retention and workforce diversity as essential elements in peak performance: 'By valuing differences in the experience, culture and background of their staff, Councils can encourage new ideas and perspectives and deliver better services' (Audit Commission, 2003).

Linstead et al. (2004) point to research which shows women acting in a more transformational way, while men are often stuck in a transactional approach, and keeping distance from their subordinates in order to maintain status. Again, linking with the Collins research, Fiona Wilson (1995) shows the characteristics of female leaders more in tune with the service of the values and mission of the organisation, rather than of themselves. Marilyn Davidson, in her work on black and minority ethnic women managers, and the 'double discrimination' that they face, fears that current practice reduces the creativity of the corporate body exponentially, and this at a time when the Equal Opportunities Commission has stated that female representation in public life is still limited (EOC, 2004) and the study by the Bristol Business School reveals women managers feel discriminated against going for the top jobs in local government (*Local Government Chronicle*, 16 May 2003).

The study by the Bristol Business School is interesting in that it appears to show that the different strands of 'modernisation' can act against each other. As councils are streamlined and cabinet government brought in, 'Traditional views of leadership are becoming more apparent as new political management arrangements place Members in more prominent leadership roles' (Bristol Report, quoted in *LGC*, 16 May 2003). When Christine Walby came in as Director for Staffordshire County Council Social Services after the Pindown crisis (see Case Study 6), one of the aspects of the corporate life which she challenged was the heavily male-dominated behaviour of senior elected members, with decisions being taken in 'smoke-filled rooms'. Walby rightly identified that the cultural problems were not simply related to social services, and that a challenge to the overall council culture was essential. It is noticeable that the chief executive, clearly in the best position to challenge this, had apparently not had the courage to do so. To do the council leader justice, he saw the need for this and made changes to his and senior members' behaviour overnight.

There are some cautionary notes to all of this. The first is that we could move from a simplistic and erroneous identification of leadership with maleness, to an equally simplistic and possibly equally erroneous reversal. The second is that, as we have discussed earlier in this chapter, leadership roles and effectiveness are partly culturally based.

As, unfortunately in Britain, we find it difficult to do 'both/and', rather than 'either/or', there is a growing tendency to use the last decade of research, not to say that there are feminine and masculine traits, which can be used congruently and constructively to create a new leadership synthesis; but rather to say that a man in a leadership role must inevitably be transactional, and a woman in a leadership role must necessarily be transformational. This simply does not accord with people's experience, and there are an increasing number of women managers at middle/senior level, with potential to move on to chief officer/chief executive, who complain of 'bullying' by female managers which is as destructive as bullying by men, but more subtle! In addition it is not helpful to say to men: 'You are transactional, women are transformational'. People have plenty of examples of senior management teams where a woman may be highly transactional, and it will be a man who will be undertaking the transformational approach. Few writers have really got to grips with this issue not least because it is so potentially divisive. Fiona Wilson (2003) is one of the few commentators to tackle this with any confidence, setting out the cultural and political issues whereby 'in societies and organisations where a male culture is prevalent, and power rests in the hands of men, women must conform to the masculine model if they want to 'keep their heads'. She then challenges us to reflect on whether 'a blend of masculine and feminine skills creates a more effective manager and that reliance on solely masculine or feminine characteristics might be counter-productive to organisational success' (155).

What is certainly still true overwhelmingly is that, as Fiona Wilson's research (2003) shows, women managers are likely to express emotions, admit vulnerability, and be less self-enhancing. Again, our own life experience tells us that men are more likely to 'blow their own trumpet', and

---

Box 4: Leadership and Ethnicity: A Personal View

Black people who are real leaders are driven to their cause for exactly the same reasons as anybody else. They have a vision of how things could be different and they are determined to realise that vision. It may be that the motivation is altruistic but then it may well be self-centred.

Like all people, black people may wish to change things because they feel passionately that they can make a difference, or they may feel that they can be **recognised** for making a difference.

It is the motivation for change that is most likely to separate BME leadership from white leadership. People from BME groups are more likely than others to be driven by the awareness of injustice, based on race, because of their personal experiences. It is also true, however, that many people from BME groups will realise the complexity of race politics.

So when asked about BME leadership, my first question is 'To what extent does racial injustice (or a perception of it) impinge on that individual's everyday life?' As one black leader put it, 'It depends on the extent to which race has left its imprint on your life and personality'.

BME leadership is, therefore, a complex mix of the personal experience of race (and racism) and the motivation to see justice and change. These factors are combined with all of the other features – likes and dislikes – that make up the personality of the leader.

It also remains true however, that race is such a defining feature, that anyone who thinks of the individual as black will think of them as a black leader. Strange, because sometimes they will not see themselves as such.

When I wrote an article about leadership for a trade magazine recently, I reflected at the end of drafting that I did not refer specifically to race. I wondered whether to change it, as I had considered using a specific example from Nelson Mandela's life early in the process of writing. The striking feature for me, was not the rights or wrongs of me dealing with race directly or indirectly, but the fact that I felt some anxiety that either black people would see me as selling out because I did not use the platform to tackle discrimination, or that white people would see me as uni-dimensional; black face, black mantra. That is the important feature of black leadership in a white society. Every outing is like stepping into a vice.

The fact is however, for black people, just like with me and my article, every act of leadership is an act of black leadership.

(Contributed by Hari Sewell,
Director of Social Care,
Camden and Islington Care Trust)

CASE STUDY NO. 10: JERSEY HEALTH AND SOCIAL SERVICES APPROACH TO CORE VALUES

Jersey Health and Social Services provide health and social care to an island population of approx. 90,000. This includes general hospital care, mental health care, social services, public health and ambulance services. A number of specialist services are purchased off-island, mainly in England.

At a workshop, which was charged with reviewing the Community and Social Services division of Jersey Health and Social Services in January 2001, discussion took place amongst senior managers about personal experiences of being a recipient of care services. It reinforced the belief that although we all expect our care providers to have the appropriate skills and qualifications for the job they are asked to do, the most fundamental need is to be treated with dignity, respect, and as an individual. Core values for Jersey Health and Social Services became one of the main agenda items in the ongoing development of the service.

The core values
Small discussion groups identifying how best to move the core values approach forward. Some 'words' were identified which culminated in the statements below:

- We aim to treat clients and colleagues with respect, consideration, dignity, courtesy and as individuals and to give service users, wherever possible, real choice and control over their lives.
- We aim to actively seek feedback from service users and treat criticism as an opportunity for service improvements and not as a trigger for defensiveness.

Identifying the words was not an excessively difficult process, making them part of everybody's everyday business and embedded within the culture proved a much greater challenge.

Three main work groups were developed and charged with looking at the issues of:

- communication
- recruitment and selection
- training and monitoring

A number of initiatives flowed from these groups which included all new staff receiving training in the principles of core values during their induction; all existing staff attending a workshop which highlighted the principles of core values; all internal and external advertising contained a slimmed down core values statement; and new contracts identified core values as one of the main competencies. During their individual performance appraisals staff were asked to rate their core values, and an audit of core values for staff and service users was carried out. Following the core values audit the senior managers carried out a 360 degree appraisal on their ability to demonstrate the process of core values.

Over time the principles of core values have become part of the language of the organisation. They are often quoted when people feel that others are not demonstrating values which, on reflection, appears to be a safe way for people to say, 'I need to be listened to and understood'.

Large complex organisations take time for philosophy and culture to change. Within any service it is important to give the workforce the infrastructure and protocols to develop effective core values, however, little will change unless they are believed in and modelled by the leader of the organisation.

(Contributed by Ian Dyer,
Director Mental Health Service,
States of Jersey)

Authors comment:
Ian Dyer has been most supportive in the setting up of a strong voluntary sector and service user/survivor forum (see Leadership Example 1).

'perform the good interview', and the executive (female or male) who is committed to developing staff, will need to work on these issues of self-confidence and appropriate self-promotion. Further research is required regarding the culture and collusive nature of all-male and all-female teams. Commenting on

recent research, featured in the *Local Government Chronical* (*LGC*, 21 April 2005: 10–11), Annie Shepperd, who was brought into trouble-torn Walsall MBC as Chief Executive several years ago, expressed scepticism at the idea of ascribing different skills to men and women and argued that more research was needed. 'It is

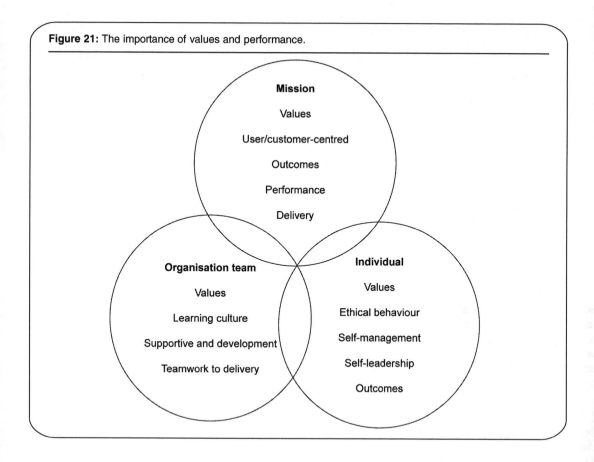

Figure 21: The importance of values and performance.

Mission

Values

User/customer-centred

Outcomes

Performance

Delivery

Organisation team

Values

Learning culture

Supportive and development

Teamwork to delivery

Individual

Values

Ethical behaviour

Self-management

Self-leadership

Outcomes

important not to label women and men as taking on certain roles. If we are going to keep the integrity of Local Government in the selection process, councils need to appoint the best person for the job.'

On the issue of culture, Linstead et al. (2004) quote Hofstede as pointing out that in some Asian cultures a more autocratic and 'Theory X' approach to motivation (see Table 5) is preferred by subordinates. The foremost thinkers in cultural approaches, indicate that the most dangerous time for a leader is when they think they have 'cracked the code'; it is usually then that cultural mistakes are made.

Rather than set up false dichotomies, it is much more constructive to create new approaches which incorporate and celebrate diversity (see Box 4). Rob Goffee and Gareth Jones (Goffee and Jones, 2000) say that their long-term investigations into leadership show that as well as leaders needing vision, authority, strategic direction, etc, they also share four unexpected qualities:

- They selectively show their weaknesses – revealing their humanity and approachability.
- They rely heavily on intuition to gauge the appropriate timing and course of their actions, as well as considering hard data.
- They manage employees with 'tough empathy' – getting alongside people to 'empathise passionately, and realistically' with the people who work for them.
- They reveal their differences – capitalising on what is unique about themselves.

We can see immediately that this links in very strongly with a positive approach to diversity and bringing on board the whole of humanity, not just small parts of it, and integrating values with performance (see Figure 21).

Moving forward

Neil Thompson in his work, *Promoting Equality* (second edn. 2003) considers discrimination at the personal, cultural and structural level, and shows that we need to work at all levels to move from oppression to creativity. While it is important that people take personal responsibility in matters of promoting diversity and equality, a personal construct is inadequate on its own. Culture, as we have seen in Chapter 6, has enormous influence in terms of 'the way we do things here'. If leaders do not get the culture of the internal organisation right, then oppression and discrimination will become commonplace. In the same way, leaders must be able to use their judgement about the cultures which appertain outside the organisation. While respect for different cultures in a community covered by a human service of any type is essential, respect does not mean not asking challenging questions. The tragedy of Victoria Climbie was partly due to cultural assumptions made by those involved in child protection in Harringay, and a failure of moral courage in challenging what were presented to them as cultural norms.

Above the cultural level comes the structural. Thompson (2003: 6–19) considers three major factors: social, issues relating to class, race, gender etc; political, the distribution of power, both formally and informally; and economic, the distribution of wealth and other material resources. As we have seen in Chapter 2 of this book, the influence of structural economic power percolates down to every level of society and has an enormous effect on the way we live. Leaders of frontline teams, for example, may not have a huge influence on structural issues but, as can be seen in Case Studies 1 and 2, even managers at a relatively junior level can look to challenge structural imbalance and injustice.

Some of the ways that we can undertake this in a leadership context are:

1. Blending the 'must do' with the 'want to do' together. There is now a considerable volume of human rights, and equal opportunities, legislation, and this needs to be aligned with clarity of values, and adherence to values. The 2003 Mori Poll on business (*The Observer*, 6 July 2003) demonstrates that even at a senior management level, companies' proclaimed values are not believed. As we saw from the Morris Report on the Metropolitan Police, there are tangible tensions between the stated policy and the actual practice.
2. On a personal level, our values and behaviours have to be authentic and congruent. The whole point about

institutional racism, for example, is based on fundamentally good people not putting good intentions into action. In a recent article in *The British Medical Journal* (19 June 2004) Dr Aneez Esmail, of Manchester University, opined that the NHS is institutionally racist because of nice people:

> Just because individuals are not racist, this does not mean that institutional racism cannot exist . . . I have rarely met doctors who are obviously bigoted, but I have met many who deny the problem but act in certain ways that result in certain groups of people being disadvantaged.

In the NHS, Sir Nigel Crisp, as Chief Executive, has taken on the job of chairing the Race Equality Action Group, and promoting action on the diversity strategy. The corollary to this is not only acting against discrimination as leaders, but also as self-leaders. As the motto in the Holocaust Museum in Washington states:

> Thou shalt not be a victim. Thou shalt not be a perpetrator. Above all, thou shalt not be a bystander.

Margaret Hefernan (see Hefernan, 2004) marks out the various roles that women are sometimes pushed into playing in corporate life. Hefernan emphasises both the duty on organisations, and on individuals facing discrimination themselves. She gives a number of tips to women who wish to succeed in the corporate world; amongst these are keeping a list of your achievements for the year; valuing your reputation with every phone call and meeting; making sure that you have a reserve of money, so that you can walk away from a job if it is doing you harm; and if your contributions are being ignored in meetings, team up with a colleague and back each other up. This last point would be true in a number of issues around discrimination. I recently talked with a black colleague who said that she was fed up with raising issues around minority ethnic groups in meetings, and feeling that she was increasingly losing her effectiveness on this. My advice was to pair up with another colleague, preferably not from an ethnic minority, who would make some of her points for her, and she could reciprocate; so that particular issues do not become stereotyped as 'belonging' to an individual from that group. Hefernan also makes the point that people usually have some choice, even limited, in how they behave; even just as Alistair Mant (1983) states that it is 'very much in the interests of men' to 'ensure that those women who are permitted to rise will provide us with a chilling example of all the most disagreeable male traits'. Hefernan alludes to how easy it is for a woman to seek power and fall into what she dubs the 'bitch' role, leaving her 'very isolated and defensive: you don't fit in with junior women or with senior men'. This role can then morph into 'the final archetype, the guy'. But, as Hefernan warns, over time, 'absorbing values which are not your own is corrosive' (see T2, *The Times*, 2 November 2004: 4–5). For people who are in complex roles, especially when new in post; or people from a minority group, outnumbered in a management team, the use of mentoring and learning sets is essential. Ryan and Haslam (2005) point to the isolation women can experience in senior positions, and this can also be true for leaders from black and minority ethnic communities, and those from a particular culture (e.g. social care) coming into a different culture (e.g. the NHS). The national learning sets for directors of social care, and for senior managers in mental health services, provides an opportunity for people to learn and develop in a safe environment and gain mutual support (see Sewell and Gilbert, 2006, forthcoming).

3. Organisational. Many organisations are now introducing human resource policies which promote diversity. Brent Social Services, for example, is moving to make the workplace more flexible, both for customers and staff. An accent on work/life balance should help the workforce bring the skills which they often leave at home into the workplace. As Hefernan again points out, 'Leadership requires ability to handle discontinuity, complexity, changes, empathy, context. Most people get most of that stuff from home, not work. The richer the life you have, the smarter the work you can do' (*The Times*, ibid.).

Tower Hamlets has received considerable positive attention for the way it is outreaching to the borough's large and growing Bangladeshi and Somali communities, through positive action schemes (see *LGC*, 16 July 2004) and working to bring these communities into the workforce with various educational and qualification schemes. This has helped Tower Hamlets Social Services become the second most diverse employer in the UK and secure Beacon Status for supporting social care workers. Noticeably, it provides pastoral care and guidance for trainees so that there is a way of working with cultural issues and expectations. Rachel Perkins, as an Executive Board Member of the St. George's and South London Mental Health Trust, and somebody who is up-front about her experiences of mental ill health, has promoted a major inclusion programme to bring people with experience of mental health issues into the workforce to increase the empathic impact of the staff group.

Some notable mentoring schemes have been introduced over the past few years, with Roy Taylor, when President of the ADSS, bringing in a mentoring scheme for black managers in partnership with the Improvement and Development Agency (I & DEA) and more recently, Sir Nigel Crisp has encouraged chief executives in the NHS to engage in a similar scheme, and has led the way on this himself.

4. One of the most encouraging approaches is through role models. People from minority groups who have succeeded, and have retained their authenticity, by leading through their uniqueness and diversity, rather than through adopting an alien approach, are enormously encouraging to those around them. We have seen in the leadership example of Jo Williams in Chapter 2, how this can work even in an originally male-dominated council. People like Professor Kamlesh Patel, who is at the time of writing Chair of the Mental Health Act Commission, National Strategic Director on BME issues for NIMHE, and a Professor at the University of Central Lancashire (besides other roles!) is very much a role model, and speaks of those who have encouraged him: 'The people I remember most fondly are those that gave me chances, encouraged me and were receptive to my sometimes fairly wacky ideas! I've always tried to return that favour by encouraging other people in their careers and supporting innovation' (quoted in *Care and Health*, 4–18 February 2004: 68).

One of the foremost advocates of a comprehensive, inclusive and congruent care system is Lord Victor Adebowale, Chief Executive of Turning Point (2004: 24–25). He combines self-deprecating humour with charisma and an evident passion for the services he champions. Engaging with such champions like Patel and Adebowale, while at the same time having the right values, policies and structures keeps diversity as a positive issue, with the accent on want to do, rather than simply need to do. After all, this is not simply a case of considering the needs of particular groups. It is much more a case of tapping, releasing and celebrating the creativity of **all** members of the staff team.

CHAPTER 11

Conclusion: 'It's Humanity – Stoopid!'

Just get the humanity right!
> (Dr Joanna Bennett, speaking about work with people from minority groups
> at the inquiry into her brother's death in care)

There's no point in having a good share price if you have no staff to run your business!
> (Business Commentator, BBC1 News, 25 August 2004)

This [Charity Award] is actually an award for my Team at Turning Point; leadership is about what happens when you're not there.
> (Lord Victor Adebowale, Chief Executive, Turning Point)

Integrity without knowledge is weak and useless, and knowledge without integrity is dangerous and dreadful.
> (Dr Samuel Johnson)

Without your wounds where would you be? In love's service, only the wounded soldiers can serve.
> (Thornton Wilder, novelist)

One may observe, in one's travels in distant countries, the feelings of recognition and affiliation that link every human being to every other human being.
> (Aristotle, *Nichomachean Ethics*)

I'm sorry if you can't dream.
> (Lance Armstrong, on winning his 7th Tour de France, and his battle with cancer, July, 2005)

Styles of leadership

A great deal of leadership is listening to people's stories and weaving these into a larger narrative tapestry. In the year of writing this book there have been major conflicts in Israel, Palestine and Iraq; and the tsunami and its devastation in the Indian Ocean countries. Out of these macro-disasters come the stories of individual and group heroism, and in the case of the tsunami, the evidence, through aid pledged, that individuals, groups and communities of all faiths and none, feel a sense of common human compassion with those victims across the world.

Leadership is about communication at times of crisis, and when Annetta Flanagan, a Northern Irish, United Nations Election Official in Afghanistan, was taken hostage by gunmen, she disarmed her kidnappers during her and her companions' 26-day ordeal, by calmly talking to her captors about herself, asking questions about themselves, and keeping up a non-verbal communication (*The Times*, 6 December 2004: 23).

In the case studies and leadership examples it is clear that leaders need to take tough decisions, and give a sense of direction, often at times of major change and confusion, but unless they can take people with them, they are unlikely to surmount the initial crisis, still less build for the future (see Collins and Porras, 2000). In the case of Antony Sheehan at NIMHE (Leadership Example 5, Chapter 5) and Connexions (Case Study 7, Chapter 7) new organisations had to be forged out of a concept, or from existing groups brought together, not always willingly; in the case of Staffordshire (Case Study 6, Chapter 6) a long-standing organisation had to be taken through a renewing cultural transformation, while at the same time major legislation had to be implemented. In the case of CAFCASS (see Case Study 9, Chapter 8) a lack of leadership from the top and a gap in understanding between those chosen to lead, and those delivering the service, led to a dangerously reduced level of service for children and the entire Board being asked to stand down, with new leadership drafted in.

At a time of such endemic change processes, when organisations are likely to be infinitely more complex, both in aims, structure, clientele, workforce and partnerships, than they were 20 years ago, good intentions without effectiveness will not be enough; and neither will short-termist macho approaches. When the new Leadership College for Local Government was set up in 2004, commentator David Walker (*The Guardian*, 19 May 2004) reminded us that there is: 'a danger that this rhetoric about leadership, unanchored to values, condones the approach of another 20th century practitioner of the "what works" school. Vote for me, Mussolini said, and I will make the trains run on time.' In Chapter 9 we considered the extreme pathology of Nazi Germany. The mass appeal of Adolf Hitler, failed soldier and failed painter, still seems extraordinary, unless, like the German journalist Konrad Heiden, who studied Hitler closely, one sees him as 'a pure fragment of the modern mass soul, unclouded by any personal qualities' (quoted in Burleigh, 2001: 100). Hitler reminded Heiden of a windless flag hanging slackly on a pole, a human 'nullity' waiting once more for the next occasion to seem a somebody.

Goleman et al. (2002) in their consideration of emotional intelligence in leadership, and the resonant and dissonant styles, admit that, partly because of the pressure to get short-term results, the old command and control style still operates in a number of places, 'yet even in today's more modernised military organisations, the commanding style is balanced by other styles in the interests of building commitment, *esprit de corps* and teamwork', Goleman et al. (2002: 97) (and see Hutton, 2004).

In fact, a study of history shows considerable emotional intelligence displayed by the most successful military commanders, even in the tough world of generalship under the Roman Empire. Adrian Goldsworthy (2004) explains that, during the winter break from campaigning, Germanicus 'paid particular attention to the health and morale of his men, **personally** touring the hospitals in the winter quarters, talking to the men as **individuals** and **praising** their feats of courage' (290, my emphases). How many managers, male or female, in our public services, demonstrate any concern for staff who are off sick, 30 per cent of whom will be off with stress-related illness (*HSJ*, 23 June 2005) or are they simply left to occupational health services. Where is that personal and visible leadership that many of the ancients had and we appear to have lost? At a financial cost to the NHS of more than £2 billion per year, and at an immeasurably high personal, service and moral cost, it is not surprising that the Chief Executive of the

Healthcare Commission, Anna Walker, states: 'that over a third of staff suffer from stress is a concern' (*HSJ*, 24 March 2005).

The BBC's *Panorama* programme (on 20th July, 2005) showed very frail, elderly patients in a general hospital being offered horrifically sub-standard, degrading and abusive care in a regime which would have been shocking if seen in a neglected, and isolated part of the developing world, let alone in the prosperous city of Brighton! The ward staff, in their turn, appeared isolated from the wider organisation, and their exile and neglect appeared to have been mirrored in the lack of care for their patients. Had I come across this situation in a residential or nursing home, while responsible for the inspection services as a director of social services, I would have had it closed down forthwith! When interviewed, the hospital CEO intoned the usual listless litany: complaints procedures, internal review, comprehensive action plan, apology. At no time was there a hint of passion for good care, let alone anger that sub-standard care had resulted in people at the end of their lives suffering pain and discomfort, and even dying alone and lonely – abandoned. At no time did you get as much as a hint that 'true leadership' might have entailed actually going out of a penthouse office, down a few stairs, seeing for oneself what was going on, getting rid of any abusive staff and supporting those who had the ability to deliver good care with guidance and support.

Our 'performance culture' appears to have led to some raising of standards in some sectors, but a dangerous reliance on the tick-box mentality, in a mirage of measurement . We have sacrificed passion for performance monitoring, and failed to use persona to boost performance. We have truly become the bland leading the bland!

If we want long-term health for organisations then we cannot afford 'hollow' men and women, people who do not have the foundation of values, but who blow like straw in the winds of ambition. I was once in the company of a highly ambitious senior manager, when he received news that a performance indicator on the safeguarding of children, had reached unacceptably low levels on his watch. Watching him pace around the room, I could see the thought coming off him: 'Whom can I scapegoat for this?', but the hard fact he had to face was that he could not dodge his own accountability! It had happened on his watch (see quote from Guiliani, p2).

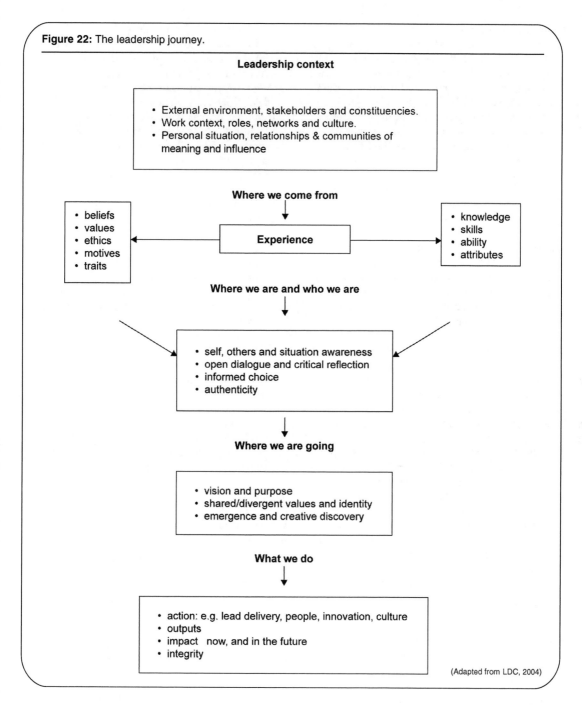

Figure 22: The leadership journey.

(Adapted from LDC, 2004)

There is much talk now about the concept of 'the wounded healer' (see, for example, Nouwen, 1994) but perhaps we also should examine the concept of 'the wounded leader' because, as Goffee and Jones (2000) and Goleman et al. (2002) and others point out, we need to know where we come from, who we are and where we are going to. Only those who

truly know themselves will truly know others. (see Figure 22).

Ethical leadership

There are some hard answers to the question, why have ethical leadership with an accent on humanity? and these are:

- Because it is right. As we move from a modern to a post-modern world (see Chapter 2) we do not feel that we have the comfort of some of the meta-narratives, the grand stories of religion and science: a better life to come in whatever world, that we once had (see Holloway, 2004). Because 'Western society now lacks a strong sense of agreement on how to understand and order the life of human communities' (121) or because we often feel that society is in a state of post-virtue (see MacIntyre, 2003) this does not absolve us from attempting to order society and social relations in a way that is not simply power to the powerful and never mind the rest. We have, therefore, to look to our humanity, and to some of the human examples we have before us. At the end of his autobiography, Nelson Mandela speaks of his television debate pre-election with outgoing President de Klerk, when Mandela reached over to take de Klerk's hand and said, 'You are one of those I rely upon. We are going to face the problem of this country *together*' (Mandela, 1994: 609, my emphasis).
- Because it works – especially in a multi-cultural and multi-faceted society. Sara Melendez (1996: 299), speaking as an entrepreneur from the Hispanic community in the United States, and writing for the Drucker Foundation, states: 'More than ever, they (leaders) will need to be able to live with ambiguity and constant change'. With a diverse customer-base, and an equally diverse workforce, the dissonant, command and control styles, or political manipulation (see Goleman et al., 2002) can no longer be considered appropriate or effective.
- Because otherwise there will not be anyone left on board! The most recent management agenda report by the Roffey Park Institute, charting work place challenges for individuals and organisations in both the private and public sectors, reveals a very worrying picture (Holbeche and McCartney, 2005). 92 per cent of managers experienced organisational change over the last 12 months. Most said that their organisation was good at initiating change but not in managing it or learning from it! The long hours culture and stress were major issues; but almost as important was a fall in the level of trust in senior managers and problems over managing diversity and developing individuals. Managers at all levels report a

lessening in commitment to the organisation, and a willingness to strike out on their own. 2004 has seen developing nations increasingly critical of the poaching of doctors and nurses. A recent investigation of hospitals in Mali (BBC News, 2004) showed a situation where qualified nurses were leeching away to the UK and USA, leaving wards understaffed or even unstaffed. This new kind of imperialism partly comes about because the UK is so careless of its own human capital, that we now strip developing nations of their human resources (See also 'Foreign Fields', *Care and Health*, 10–16 August 2004).

Unless we learn to bring into the workforce those within our own communities, as Tower Hamlets has with its Bangladeshi and Somali communities (see *Community Care*, 18–24 November 2004: 32–33) support, develop and retain those we do have within services; and draw back into services those who have left on a temporary basis, then we simply will not have enough people to steer the ship!
- Because new models require new leaders. As we have seen from Case Study 7 of Connexions (Chapter 7) the new service configurations require leaders to be very strong on vision, on directions, and on taking people with them. The effects of globalisation give clear messages concerning a style which connects rather than separates.

When Antony Sheehan set up NIMHE, he appointed Professor Bill Fulford to lead on values-based practice. This model is also reinforced from research from the business schools, with Dr. Linda Holbeche, asserting that values 'will become central to organisations achieving sustainable high performance'. With workers in both the public and private sector becoming disenchanted with the lack of values or 'false' values in their employing organisations and 'the damaging effects of company politics, lack of genuine support for learning and innovation, a loss of meaning and a sense of being under-valued as individuals, poor management practice and lack of leadership' (*Research at Roffey Park*, Issue 15, July 2005: 2) many workers are leaving organisations in droves. Holbeche argues that being a values-based organisation will become a key definition of a high performance organisation and that 'organisations that fail to embrace a values-based approach run two key risks: loss of talent and loss of reputation' (see also Holbeche,

2005). Julia Cleverdon, CEO of Business in the Community, echoes this sentiment: 'Companies now know that to attract and retain employees they must share the same values' (*The Times*, 'Public Agenda': 5).

There is a cancer of complacency in much of the public sector, including high profile and well-regarded voluntary organisations, where: 'we are a values-based organisation' can be used as an empty mantra which hides oppressive practice. True leadership means that the values are *espoused and lived out* at all levels; and leaders need to be challenging themselves and challenging others around them on a constant basis.

Discussions around the new vision for Adult Social Care Services in the Autumn of 2004, were very much around issues of shared and dispersed leadership – with the real emphasis on leadership by service users and carers (see Leadership Example No. 6, Chapter 9). Work on citizenship models of assessment and service delivery, rather than 'the professional gift model' (see Duffy, 2004) person-centred planning, through developing person-centred teams (see Sanderson, 2003) and building capacity by augmenting rather than substituting, and supporting rather than direct caring (see Dowson and Bates, 2004) will necessitate a leadership style which shares and distributes leadership, rather than micro-manages.

'Ask any patient', writes Gill Morgan (*The Times*, 2004) Chief Executive of the NHS Confederation, 'about their contact with the NHS, good or bad, and you will find one thing in common: it is not their medical treatment that really shapes their experience, but the way they were treated by individual members of staff – from receptionists and porters to nurses and GPs'.

What is also clear is that there are strong 'connections between how staff are managed, how they feel about their work and the outcomes for patients', as says Jocelyn Cornwell (*Society Guardian*, 2004: 9) former Chief Executive of the Commission for Health Improvement, an opinion echoed by Sir Ian Kennedy, the incoming Chair of the Health Inspectorate, who expressed concerns about professionals feeling that 'they have no control', and that 'you cannot serve the interest of patients without also taking proper account of the interest of those who look after them' (Society Guardian, 21 July 2004). Unfortunately,

according to Professor Beverly Alimo-Metcalfe and John Alban-Meltcalfe (*Health Service Journal*, 26 June 2003) senior managers often appear to rely on their status, and while backing leadership programmes for more junior members of staff, are not open to development themselves. The NHS Leadership in particular scores badly on: enabling and empowering staff; being accessible, and not overly status-conscious; and being able to resolve a wide range of complex problems using listening, talking and creativity. The same researchers make the point, which echoes that of Roffey Park's research into global leadership (Sinclair and Agyeman, 2004), that the role of leadership in the public sector has a 'staggering complexity', and that while 'the transactional competencies of management' are crucial, they 'are simply not sufficient on their own' (Alimo-Metcalfe and Alban-Metcalfe, 2000).

In a performance-driven public sector, one of the factors in a successful approach towards empowerment and devolved responsibility to the front line, is clarity and ownership of the relevant performance indicators. Russell Mannion et al., in their study of *Cultures for Performance in Health Care* (Mannion et al., 2005) found that, especially with the mergers of Trusts and new Partnerships, many high-performing organisations in the NHS were characterised by strong drivers from the top, and the establishment of sound systems for monitoring, evaluating and improving performance. Low-performing Trusts in the acute sector were notable for a lack of strategic direction, and poor systems. Those organisations which were performing well, however, had identified that a continuation of top down approaches and transactional methods, was about to both lose its effect, and indeed become counter-productive. They were now moving towards a greater emphasis on transformational approaches. In the social care sector, the London Borough of Tower Hamlets has been featured recently, not only because of its imaginative recruitment processes, but because it has gained a third star, after a history of under-performance, political tensions affecting service delivery, and a tendency to opt for structures which impeded rather than aided core business. In recent years, strong backing from elected members, which has seen a priority given to social services spending, even when the central government settlement was unfavourable, and a stable management team has enabled the director to work with staff: 'Getting people to focus on the right things', (Leason, 2004). It is perhaps not surprising that the director is a regular visitor to front-line teams: 'Staff do not always feel appreciated, especially by directors, so it is good to get out there and tell them'. Director, Ian Wilson (*Local Government Chronicle*, 2004: 26) mentions receiving an e-mail that referred to a 'jester' of appreciation and muses that 'perhaps that is what I should be described as for the purpose of these visits'!

Towards the future

It is now worth bringing ourselves back to where we began. Where are we coming from? Who do we feel we are? What is the situation we face? Who are the people we have the responsibility of leading? Who are the people we look to from our present or our past, whom we see as leaders, who might help us in our current role?

Leadership is not simply about conventional leadership roles. It can be about hidden, unsung heroes, like those, many of whom are just coming to light, who helped Jews escape the Holocaust (see Gilbert, M., 2002); it might be an academic and service user champion, like Peter Beresford (*Society Guardian*, 2005: 6–7) or social researchers, such as Maureen Oswin (Philpot, 2001) or anyone who has inspired you. For as George Eliot reminds us in *Middlemarch*:

> *But the effect of her being on those around her was incalculably diffusive, for the growing good of the world is partly dependent on unhistoric acts, and that things are not so ill with you and me as they might have been is half owing to the number who lived faithfully a hidden life and rest in unvisited tombs.*
>
> (811)

For me, it is as much about my first team manager in Social Services, Jean Carruthers, who was always pushing me that little bit more; Mick Hunt, my first sergeant in the Army, who managed us junior officers as we tried to lead (!) visionary academics like Maurice Keen and Patrick Wormald; front line managers and staff who had to carry forward service changes against difficult financial backdrops; as much as generals and senior managers I worked for.

At the end of the day, leadership is, as Sir John Harvey-Jones describes it, 'A priceless gift which you have to earn from the people who

work with you' (op. cit.) and we have to ask ourselves the ultimate face-in-the-mirror question: Why would anybody wish to be led by us? (see Exercise 8).

Exercise 8: So, Ask Yourself!

So why?!

1. It is worth asking yourself in any leadership role you undertake: 'Why would people wish to be led by you?' What is it that you have to offer this leadership challenge and the people who are looking to you for leadership?

2. Why do you wish to be led by the person who is leading you? Do they share your values? Do you trust them to lead you in the right direction, with the right values, and to support you when the going gets tough?

At the same time we are also entitled to ask whether the people we are working for are worth our loyalty and hard work. As Alford and Naughton pose the question 'What kind of person should I as a manager or employee strive to become?'

The second question is at the level of organisational integrity.

> *What kind of organisational community should I as a manager or employee strive to build and maintain?*
>
> (Alford and Naughton, 2001: 8)

If the person or organisation we are working for is not in tune with who we believe we are, then it is better to walk away and work for people we can trust, or carve out a career which relies on making partnerships with people with similar values. Leaving local government after 26 years was scary; but the great freedom and the joy is that now I am very choosy about who I work for.

We need to take that priceless gift, which is a lantern raised for light and hope, and carry it into the onrushing winds and storms of change, holding it aloft as we walk together with those whose complementary skills we recognise, value and celebrate. We have to show the way, though there is no shame in sometimes asking for directions or looking at the compass. We do not have to be in the lead the whole time: like a flight of geese, we may be at the point of the V for a while, and then support from the wings; but above all, we have to do what only we can do: to be ourselves with the values, attributes and skills that we have, and lead into the dark with respect for the past and hope for the future.

We have to serve **and** lead , and serve **to** lead. May you go well on the journey.

PART FOUR

Resources

Organisations

Centre for Health and Spirituality Staffordshire University, Brindley Building, Leek Road, Stoke on Trent, ST4 2DF. b.r.moss@staffs.ac.uk

Centre for Spirituality Worth Abbey, Paddockhurst Road, Turner's Hill, West Sussex, RH10 4SB. Tel: 01342 710318 spirituality@worth.net www.worthabbey.net
A centre which runs a number of courses which look at spirituality in the workplace.

Chartered Institute of Personnel and Development CIPD House, Camp Road, Wimbledon, London, SW19 4UX. Tel: 020 8971 9000 Fax: 020 8263 3333

Institute of Management Cottingham Road, Corby, Northamptonshire, NN17 1TT. Tel: 01536 207400 Fax: 01536: 201651 www.inst-mgt.org.uk
An organisation devoted to the 'art and science of management'.

Local Government Leadership Centre Local Government House, Smith Square, London, SW1P 3HZ.
Tel: 020 7664 3000 Fax: 020 7664 3030 info@lga.gov.uk www.lga.gov.uk

NHS Leadership Centre Richmond House, 79 Whitehall, London, SW1A 2NS. Tel. 0845 607 4646 www.dh.gov.uk

National College for School Leadership (NCSL) Triumph Road, Nottingham, NG8 1DH. Tel: 0870 001 1155 www.ncsl.org.uk

National Institute for Mental Health in England (NIMHE) Blenheim House, W1, Duncombe Street, Leeds, LS1 4PL. Tel: 01132543813 www.nimhe.org.uk
(NIMHE is now part of the Care Services Improvement Partnership (CSIP), which also includes a number of other Government initiatives aimed at developing services, e.g. the Valuing People Programme.)

Social Care Institute for Excellence (SCIE) First Floor, Goldings House, 2 Hayes Lane, London, SE1 2HB. Tel: 020 7089 6840 www.scie.org.uk
SCIE is charged with developing the knowledge base in the social care sector. It commences a leadership programme in 2005.

Work Foundation (formerly The Industrial Society) Peter Runge House, 3 Carlton House Terrace, London, SW1Y 5DS. Tel: 0870 400 1000 Fax: 0870 400 1099 customercentre@indsoc.co.uk Also offices in Belfast, Birmingham and Glasgow.
A pioneering organisation which concerns itself with workbase issues, including professional development and leadership.

Internet resources

The following Internet sites contain extensive information relating to supervision, leadership and related matters:

The Chartered Institute of Personnel and Development www.cipd.co.uk
The website of the foremost professional organisation relating to human resource development. A very useful starting point for information about a wide range of issues relating to human resources.

The Institute of Training and Occupational Learning www.itol.co.uk
A relatively new professional organisation geared towards promoting high standards in occupational education and training.

National Nursing Leadership Project www.nursingleadership.co.uk
An invaluable site for anyone interested in leadership in nursing and health care.

NB These sites are correct at the time of publication, but may be liable to change over time.

Recommended reading

The following texts are helpful in exploring specific areas of leadership.

A general overview of management theory

Gilbert, P. and Thompson, N. (2002) *Supervision and Leadership Skills: A Training Resource*, Wrexham: Learning Curve Publishing.

Handy, C. (1985) *Understanding Organisations*, Harmondsworth: Penguin.

Lawrence, P. and Elliott, K. (1985) *Introducing Management*, London: Penguin Business.

Scragg, T. (2001) *Managing at the Front Line: A Handbook for Managers in Social Care Agencies*, Brighton: Pavilion.

Texts relating to leadership as a specific issue

Adair, J. (2002) *Inspiring Leadership*, London: Thorogood.

Blanchard, K., Zigarmi, P. and Zigarmi, D. (1986) *Leadership and the One Minute Manager*, London: William Collins.

Collins, J. (2001) *Good to Great*, London: Random House.

Kotter, J.P. (1996) *Leading Change*, Boston: Harvard Business School Press.

Storey, J. (Ed.) (2004) *Leadership in Organisations: Current Issues and Key Trends*, London: Routledge.

Organisational culture

Hampden-Turner, C. (1990) *Corporate Culture*, London: Hutchinson.

Mannion, R., Davies, H. and Marshall, M. (2005) *Cultures for Performance in Health Care*, Berkshire: Open University Press.

Newman, J. (1996) *Shaping Organisational Cultures in Local Government*, London: Pitman.

Schein, E. (2004) *Organizational Culture and Leadership*, 3rd edn, San Francisco: Jossey-Bass.

Smith, P. and Peterson, M. (1988) *Leadership, Organisations and Culture*, London: Sage.

Changing organisations

Attwood, M., Pedler, M., Pritchard, S. and Wilkinson, D. (2003) *Leading Change: A Guide to Whole Systems Working*, Bristol: The Policy Press.

Martin, V. (2003) *Leading Change in Health and Social Care*, London: Routledge.

Proehl, R.A. (2001) *Organisational Change in the Human Services*, California: Sage.

The interaction between management and leadership

Goleman, D., Boyatzis, R. and McKee, A. (2002) *The New Leaders: Transforming the Art of Leadership into the Science of Results*, London: Little Brown.

Kotter, J.P. (1990) *A Force for Change: How Leadership Differs from Management*, New York: The Free Press.

Peters, T. and Austin, N. (1985) *A Passion for Excellence: The Leadership Difference*, London: William Collins.

Strategic management

Adair, J. (2003) *Effective Strategic Leadership*, London: Pan.

Johnson, G. and Scholes, K. (1989) *Exploring Corporate Strategy: Text and Cases*, London: Prentice-Hall.

Lynch, R. (2000) *Corporate Strategy*, 2nd edn, Harlow: Pearson Education.

Supervision

Betts, P.W. (1993) *Supervisory Management*, London: Pitman.

Morrison, T. (2001) *Supervision in Social Care*, 2nd edn, Brighton: Pavilion.

Thompson, N. (2002) *People Skills*, 2nd edn, Basingstoke: Palgrave.

Staff care

Thompson, N. (1999) *Stress Matters: A Personal Guide*, Birmingham: Peppar.

Thompson, N., Murphy, N. and Stradling, S. (1996) *Meeting the Stress Challenge*, Lyme Regis: Russell House Publishing.

Managing yourself and self-managed learning

Cunningham, I., Bennett, B. and Dawes, G. (Eds.) (2000) *Self Managed Learning in Action*, Aldershot: Gower.

Parikh, J. (1991) *Managing Yourself: Management by Detached Involvement*, Oxford: Blackwell.

Pedlar, M., and Boydell, P. (1999) *Managing Yourself*, London: Lemos and Crane.

Some interesting ways of looking at leadership

Birch, P. and Clegg, B. (1996) *Imagination Engineering: The Toolkit for Business Creativity*, London, Pitman.

Corrigan, P. (1999) *Shakespeare on Management*, London: Kogan Page.

Cranwell-Ward, J., Bacon, A. and Mackie, R. (2002) *Inspiring Leadership: Staying Afloat in Turbulent Times*, London: Thomson.

Gardner, H. (1996) *Leading Minds: An Anatomy of Leadership*, London: HarperCollins.

Keegan, J. (1987) *The Mask of Command*, London: Jonathan Cape.

Wheatley, M. (1999) *Leadership and the New Science*, San Francisco, Berrett-Koehler.

An overview of project management

James, P. (2004) *Get it Right First Time: A Self Help and Training Guide to Project Management*. Lyme Regis: Russell House Publishing.

Turner, R. (1993) *The Handbook of Project-based Management*, Maidenhead: McGraw-Hill.

References

Adair, J. (1983) *Effective Leadership*, Aldershot: Gower.

Adair, J. (2002) *Inspiring Leadership*, London: Thorogood.

Adair, J. (2003) *Effective Strategic Leadership*, London: Pan Macmillan.

Adair, J. (2005) *How to Grow Leaders: the Seven Key Principles of Effective Leadership Development*, London: Kogan Page.

Adair, J. and Nelson, J. (Eds) (2004) *Creative Church Leadership*, Norwich: Canterbury Press.

Adams, S. (1997) *The Dilbert Principle*, London: Macmillan.

Adebowale, Lord V. (2004) Marginal Points, *Health Service Journal*, 3 Jun.

ADSS/NIMHE (2003) (Gilbert, P. and Joannides, D.) *Positive Approaches to the Integration of Health and Social Care in Mental Health Services*, ADSS/NIMHE.

Alford, H. and Naughton, M. (2001) *Managing as if Truth Mattered*, Indiana: University of Notre Dame Press.

Alimo-Metcalfe (2003) *website*, Leeds University.

Alimo-Metcalfe, B. and Alban-Metcalfe, J. (2000) Heaven Can Wait, *Health Service Journal*, 12 Oct.

Alimo-Metcalfe, B. and Alban-Metcalfe, J. (2004) Leadership in Public Sector Organisations, in Storey, J. (Ed.) *Leadership in Organisations: Current Issues and Key Trends*, London: Routledge.

Anderson, D. (1991) in Keegan, J. (Ed.) *'Slim'*, *Churchill's Generals*, London: Abacus.

Argyris, C. (1953) *The Personnel Journal*. 32: 2.

Audit Commission (2003) *Managing People*, London: Audit Commission.

Austin, D.M. (2002) *Human Services Management*, New York: Columbia Services Press.

Bamford, T. (2001) *Commissioning and Purchasing*, London: Routledge.

Bass, B. and Avolio, B. (1994) *Improving Organisational Effectiveness Through Transformational Leadership*, London: Sage.

Bauman, Z. (2000) *Liquid Modernity*, Cambridge: Polity Press.

Bauman, Z. (2004) *Identity*. Cambridge: Polity Press.

Belbin, R.M. (1981) *Management Teams*, Oxford: Heinemann.

Belbin, R.M. (1993) *Team Roles at Work*, London: Butterworth Heinemann.

Benedict of Nursia (circa. 540 AD) Translation Fry, T. (Ed.) (1982) *The Rule of St. Benedict*, Minnesota: The Liturgical Press.

Bennett, D. (2000) Strategic Learning, in Cunningham, I., Bennett, D. and Dawes, G. *Self-Managed Learning in Action*. Aldershot: Gower.

Beresford, P. (2005) Out in the Lead, *Society Guardian*, 5 Jan.

Berry, L. (2004) Stand Up and Be Counted, *Care and Health*, 6-12 Jul.

Blanchard, K. and Johnson, S. (1983) *The One Minute Manager*, London: HarperCollins.

Blanchard, K. et al. (1986) *Leadership and the One Minute Manager*, London: HarperCollins.

Blofeld, Sir John (2003) *Independent Inquiry into the Death of David Bennett*, Cambridge: Norfolk, Suffolk and Cambridgeshire SHA.

Bose, P. (2003) *Alexander the Great's Art of Strategy*, London: Profile Books.

Briggs-Myers, I. (1992) *Gifts Differing*, California: Consulting Psychologists Press.

Brindle, D. (2004) It's time to look at the big picture, *The Guardian*, 14 Jul.

Bristol Business School (2003) Bristol Report, quoted in *Local Government Chronicle*, 16 May.

Brooke, C. (1971) *The Saxon and Norman Kings*, London: Fontana.

Bryman, A. (1996) Leadership in Organisations, in Clegg, S.R., Harvey, C. and Nord, W.R. (Eds) *Handbook of Organisational Studies*, London: Sage.

Burleigh, M. (2001) *The Third Reich: A New History*, London: Pan Macmillan.

Burns, J. MacGregor and Dunn, S. (2001) *The Three Roosevelts: The Leaders Who Transformed America*, New York: Atlantic Monthly Press.

Butler, C. (Ed.) (1999) *Basil Hume: By His Friends*, London: HarperCollins.

Cabinet Office (2001) *Choosing the Right Fabric: A Framework for Performance Information*, London: HMSO.

Cabinet Office, Performance and Innovation Unit (2001) *Strengthening Leadership in the Public Sector*, London: HMSO.

Cartledge, P. (2004) Alexander the Great, Hunting for a New Past?, *History Today*, 54: 7, Jul.

Caulkin, S. (2005) Morris's Labour of Love, *The Observer*, 3rd July.

Cayton, H. (2004) A Doctor's Dilemma, *Health Service Journal*, 9 Dec.

Chang, J. and Halliday, J. (2005) *Mao: The Unknown Story*, London: Jonathan Cape.

Chartered Institute of Personnel Development (2003) *Reorganising for Success*, London: CIPD.

Chartered Management Institute and DTI (2004) *Inspired Leadership: An Insight into People who Inspire Exceptional Performance*, London: CMI.

Clutterbuck, D. and Crainer, S. (1990) *Makers of Management*, London: Macmillan.

Collins, J. (2001) *Good to Great*, London: Random House.

Collins, J. and Porras, G. (2000) *Built to Last*, 3rd edn, London: Random House.

Corrigan, P. (1999) *Shakespeare on Management: Leadership Lessons for Today's Managers*, London: Kogan Page.

Covey, S. (1992) *Principle-centred Leadership*, London: Simon and Schuster.

Cox, J., Campbell, A. and Fulford, K.W.M. (2005/6, forthcoming), *Medicine for the Person: Faith, Values and Science in Healthcare Provision*, London: Jessica Kingsley.

Cranwell-Ward, J. Bacon, A. and Mackie, R. (2002), *Inspiring Leadership: Staying Afloat in Turbulent Times*, London: Thomson.

Cunningham, I. (1999) *The Wisdom of Strategic Learning: The Self-managed Learning Solution*, 2nd edn, Maidenhead: McGraw-Hill.

Cunningham, I., Bennett, D. and Dawes, G. (2000) *Self-Managed Learning in Action*, Aldershot: Gower.

Dalai Lama, The (2001) *The Art of Living*, London: Thorsons.

Darley, G. (1990) *Octavia Hill: A Life*, London: Constable.

Davidson, M. (1997) *The Black and Ethnic Minority Woman Manager: Cracking the Concrete Ceiling*, London: Paul Chapman Publishing.

Davis, A. (2004) Integration: What's in it for Service Users?, *Integration of Health and Social Care*, SPN Study Day Paper, 20 Apr.

Deal, T. and Kennedy, A. (1988) *Corporate Cultures*, Reading, MA: Addison-Wesley.

De Botton, A. (2004) *Status Anxiety*, London: Hamish Hamilton.

De Mello, A. (1988) *Walking on Water*, Dublin: Columba Press.

De Toqueville, A. (1864) *Democracy in America*, Paris.

Dibdin, M. (2003) *Medusa*, London: Faber & Faber.

Dickens, P. and Gilbert P. (1979) *The State and the Housing Question*, Sussex: University of Sussex Monograph.

DoH (2000) *The NHS Plan: A Plan for Investment, a Plan for Reform*, London: DoH.

DoH (2005) *Delivering Race Equality in Mental Health Care: An Action Plan for Reform Inside and Outside Services and the Government's Response to the Independent Inquiry into the Death of David Bennett*, London: DoH.

Dowson, S. and Bates, P. (2004) *Building Capacity: The Role of Specialist Services*, Manchester: National Development Team.

Duffy, S. (2004) In Control, *Journal of Integrated Care*, 12: 6, Dec.

Drucker, P. (1967) *Managing for Results*, London: Heinemann.

Edwards, R. and Townsend, H. (1965) *Business Enterprise: Its Growth and Organisation*, London: Macmillan-Palgrave.

Ejo, Y. (2004) Managing Practice in Black and Minority Ethnic Organisations, in Statham, D. (Ed.) *Managing Front Line Practice in Social Work*, London: Jessica Kingsley.

Eliot, G. (1872, this edn 1964) *Middlemarch*, Chicago: Signet Classics.

Equal Opportunities Commission (2004) *Who Runs Britain?* London: EOC.

Evans, R.J. (2003) *The Coming of the Third Reich*, London: Allen Lane.

Fairclough, A. (1990) *Martin Luther King Junior*, Athens, Georgia: University of Georgia Press.

Ferns, P. (2005) Finding a Way Forward: A Black Perspective on Social Approaches to Mental Health, in Tew, J. (Ed.) *Social Perspectives in Mental Health*, London: Jessica Kingsley.

Fiedler, F.E. (1967) *A Theory of Leadership Effectiveness*. New York: McGraw-Hill.

Field, J. and Peck, E. (2003) Mergers and Acquisitions in the Private Sector: What are the lessons for Health and Social Services? *Social Policy and Administration*, 37: 7, Dec.

Flamholtz, E. and Randle, Y. (1989) *The Inner Game of Management*, London: Hutchinson.

Foundation for Church Leadership (2005) *Focus on Leadership*, FCL.

Fowler, A. (1988) *Human Resource Management in Local Government*, London: Longman.

Frankl, V.E. (1959 – first published 1946) *Man's Search for Meaning*, Hodder and Stouton.

Fraser, D. (1994) *Knight's Cross: A Life of Field Marshall Erwin Rommel*, London: HarperCollins.

Fraser, Macdonald G. (1992) *Quartered Safe Out Here*, London: HarperCollins.

Fromm, E. (1976) *To Have or To Be?* London: Abacus.

Fulford, K.W.M. and Woodbridge, K. (2004) Right, Wrong and Respect, *Mental Health Today*, Sep.

Furedi, F. (2004) *Therapy Culture*, London: Routledge.

Gardner, H. (1997) *Leading Minds: An Anatomy of Leadership*, London: HarperCollins.

Gilbert, M. (1991) *Churchill: A Life*, London: Heinemann.

Gilbert, M. (2002) *The Righteous: The Unsung Heroes of the Holocaust*, London: Doubleday.

Gilbert, P. (1983) New Services, New Strategies, *Community Care*, 31 Mar.

Gilbert, P. (1985) *Mental Handicap: A Practical Guide for Social Workers*, Sutton: Reed Business.

Gilbert, P. (2003a) *Integrity and Integration*, presentational material for the NIMHE/SCIE Fellowship.

Gilbert, P. (2003b) *The Value of Everything: Social Work and its Importance in the Field of Mental Health*, Lyme Regis: Russell House Publishing.

Gilbert, P. (2004a) Integrity and Integration: Producing Better Outcomes for Service Users and Carers, *SPN Study Day Paper: The Integration of Health and Social Care*, 20 Apr, London: SPN.

Gilbert, P. (2004b) Every Day is D-Day, *Care and Health*, Jun 29 to Jul 5.

Gilbert, P. (2004c) It's Humanity, Stoopid!, Inaugural Professorial Lecture, *Staffordshire University*, 29 Sep.

Gilbert, P. (2005a) *The Language of the Heart*, Conference Presentation to Mental Health communities in Jersey, March.

Gilbert, P. (2005b) Keep up Your Spirits! *Openmind*, Autumn.

Gilbert, P. and Jolly, L. (2004) *Serving to Lead: St. Benedict and Servant Leadership*, Worth Abbey Centre for Spirituality pamphlet, Sussex: Worth Abbey, Jul.

Gilbert, P. and Spooner, B. (1982) Strength in Unity, *Community Care*, 28 Oct.

Gilbert, P. and Scragg, T. (1992) *Managing to Care*, Sutton: Reed Business Publishing.

Gilbert, P. and Farrier-Ray, S. (1995) Stressed Out, *Community Care*, 19-25 Jan.

Gilbert, P. and Palmer, K. (1995) The Business of Caring, *Care Weekly*, 2 Feb.

Gilbert, P. and Thompson, N. (2002) *Supervision and Leadership Skills: A Training Resource*, Wrexham: Learning Curve Publishing.

Giuliani, R. (2002) *Leadership*, London: Time Warner.

Glasby, J. and Peck, E. (2004) *Care Trusts: Partnership Working in Action*, Oxford: Radcliffe Medical Press.

Glasby, J., Peck, E. and Davis, M. (2005) Joined-up Solutions to Joined-up Problems?: Alternatives to Care Trusts, *Journal of Integrated Care*, 13: 1, Feb.

Glynn, C. and Holbeche, L. (2001) *The Management Agenda 2001*, Horsham: Roffey Park Management Institute.

Goffee, R. and Jones, G. (2000) Why Should Anyone Be Led by You?, *Harvard Business Review*, Sep/Oct.

Goldsworthy, A. (2004) *In the Name of Rome*. London: Phoenix.

Goleman, D., Boyatzis, R. and Mckee, A. (2002) *The New Leaders: Transforming the Art of Leadership into the Science of Results*, London: Little Brown.

Gould, N., and Baldwin, M. (2004) *Social Work, Critical Reflection and the Learning Organisation*, Aldershot: Ashgate.

Graham, J. (1997) *Outdoor Leadership*, Seattle, WA: The Mountaineers.

Greene, G. (1955) *The Quiet American*, London: Penguin.

Greenleaf, R. K. (1977) *Servant Leadership: A Journey into the Nature of Legitimate Power and Greatness*, New Jersey: Paulist Press.

Grey-Thompson, T. (2001) *Seize the Day*, London: Hodder and Stoughton.

Hampden-Turner, C. (1990) *Corporate Culture: From Vicious to Virtuous Circles*, London: Hutchinson Business.

Hampden-Turner, C. (1992) *Creating Corporate Culture: From Discord to Harmony*, California: Addison-Wesley.

Hampden-Turner, C. and Trompenaars, A. (1993) *The Seven Cultures of Capitalism*, New York: Doubleday.

Hampson, M. (2005) *Head versus Heart*, London: John Hunt.

Handy, C. (1978) *Gods of Management*, London: Pan.

Handy, C. (1985) *Understanding Organisations*, 3rd edn, London: Penguin Books.

Handy, C. (1989) *The Age of Unreason*, Boston: Harvard Business School Press.

Hardy, B., Turrell, A. and Wistow, G. (1992) *Innovations in Community Care Management*: Aldershot Avebury.

Harrison, R., Mann, G., Murphy, M., Taylor, A., and Thompson, N. (2003) *Partnership Made Painless*, Lyme Regis: Russell House Publishing.

Harrison, R. and Stokes, H. (1990) *Diagnosing Organisational Culture*, Sussex: Roffey Park Management Institute.

Harvey, D. (1990) *The Condition of Post Modernity: An Enquiry into the Origin of Cultural Change*, Oxford: Blackwell.

Harvey, A.D. (2003) Gustav III of Sweden: The Forgotten Despot of the Age of Enlightenment, *History Today*, Dec.

Harvey-Jones, Sir J. (1988) *Making it Happen: Reflections on Leadership*, London: Collins.

Health Education Authority (1999) *Happy Ever After?: Supporting Staff through Mergers and Beyond*, London: HEA.

Hefernan, M. (2004) *The Naked Truth: A Working Woman's Manifesto on Business and What Really Matters*, New York: Jossey Bass.

Hefernan, M. (2004) T2, *The Times*, 2 Nov.

Henderson, J. and Atkinson, D. (Ed.) (2003) *Managing Care in Context*, London: Routledge/The Open University.

Hersey, P. (1984) *The Situational Leader*, New York: Prentice-Hall.

Herzberg, F. (1960) *The Motivation to Work*, Chichester: John Wiley.

Hewison, A. (2004) *Management for Nurses and Health Professionals: Theory into Practice*, Oxford: Blackwell.

Hickey, M. (1992) *The Unforgettable Army*, Tunbridge Wells: Spellmount.

Hoffman, E. (1989) *Lost in Translation*, London: William Heinemann.

Hofstede, G. (1980) *Cultures, Consequences*, Beverly Hills: Sage.

Hofstede, G. (1992) *Cultures and Organisations*, London: Harper Collins.

Holbeche, L. (2005) *The High Performance Organisation*. London: Butterworth-Heinemann.

Holbeche, L. and McCartney, C. (2005) *The Management Agenda 2005*, Horsham: Roffey Park Management Institute.

Holbeche, L. with Springett, N. (2004) *In Search of Meaning at Work*, Horsham: Roffey Park Management Institute.

Holloway, R. (2004) *Looking in the Distance: The Human Search for Meaning*, London: Canongate Books.

Horne, A. (1989) *Macmillan 1957-1986*, Vol. ii of the Official Biography, London: Macmillan.

Howard, A. (2005) *Basil Hume: The Monk Cardinal*. London: Headline.

Hudson, B. (2005) Partnership Working and the Children's Services Agenda: is it feasible? *Journal of Integrated Care*. 13: 2, April.

Hunt, J.G. (1991) *Leadership: A New Synthesis*, London: Sage.

Hunter, T. (2002) Stars in Their Eyes, *Care and Health*, Oct. 16-29.

Hutchinson, F., Mellor, M. and Olsen, W. (2002) *The Politics of Money: Towards Sustainability and Economic Democracy*, London: Pluto Press.

Hutton, W. (2004) Can We Trust Our Officer Class? *The Observer*, 30 May.

Insley, C. (2006, forthcoming) *Athelstan*, London: Longman.

Janki Foundation (2004) *Values in Health Care: A Spiritual Approach*, London: The Janki Foundation for Global Health Care.

Jenkins, S. (1995) *Accountable to None: the Tory Nationalization of Britain*, London: Hamish Hamilton.

Johnson, G. and Scholes, K. (1989) *Exploring Corporate Strategy: Text and Cases*, London: Prentice-Hall.

Jones, K. (1972) *A History of the Mental Health Service*, London: Routledge, Keegan, Paul.

Kanter, R.M. (1983) *The Change Masters*, London: Unwin.

Kaplan, R. and Norton, D. (1996) *The Balanced Score Card: Translating Strategy into Action*, Boston: Harvard Business School Press.

Keegan, J. (1987) *The Mask of Command*, New York: Viking Penguin.

Kelley, R. (1988) In Praise of Followers, *Harvard Business Review*, Nov/Dec.

Kenny, A. (2004) Forty Years On, *Oxford Today*.

Kilmann, R. (Ed.) (1985) *Gaining Control of the Corporate Culture*, New York: Jossey-Bass.

Knights, D. and Willmott, H. (1999) *Management Lives*, London: Sage.

Kocher, P. (1974) *Master of Middle Earth: The Achievement of J.R.R. Tolkien*, London: Penguin Books.

Kotter, J.P. (1988) *The Leadership Factor*, New York: The Free Press.

Kotter, J.P. (1990) What Leaders Really Do, *Harvard Business Review*, May/Jun.

Kotter, J.P. (1990) *A Force for Change: How Leadership Differs from Management*, New York. The Free Press.

Kotter, J.P. (1996) *Leading Change*, Boston: Harvard Business School Press.

Kouzes, J. and Posner, B. (1990) The Credibility Factor: What followers expect from their leaders. *Management Review.* January.

Lawrence, P. and Elliott, K. (1988) *Introducing Management*, London: Penguin Business.

Layard, R. (2005) *Happiness: Lessons From a New Science*, London: Allen Lane.

Leadbeater, C. (2000) *Living on Thin Air: the New Economy.* 2nd edn, London: Penguin Books.

Leadership Development Commission (2004) *An Emerging Strategy for Leadership Development in Local Government*, London: LDC .

Leason, K. (2004) Then There Were Three, *Community Care*, 18-24 Nov.

Le Guin, U. (1971) *The Lathe of Heaven*. London: Penguin.

Le Guin, U.K. (1973–1993 Quartet Edition) *The Farthest Shore*, London: Penguin.

Levy, A. and Kahan, B. (1991) *The Pindown Experience and the Protection of Children, the Report of the Staffordshire Childcare Inquiry, 1990*, Stafford: Staffordshire County Council.

Linstead, S., Fulop, L. and Lilley, S. (2004) *Management and Organization: A Critical Text*, Basingstoke: Palgrave Macmillan.

Locke, E. (1991) *The Essence of Leadership*, New York: Lexington.

Lodge, D. (1989) *Nice Work*, Harmondsworth: Penguin.

Lovelock, R., Lyons, K. and Powell, J. (2004) *Reflecting on Social Work: Discipline and Profession*, Aldershot: Ashgate.

Lynch, R. (2000) *Corporate Strategy*, 2nd edn, Harlow: Pearson Education.

Machiavelli, N. (1514, Penguin edn 1961) *The Prince*, Harmondsworth: Penguin.

MacIntyre, A. (2003) *After Virtue*, London: Gerald Duckworth.

Mandela, N. (1994) *Long Walk to Freedom*, London: Little, Brown and Company.

Mangham, I. (2004) Leadership and Integrity, in Storey, (Ed.) *Leadership in Organisations: Current Issues and Key Trends*, London: Routledge.

Mannion , R. et al. (2005) *Cultures for Performance in Health Care*, Buckingham: Open University Press.

Mant, A. (1984) *Leaders We Deserve*, Oxford: Basil Blackwell.

Martin, V. (2002) *Managing Projects in Health and Social Care*, London: Routledge.

Martin, V. (2003) *Leading Change in Health and Social Care*, London: Routledge.

McLean, A. and Marshall, J. (1988) *Cultures at Work*, London: LGMB.

Melendez, S. (1996) 'Outsiders' View of Leadership, in Hesselbein et al. *The Leader of the Future*, San Francisco: Jossey-Bass.

Midwinter, E. (1994) *The Development of Social Welfare in Britain*, Buckingham: Open University Press.

Mintzberg, H. (1994) The Fall and Rise of Strategic Planning, *Harvard Business Review*, Jan/Feb.

Mirza, H.S. (1992) *Young, Female and Black*, London: Routledge.

Morgan, G. (1997) *Images of Organisation*, London: Sage.

Morgan, G. (2004) Public Agenda, *The Times*, 22 Jun.

Morrell, M. and Capparell, S. (2001) *Shackleton's Way: Leadership Lessons from the Great Antarctic Explorer*, London: Nicholas Brealey.

Moullin, M. (2002) *Delivering Excellence in Health and Social Care*, Buckingham: Open University Press.

Morris, Sir W. (2004) *The Morris Inquiry Report*, Metropolitan Police Authority, 14 Dec.

Mullins, L. J. (2002) *Management and Organisational Behaviour*, 6th edn, Harlow: Prentice-Hall.

National College for School Leadership (2004) *Learning to Lead: NCSL's Strategy for Leadership Learning*, Nottingham: NCSL.

Newman, J. (1996) *Shaping Organisational Cultures in Local Government*, London: Pitman.

Nicholls, J. (1999) Value-centred Leadership: Applying Transforming Leadership to Produce Strategic Behaviour in Depth, Part 2, *Strategic Change.* 8 Nov.

NIMHE (2002) *First Year Strategy for NIMHE: Meeting the Implementation Challenge in Mental Health*, Leeds: NIMHE.

Nouwen, H. (1994) *The Wounded Healer*, London: Darton, Longman and Todd.

O'Connor, J. and Seymour, J. (1993) *Introducing NLP*, London: Aquarian Press.

Onyett, O. (2003) *Team Working in Mental Health*, London: Palgrave Macmillan.

Ouchi, W. (1981) *Theory Z: How American Business Can Meet the Japanese Challenge*, Boston: Addison-Wesley.

Palmer, H. (1995) *The Enneagram in Love and Work*. San Francisco: Harper Collins.

Parikh, J. (1991) *Managing Yourself: Management by Detached Involvement*, Oxford: Blackwell.

Peck, E., Gulliver, P. and Towell, D. (2001) Evaluation of the Implementation of The Mental Health Review in Somerset, *Managing Community Care*, 9: 1, Feb.

Peck, E. and Crawford, A. (2002) You Say Tomato: Culture as a Signifier of Difference Between Health and Social Care, *The Mental Health Review*, 7: 3, Sep.

Pedersen, S. (2004) *Eleanor Rathbone and the Politics of Conscience*, Connecticut: Yale University.

Pedlar, M. and Boydell, T. (1999) *Managing Yourself: How to Develop and Sustain Your Skills, Action, Health and Identity at Work*, London: Lemos and Crane.

Peters, T. (1989) *Thriving on Chaos*, London: Pan.

Peters, T. and Austin, N. (1985) *A Passion for Excellence: The Leadership Difference*, Glasgow: William Collins.

Peters, T. and Waterman, R. (1982) *In Search of Excellence: Lessons from America's Best-run Companies*, New York: HarperCollins.

Philpot, T. (2001) Maureen Oswin, An Obituary, *The Guardian*, 17 Jul.

Pierson, J. (2002) *Tackling Social Exclusion*, London: Routledge.

Pollitt, C. (2003) *The Essential Public Manager*, Maidenhead: Open University Press/McGraw-Hill Education.

Porter, M.E. (1985) *Competitive Advantage*, New York: Free Press.

Pratchett, T. (1996) *Maskerade*, London: Corgi Books.

Pratchett, T. (1998) *The Last Continent*, London: Doubleday.

Pratchett, T. (2001) *Thief of Time*, London: Doubleday.

Proehl, R.A. (2001) *Organisational Change in the Human Services*, California: Sage.

Putnam, D. (2000) *Bowling Alone: the Collapse and Revival of American Community*. New York: Simon & Schuster.

Rappaport, H. (2005) The Invitation That Never Came: Mary Seacole After the Crimea, *History Today*, Feb.

Rawlinson, D. and Tanner, B. (1989) *Financial Management in the 1990s*, Harlow: Longman.

Reed, A. (2004) Health Care is from Mars, Social Care is from Venus, *Care and Health*, 7-20 Jan.

Rees, W. (1984) *The Skills of Management*, London: Crown Books.

Rolheiser, R. (1998) *Seeking Spirituality*, London: Hodder and Stoughton.

Rowe, D. (1988) *The Successful Self*, London: Fontana.

Rowntree, J. (2004) *Joseph Rowntree Report, Inter-agency Work and the Connexions Strategy*, Dec.

Ryan, M. and Haslam, A. (2005) The Glass Cliff: Evidence That Women are Over-Represented in Precarious Leadership Positions. *British Journal of Management*. 16, 81–90.

Sackmann, S. (1991) *Cultural Knowledge in Organisations*, London: Sage.

Sacks, J. (2002) *The Dignity of Difference: How to Avoid the Clash of Civilisations*, London: Continuum.

Sacks, J. (2005) *To Heal a Fractured World: the Ethics of Responsibiltiy*. London: Continuum.

Sanderson, H. (2003) Implementing Person-Centred Planning by Developing Person-Centred Teams, *Journal of Integrated Care*, 11: 3, Jun.

Schein, E. (1985) *Organisational Culture and Leadership*, San Francisco: Jossey-Bass School Press.

SCIE (2005) *Learning Organisations: A Self Assessment Resource Pack*, London: SCIE.

SCIE (2005) *Leading Practice: A Development Programme for Front-line Managers*, London: SCIE.

Scott, M.C. (2000) *Re-inspiring the Corporation*, Chichester: John Wiley.

Scragg, T. (2001) *Managing at the Frontline: A Handbook for Managers in Social Care Agencies*, Brighton: Pavilion.

Seabrook, J. (1988) *The Leisure Society*, Oxford: Blackwell.

Senge, P. (1990) *The Fifth Discipline: The Art and Science of the Learning Organization*, New York: Doubleday.

Sewell, H. (2004) Leadership and Pro-Activity, *Care and Health*, 22-28 Jun.

Sewell, H. and Gilbert, P. (2006, forthcoming) Leading and Learning: the Social Care Learning Set. *British Journal of Leadership*.

Shaw, P. (2002) *Changing Conversations in Organisations: a Complexity Approach to Change*. London: Routledge.

Sinclair, A. and Agyeman, B. (2004) *Building Global Leadership: Strategies for Success*, Horsham: Roffey Park Management Institute.

Singleton, D. (2005) New Leaders for New Schools. *Children Now*. 22–28 June.

Small, H. (1998) *Florence Nightingale: Avenging Angel*, London: Constable.

Smith, J. et al. (2004) *A Review of the Effectiveness of Primary Care-led Commissioning and its Place in the NHS*. London: The Health Foundation.

Smith, P. and Peterson, M. (1988) *Leadership, Organisations and Culture*, London: Sage.

Snell, J. (2002) Where does the buck stop?, *Community Care*, 21-27 Feb.

Spreckley, P. and Hart, T. (2001) Reigning Cats and Dogs, *The Health Service Journal*, 24 May.

Starkey, D. (2004) *The Monarchy of England: The Beginnings*, London: Chatto & Windus.

Steare, R. and Jamison, C. (2003) *Integrity in Practice*, London: Financial Services Authority/The Soul Gym/Skills Council for Financial Services.

Storey, J. (Ed.) (2004) *Leadership in Organisations: Current Issues and Key Trends*, London: Routledge.

Sturges, J. (2004) The Individualisation of the Career and its Implications for Leadership and Management Development, in Storey, J. (Ed.)

Stewart, R. (1986) *The Reality of Management*, 2nd edn, London: Heinemann.

Tacey, D. (2004) *The Spirituality Revolution: The Emergence of Contemporary Spirituality*, London: Brunner: Routledge.

Tannenbaum, R. and Schmidt, W. (1958) How to Choose a Leadership Pattern, *Harvard Business Review*, 36: 2, Mar/Apr.

Tannenbaum, R. and Schmidt, W. (in Stewart 1986) *The Reality of Management*, London: Heinemann.

Tew, J. (Ed.) (2005) *Social Perspectives in Mental Health*, London: Jessica Kingsley Publishers.

Thompson, N. (2000) *Tackling Bullying and Harassment in the Workplace*, Birmingham: Pepar.

Thompson, N. (2001) *Anti-Discriminatory Practice*, 3rd edn, Basingstoke: Palgrave.

Thompson, N. (2003) *Promoting Equality: Challenging Discrimination and Oppression in the Human Services*, 2nd edn, London: Palgrave Macmillan.

Thompson, N. (2005 forthcoming) *People Problems*, London: Palgrave Macmillan.

TOPSS (2004) *Leadership and Management: A Strategy for the Social Care Workforce*, Leeds: TOPSS.

Vardy, P. (2003) *Being Human: Fulfilling Genetic and Spiritual Potential.* London: Darton, Longman & Todd.

Veal, D. (2004) *Roffey Park Newsletter*, Autumn 2004, Roffey Park Management Institute.

Walsh, K. (1989) *Marketing in Local Government.* Harlow: Longman.

Wanless, D. (2002) Wanless Report on the NHS, *Health Service Journal*, 25 Apr.

Webster, A. (2002) *Wellbeing.* London: SCM Press.

Webster, C. (2002) *The National Health Service: A Political History*, 2nd edn, Oxford University Press.

Weinberg, D.B. (2003) *Codegreen: Money-driven Hospitals and the Dismantling of Nursing*, New York: Cornell University Press.

Welch, J. with Byrne, J. (2001) *Jack: What I've Learned Leading a Great Company and Great People*, Headline Press.

Wheatley, M. (1999) *Leadership and the New Science: Learning about Organizations from an Orderly Universe*, San Francisco: Berett-Koehler.

Wilson, F. (2003) *Organisational Behaviour and Gender*, 2nd edn, Aldershot: Ashgate.

Woodward, C. (2004) *Winning! The Story of England's Rise to Rugby World Cup Glory*, London: Hodder and Stoughton.

Zohar, D. and Marshall, I. (2000) *S.Q: Spiritual Intelligence, The Ultimate Intelligence*, London: Bloomsbury.